Recipes for this Micro Menus Cookbook were developed for use in a microwave oven by the Better Homes and Gardens Test Kitchen (above). Here, editor Pat Jester puts the finishing touches on *Clambake for Two* for a taste panel.

The kitchen of the photography studio buzzes with activity as food stylist Mable Hoffman and editors prepare the food for the photos in microwave ovens (above). Each food setup is carefully "propped" with appropriate dishes and accessories to give you attractive serving ideas as well as complementary menu item suggestions.

In the studio, photographer George de Gennaro discusses the setup for the *Clambake for Two* photograph with the editors. This was just one of over forty photographs taken for this book. For a look at the final photo, turn to page 130. We think you'll agree it looks appetizing—and it tastes as good as it looks!

CONTENTS

1

Total cooking time: 13 minutes

3	10					

Time capsules—each recipe begins with these easy reference time capsules. At the top of each box is the total cooking time. The time breakdown for each recipe step is listed in the individual boxes. For example a dish which cooks for 3 minutes in one step and then 10 minutes in another step would have a 3 in the first box, a 10 in the second box, and the total cooking time listed would be 13 minutes. You'll also notice the times are listed as they would appear on a digital timer—3:30 means 3 minutes 30 seconds cooking time.

2 TEST KITCHEN TIPS

Here are 19 helpful hints to help you use your microwave oven. There's everything from making drinks right in the serving mugs, to baking cupcakes in a matter of minutes, and combining microwave and barbecuing. See pages 38 to 40 for a summary of tip boxes.

3 MICRO MENU PLANNER

This mini index by chapter is on each divider tab. Not only can you see all the recipes at a glance, it's a fun way to plan menus, too. Try mixing and matching meats, salads, vegetables, and desserts for easy meals.

4 TIMETABLE

Step-by-step ideas for cooking each menu are given in the timetables. Dovetailing times is a little different in microwave cooking, so these helpful timetables will get you off to a smooth start. There's a whole new world of possibilities for meal planning when you think about how effortlessly your microwave oven reheats foods to their original freshness. On the other hand some foods require a standing time to finish cooking. Follow a few of our timetables to get in the swing of things.

5 MENU

Over 40 menus will help you learn to use your microwave oven as effectively as possible. The menus are planned to have both eye appeal and good nutrition for your family. In addition, you'll want to create your own menu ideas—and we help you do that, too. The Micro Menu Planners at the beginning of each chapter make it easy to plan meals within or between chapters. In addition, the index has recipes listed by category, such as vegetables, as well as alphabetically to aid in your planning.

6 ABC's

The ABC's of microwave cooking, starting on page 8, get down to the nuts and bolts of how microwave cooking works and how it differs from conventional cooking. It's a fascinating story that you'll enjoy reading while you're cooking this "short course". And once you understand the functions of microwave cooking, using these principles will just come naturally.

7 INDEX

There are 16 pages of index to help you find what you're looking for. You'll find recipes listed several times under different headings to help you locate them more easily. There is also a mini index on the tabbed divider for each chapter. Wonder where you saw a tip box? Remember the tips summary starting on page 38. In addition all of the tips are indexed on the front of the index tab.

8 LIFESTYLE

Lifestyle means the way you live—doing your own thing. And microwave cooking fits right in. You'll find a chapter for old-time favorites, entertaining, cooking when there's just one or two, fast meals that beat the clock, and foods that go from freezer to table in just a matter of minutes. So vary your lifestyle and pick the chapter to go along with it.

9 UTENSIL CHART

On pages 12 and 13 you will find the most up-to-date information concerning microwave utensils. Be sure to look at this chart carefully. You'll find that you already own many utensils that you can use in your microwave oven. Take a look at the photograph on page 11. This shows some of the specialized microwave cooking utensils that are available to make microwave cooking more enjoyable.

10 BASIC COOKING

Basic Cooking means just that. You don't need a recipe. You just want to know how to cook, for example, a plain broiler-fryer chicken, or a hamburger, or maybe you just want to scramble an egg. You already know how to do it conventionally. All you want to know is how long does it take in the microwave. Right? Then the basic cooking section is for you. It begins on page 22 and is divided into basic cooking for beef, pork, lamb, veal, poultry, fish, eggs, vegetables, salads, desserts, breads, beverages, soups, sauces, appetizers, and sandwiches.

11 CHARTS

Charts put information at your fingertips. And because you will use them a lot, they are color-coded to help you locate them. If you thumb through the end of the book, you will discover that vegetable charts are green, the roasting chart red, defrosting is blue, cakes are designated by yellow, frozen convenience foods have an orange tone, and packaged convenience foods go with purple.

12 USE & CARE

Use and Care of your new microwave oven is very important. Be sure that you carefully read and understand the Use and Care Guide that came with your microwave oven before starting to use the oven.

MICROWAVE COOKING

The fascinating world of microwave cooking is at your fingertips. And what easier way to learn the hows and whys of micro-cooking than by making this luscious meal. We'll help you select utensils off your shelf to cook this Spicy Meat Loaf (page 17), Twice Baked Potatoes and Broccoli with Cheese Sauce (page 19), Apple-mandarin Salad Mold (page 15), and S'more Pudding (page 21). We guarantee your first meal can be a smashing success—and you can be a master micro-chef!

THE ABC'S OF MICROWAVE COOKING

Meet the Microwave

Micro means tiny, very small, short. In the case of microwaves, we're talking about short energy waves. You're more familiar with energy waves than you may think. A bass drum produces relatively long energy waves. Waves become progressively shorter as we go from the drum to the piccolo to radio waves to visible light waves.

Waves of different lengths have different characteristics. Holding up your hand won't stop sound waves, but it can stop light waves. You use different kinds of energy waves every day. But, right now let's think only about microwaves.

Small waves with big cooking power

Three important characteristics of microwaves are:
1. Microwaves bounce off metal.
2. Microwaves pass through most glass, paper, and plastic objects.
3. Microwaves are absorbed by food.

When microwaves are absorbed by food, what happens? The molecules in the food begin to vibrate. The vibrating molecules bump into each other causing friction. It is this friction that produces heat instantly within the food. You can get an idea of heat produced by friction by rubbing your hands together quickly.

How does microwave cooking differ from conventional cooking? With conventional range cooking, you heat the air in the oven. The hot air heats the surface of the food. From here, the heat is conducted slowly to the inside of the food.

Microwaves also cook food from the outside in. The greatest amount of microwave energy is absorbed near the surface of the food. Where this absorption occurs, cooking begins immediately. The waves lose power as they go deeper into the food. That's why there's more cooking taking place at a depth of 1 to 2 inches.

Thus thin foods cook fairly rapidly and evenly throughout, while thicker foods, such as roasts, cook faster in the area nearest the surface where the microwaves are absorbed. The center of the roast cooks by conduction of heat which is much slower. Remember, the heat is produced only in the food, not in the cavity of your microwave oven. This makes for cool cooking.

Microwave utensils

Why shouldn't you cook in metal pans? Food must absorb microwaves in order to cook. Therefore, the microwaves must first pass through the cooking utensil. Most glass, paper, and plastic containers allow microwaves to do just that. Remember, microwaves bounce off metal. Therefore, if you would use metal pans, few microwaves would reach the food and the food would heat very slowly. So remember: use microwave-safe glass, paper, and plastic utensils for cooking in your microwave oven. The photo at right shows a sample of the many utensils that you can use in the microwave oven. For more details, see the utensil chart on pages 12 and 13 and the microwave utensil test on page 11.

Look for labels on cooking utensils that indicate they are recommended for microwave oven use. If your dinnerware is described by the manufacturer as ovenproof, such as Temperware by Lenox or casual china by Franciscan, it is usually safe for use in the microwave oven. Some glass and ceramic items could contain a glaze or other material that absorbs microwaves, such as Centura dinnerware by Corning Glass. These items should not be used in the microwave oven. Use the dish test on page 11 to check the dishes you wish to use.

Avoid chipped or cracked utensils. Do not use casseroles and covers with metal screws on handles and glued on parts. Do not use delicate glassware and lacquerware.

Glass measuring cups (especially the 2-cup and 4-cup sizes) are handy for cooking sauces and soups. You can warm beverages right in the cups provided they are made of microwave-safe material. See the dish test on page 11. It's also convenient to warm baby bottles. Remove the cover and nipple before heating in the microwave oven.

Microwave cooking can still burn

Be careful when removing ovenware, dishes, and other food containers from the microwave oven. They may get hot enough that you will need to use hot pads.

Use caution when removing a cover. Steam builds up in the container and can burn you. Always tilt the cover away from you or poke a hole in a paper covering.

Cook foods according to the times and quantities given in the cookbook. Do not overcook foods or they may burn. Shorten cooking time for smaller quantities. As in conventional cooking, overcooking will burn food and may flame.

A microwave oven is different from a conventional oven. For best results, use the cookbook directions. Some foods such as potatoes and snacks may smoke and burn if they are overcooked.

SPECIAL MICROWAVE UTENSILS

Browning dish—tips for use:
1. Do not use paper toweling or waxed paper for covering. They could catch fire due to the high heat from the dish.
2. Do not preheat for more than 8 minutes.
3. Use hot pads when handling the browning dish.
4. Preheat the browning dish empty and uncovered.
5. Do not use non-stick vegetable coatings with the browning dish.
6. Dish will become hot. Set on a heat resistant surface to avoid damage to counter.

Microwave thermometer or probe—tips for use:
1. Avoid touching the oven walls to prevent arcing.
2. Remove from cooked food with hot pads.
3. Do not store in the microwave oven.
4. Do not wash in the dishwasher.
5. Do not use microwave thermometers or probes in conventional ovens.

IS IT SUITABLE FOR USE IN A MICROWAVE OVEN?

Use this simple test to see if a dish should be used in the microwave oven.

1. Place the dish beside a cup of water in the microwave oven.
2. Turn the oven to the **HIGH** setting for one minute. If the dish gets hot, it is absorbing microwave energy and should not be used in the microwave oven.
3. Do not use plastic utensils when cooking foods high in fat or sugar, unless recommended by the utensil manufacturer. Read the directions that come with plastic utensils carefully.

MICROWAVE UTENSILS

You may already have utensils that will be acceptable for microwave oven cooking. Many new utensils are being developed specifically for use in a microwave oven. Look for labels on cooking utensils that indicate they are recommended for microwave oven use. Use all utensils with care.

Do not store utensils in the oven. Use hot pads. Some utensils may be hot after cooking. Do not overcook foods (especially foods cooked in plastic or paper utensils). Below is a summary of utensils, their characteristics, and tips for use.

Utensil Material	Characteristics	Tips for Use
Glass and Ceramics	Microwaves pass through most glass and ceramics. Oven proof glass and ceramics can withstand high temperatures. Typical shapes: casseroles, custard cups, loaf dishes, pie plates, measuring cups, dinnerware serving dishes, serving bowls, mugs.	**Don't use glass or ceramic dishes with metallic trim or metal bands.** Do not use utensils with metal handles, screws, or other metal parts that cannot be removed. Use 1 minute dish test (page 11) to check each item. Use for recipes high in fat and sugar. These foods become very hot in the microwave oven. Avoid using chipped or cracked utensils. Do not use bottles with narrow openings. Do not use jars which are not heat tempered. Look for labels on the utensils that indicate they are recommended for microwave oven use.
Metal	Microwaves bounce off metal. Metal can cause arcing—a sparking lightning-like effect that you can see and hear. If arcing occurs, reposition the food and metal in the oven. If arcing continues, remove the metal from the oven. Typical utensils: microwave thermometers, frozen dinner trays, and poultry clamps.	Use aluminum foil for shielding. If part of a food is cooking too fast, secure a piece of aluminum foil over that area with toothpicks. Poultry clamps may be used with large food quantities. Don't use metal saucepans, pie plates, baking pans, standard meat or candy thermometers, or frozen dinner trays over ¾ inch deep. To avoid damage to the oven walls, metal should not touch the walls. **Don't use glass, paper, or ceramic containers with metallic trim or metal bands.** When using foil frozen dinner trays: 1. Remove foil cover. 2. Return container to carton if a cover is needed. 3. Place tray in center of oven. Do not let metal or carton touch oven walls. 4. Cook only one tray at a time. Remove all twist ties and metal lids to avoid arcing and possible flames.

Utensil Material	Characteristics	Tips for Use
Paper	Microwaves pass through most paper containers. Typical utensils: paper plates, cups, paper towels, napkins, freezer paper, baking parchment, waxed paper, and paper from frozen food packages.	Use of paper should be limited to cooking times up to 4 minutes or frozen food cooking times up to 10 minutes. Paper towels help absorb grease or moisture and help prevent spattering. Defrost frozen juice in paper containers. Remove one metal end. Do not attempt to pop corn in a paper bag. Do not use paper fast food containers with metal handles, foil lining, or foil wrapping. Remove all twist ties and metal lids to avoid arcing and possible flames.
Plastic	Microwaves pass through most plastic containers. Some plastics may melt or soften from the heat of the food. Typical utensils: boil-in-the-bag pouches, cake dishes, cupcake holders, trays, roasting racks, bacon racks, pie plates, oven cooking bags.	Use 1 minute dish test (page 11) to check each item. Do not use plastic containers when cooking foods high in fat or sugar, unless recommended by utensil manufacturer. Use plastic utensils that have been recommended for safe microwave oven use by the utensil manufacturer. Cut a slit in the top of boil-in-the-bag pouches before heating so steam can escape. Do not use thin plastic sandwich bags. Oven roasting bags can be used according to manufacturer's directions. Slit before heating and close with string. Do not use melamine utensils and dishes. Lightweight freezer containers may distort because of high food temperatures and should not be used. Use plastic wrap only if it has been recommended for safe microwave oven use by the wrap manufacturer. Use plastic wrap for a tight cover. Be careful when removing the cover. Steam builds up in the container and can burn you. Lift cover away from you or leave opening for steam to escape.
Straw and wood	Typical shapes: wooden skewers, woven straw baskets, wooden bowls, spoons, platters	Select items without metal wires or metallic trim. Use only for short cooking times. Straw and wood will dry out and may crack from long cooking times or continued use.

Apple-mandarin Salad Mold

Cooking with the Cook Power control will come naturally. Why? It can be as easy as boiling water on top of your
range. For example, if you start at **HIGH**, the water boils
quickly. After adding food, you can turn the setting down
to simmer gently or lower the setting even more to just
keep food warm. Your Cook Power control is designed to
operate the same way—from **HIGH** to **MEDIUM (5)** to
LOW (1). It's the same idea with a new face.

If fruit-flavored gelatin isn't your cup of tea, think of all
the other tasty things you can make with 1 cup of boiling
water: instant coffee, spiced tea, bouillon, instant cocoa,
one-serving-size dry soup mix, to name a few. And you can
boil the water right in the heat-proof mug you're going to
serve it in. No mess, no fuss. Just an easy refreshment to
sit back and enjoy while you read the rest of this ABC's of
Microwave Cooking chapter.

14

Cook Power control spells convenience

Think of the control on your microwave oven as a friend. Its operation is similar to the control knob on the surface units of your range. For example, a low setting means low power and slow cooking.

For quick heating of convenience foods, beverages, vegetables, fruits, burgers, cupcakes, and sauces, use **HIGH**. Choose **MEDIUM HIGH (7)** for tender meats, poultry, meat loaves, and casseroles that require quick cooking to retain moisture and tenderness. **MEDIUM (5)** is recommended for less tender meats that need to simmer, such as pot roast and stew, or for even cooking of baked goods such as cakes. Turn to **MEDIUM LOW (3)** for defrosting frozen foods. **LOW (1)** works best for softening butter, raising yeast breads, and holding foods at serving temperature.

Some foods can be cooked at more than one power setting. Choose the one that best fits your needs or your time schedule. Foods can be thawed quickly at **HIGH** or **MEDIUM HIGH (7)**, but need more watching and care than the same item done at **LOW (1)** or **MEDIUM LOW (3)**.

Reheating foods can also be done at a wide range of settings. You can reheat quickly at **HIGH** but you'll need to open the door and stir, turn, or rotate the food a few times while it's heating. On the other hand, you can reheat items more evenly at a lower setting—without as much stirring—but it will take a longer heating time.

You can roast at **HIGH** but you will need to check and rearrange the food periodically to ensure even cooking. A lower setting for roasting requires less watching, but it will take a longer time to cook. Use the setting and method that fits best into your schedule.

The wide variety of Cook Power control settings allows for cooking versatility. Use good cooking sense. Turn power down if food is cooking too quickly. Use a higher setting and stir a few times if you want a casserole to heat more quickly. The recipes are a guideline. You'll find specific settings mentioned in each recipe. We found these settings gave the best results when we prepared the recipes in our test kitchens.

Greet your microwave oven with open arms

Your microwave oven has exciting sights and sounds you'll want to get to know. Let's take a look at what you can expect when you use your microwave oven.

Place a 4-cup glass measure filled with 1 cup of cool tap water in your microwave. Close the door. Set the timer for 4 minutes. Set the Cook Power control at **HIGH**. Push the start button.

The power comes on instantly. The water begins heating. Open the door—the timer and power stop. Close the door and push the start button. The timer picks up where it left off.

After 2½ minutes (the timer will read 1½ minutes, the amount of time left from your original 4-minute setting) the water will be close to boiling. When it starts to boil, turn the Cook Power control to **MEDIUM (5)**, then to a lower setting.

Watch the water carefully—it boils more slowly, then simmers, and barely forms bubbles at all as you lower the Cook Power setting. Remember, lower power means slower cooking.

After 4 minutes a bell sounds and the power shuts off automatically. Reach in and touch the handle of the measuring cup—it's not boiling hot, but the water is. Utensils will stay cool except for any heat transferred from the hot food to the dish.

Now that you have successfully boiled a cup of water, dump in a package of gelatin and make a simple molded salad for dinner!

Recipe style makes cooking easy

Every recipe begins with total cooking time. A glance at the boxed Time Capsules at the top of each recipe tells you the breakdown in time for major cooking steps. The Cook Power control is provided with large type so it's easy to read. You'll also find directions for selecting utensils, covering, and stirring to ensure a delicious recipe every time you make it.

Recipes have been tested for consistent results and quality. However, it's a good idea to visually check for doneness shortly before the recommended cooking time is up to avoid overcooking. Remember a few minutes in the microwave oven at **HIGH** is equal to about four times the conventional cooking time. Therefore, overcooking can happen quickly. Add more cooking time in small amounts (1 minute or less) and check for doneness.

APPLE-MANDARIN SALAD MOLD

Total cooking time: 2 minutes 30 seconds

2:30							

1 cup water
1 3-ounce package lime-flavored gelatin
1 11-ounce can mandarin orange sections
¾ cup diced unpared apple

Place 1 cup water in 4-cup glass measure. Cook, uncovered, at **HIGH** for 2½ to 3 minutes, till boiling. Stir in gelatin to dissolve. Drain mandarin oranges, reserving syrup. Add enough water to reserved fruit syrup to make 1 cup; stir into dissolved gelatin.

Chill till partially set. Fold in mandarin oranges and diced apple. Turn into 4-cup mold. Chill till firm. Unmold and garnish with endive and apple slices, if desired. Makes 4 to 6 servings.

MOLDED SALAD VARIATIONS

Be a creative cook and come up with more molded salad concoctions. For each 3-ounce package of gelatin, use 2 cups liquid (slightly less for a large mold) and up to 2 cups fruit. How about:

- raspberry-flavored gelatin with frozen raspberries and cranberry-orange relish
- cherry-flavored gelatin with pitted dark sweet cherries and port wine
- orange-flavored gelatin with grapefruit and orange sections along with ginger ale and candied ginger
- lemon-flavored gelatin with pineapple, marshmallows, nuts, and lemon yogurt

Spicy Meat Loaf

It's back to school for a crash course in microwave cooking! And you'll go to the head of the class when you learn that cooking times vary, depending on:
1. amount of food
2. starting temperature of food
3. shape of food
4. composition of food

Shape this savory Spicy Meat Loaf recipe to suit your time schedule. The traditional loaf shape micro-cooks in just 24 minutes. Form it into a ring and it's done in 16 minutes. And, if you're really in a rush, make individual meat loaves—from mixing bowl to table in a mere 12 minutes! Remember these three shapes for your other favorite meat loaf recipes, too.

16

Food temperature, shape, and composition all affect the cooking time. Let's take a closer look at all three and see why.

Starting temperature

It's reassuring to know that even with the speed of microwave, warm water still comes to a boil faster than cold water. By the same token, refrigerated foods take longer to heat than the same foods starting at room temperature. Keep in mind we tested our recipes with the ingredients taken directly from proper storage—refrigerated meats, room temperature canned goods, etc. So you can feel free to substitute canned peas for frozen, but remember to reduce the cooking time.

Shape

Thinner foods cook faster in the microwave than thicker foods. Why? Remember that microwaves lose power as they go deeper into food. Therefore, thinner foods and outside layers of thick foods cook by microwave while the center of thick foods cooks by conduction of heat.

Look at shape in a different way. The corners of a square baking dish tend to cook faster than the center. Why? The corners receive microwave energy from the top, bottom, and two sides. The center of the food cooks more slowly because it receives microwave energy only from the top and bottom. This also explains why you stir during cooking—to distribute the heat evenly throughout the food.

The doughnut wins the award for being the best shape for microwave cooking. It has no corners, no center. Cooking can take place all around—through the top, bottom, sides, and center. That's why some recipes suggest shaping food into a ring or putting a custard cup in the center of a dish. This creates the ideal doughnut shape.

There are other ways to choose or change the shape of food. Choose a pot roast that is the same thickness throughout with no jagged corners. Cut meat and vegetables for stew or stir-frying into uniform-size pieces. Remember, the larger the chunks, the longer the cooking time. Similarly, sliced ham heats more quickly than the whole unsliced ham.

Composition

You'll find some foods cook faster than others because of the ingredients they contain. Take a jelly-filled doughnut, for example. After heating, the doughnut may feel cool to the touch while the sugary jelly inside the doughnut may be very hot.

MEAT LOAF POINTERS

There is a secret to success in making a tender, juicy meat loaf. First of all, mix the egg, liquid, crumbs, and seasoning ingredients together in a bowl. Then crumble in the meat mixture and mix lightly till well combined. Overmixing will result in a compact loaf. When shaping the loaf, handle only as much as necessary.

For more meat loaf ideas, try *Italian Meat Loaf* (recipe on page 56), *Meat Roll Spaghetti Dinner* (recipe on page 57), *Curried Fruit Ham Ring* (recipe on page 127), and *Stroganoff Meat Ring* (recipe on page 127).

SPICY MEAT LOAF

Total cooking time: 21 minutes 30 seconds

20	1:30						

2 beaten eggs
¾ cup milk
⅔ cup fine dry bread crumbs
2 tablespoons finely chopped onion
1 teaspoon salt
½ teaspoon chili powder
  Dash pepper
1½ pounds ground beef
¼ cup hot-style catsup
1 tablespoon brown sugar
½ teaspoon dry mustard

In mixing bowl, combine egg, milk, bread crumbs, onion, salt, chili powder, and pepper. Add beef; mix well. Shape into a loaf in a 10×6×1½-inch baking dish or in an 8½×4½×2½-inch dish. Cook, covered, at **MEDIUM HIGH** (7) for 20 to 22 minutes, giving dish a half turn once. Drain off excess fat.

In bowl, combine catsup, brown sugar, and dry mustard; spread or spoon atop meat. Cook, uncovered, at **MEDIUM HIGH** (7) for 1½ to 2 minutes. Let stand 5 minutes before serving. Makes 6 servings.

Ring Loaf: Shape meat into a ring in an 8-inch round baking dish; cook, covered, at **MEDIUM HIGH** (7) for 12 to 14 minutes. Drain, glaze, and let stand as above.

Individual Loaves: Shape meat mixture into 6 individual loaves. Place in 12×7½×2-inch baking dish. Cook, covered, at **MEDIUM HIGH** (7) for 10 minutes, rearranging loaves once. Drain, glaze, and let stand as above.

CHEESY HERBED BEEF LOAF

Total cooking time: 41 minutes

3	38						

½ cup chopped onion
¼ cup chopped green pepper
½ cup water
1 8-ounce can tomato sauce
2 beaten eggs
2¼ cups soft bread crumbs (3 slices)
½ teaspoon salt
¼ teaspoon dried thyme, crushed
1 cup (4 ounces) diced process American cheese
2 pounds ground beef

In mixing bowl, combine onion and green pepper with water. Cook, covered, at **HIGH** for 3 minutes; drain off water. Stir in tomato sauce, eggs, crumbs, salt, dash pepper, and thyme. Add cheese and ground beef; mix well. Pat into 9×5×3-inch loaf dish. Place loaf dish on glass pizza plate in microwave oven to catch juices. Cook, covered, at **MEDIUM HIGH** (7) for 38 to 40 minutes, giving dish half turn once. Let stand covered 10 minutes before serving. Makes 8 servings.

Twice Baked Potatoes

For more even cooking in the microwave oven:
1. Cover utensils with lids or waxed paper.
2. Stir foods from the outside in.
3. Arrange and rearrange foods as needed.
When adjusting the size of recipes:
1. Increase cooking time as food amount increases.
2. Decrease cooking time as food amount decreases.

Keep this lazy-day method for frozen vegetables in mind. Simply loosen the wrapping and cook right in the original carton. Or, if you buy vegetables in cooking pouches, cut a few slits in the top side of the pouch and cook as is. What could be easier? Maybe baked potatoes are—and you can give them a new twist with our special toppers on page 113. Baked potatoes never had it so good.

THE ABC'S OF MICROWAVE COOKING *(continued)*

We want you to serve your microwave recipes with pride. That's why we've tested and retested our recipes until we had top-notch results. During our testing we've also come up with some additional pointers that will help ensure your microwave cooking success.

Varying quantity and volume
When the *amount* of food varies, the *cooking time* varies also. For example, 1 potato may take 4 minutes to bake while 2 potatoes take 7 minutes. Likewise, 1 cup of cool tap water boils in about 2½ minutes but 2 cups take approximately 4¾ minutes.

Here are some rules of thumb to follow when you adjust a recipe to suit your family's size. Remember when cooking smaller amounts of food that *half* the quantity doesn't necessarily cook in *half* the time. Instead, we suggest you reduce the time by slightly less than half. Then check for doneness, and add a little more cooking time if necessary. To double a recipe add a little more than half the original cooking time. Check for doneness, and then add more time in small portions if necessary.

Covering foods while cooking
You'll find glass casserole lids and ordinary waxed paper handy for covering foods in your microwave oven. Covering prevents spattering and ensures more moist, even heating throughout.

Stirring from the outside in
In conventional cooking, you stir a cheese sauce to keep it from scorching on the bottom of the hot pan. Food in a microwave oven is heated directly by the microwaves, so there's little chance of scorching the bottom. We stir for a different reason. Remember that microwaves cook from the outside in. Therefore, when you stir you are redistributing the heat—moving the hot outside sauce inward to replace the cooler sauce in the center of the dish.

For food that can't be stirred, such as a roast, turn it over about halfway through cooking or defrosting. In the case of meat loaf or cake, you can't stir or turn it over. So, rotate the baking dish a quarter or half turn in the microwave oven about halfway through the cooking time.

What happens if you are too busy to stir during cooking or you stir fewer times than suggested? Chances are the recipe will still turn out satisfactorily, but you can expect the food to be cooked less evenly.

Arranging and rearranging foods
Irregularly shaped foods cook less evenly. Remember to put the thicker, meatier parts of drumsticks or pork chops toward the outside of the dish, the bonier parts toward the center. When you reheat a plate of food, make sure the thick, more dense foods such as meat are toward the outside of the plate. Place porous, easily heated foods like rolls in the center.

Rearrange meat patties, cupcakes, and muffins within the microwave oven if one seems to be cooking more slowly than the others. Keep this in mind, too, when cooking chicken rolls in a rectangular baking dish. You may find the rolls in the center will not cook as quickly as the rolls at the ends. A quick trading of places in the dish remedies that.

BAKED POTATOES
Scrub medium-size potatoes; prick with fork. Place in a spoke pattern in microwave oven, leaving one inch between potatoes. Cook, uncovered, at **HIGH** until slightly firm. Wrap in foil. Let stand 5 minutes to complete cooking.

POTATOES	COOKING TIME
1	4 to 6 minutes
2	7 to 8 minutes
3	9 to 10 minutes
4	12 to 13 minutes
5	14 to 15 minutes
6	16 to 17 minutes
7	18 to 19 minutes
8	19 to 20 minutes

TWICE BAKED POTATOES

Total cooking time: 4 minutes

4							

Bake 6 potatoes according to recipe above; let stand 5 minutes. Slice the top off each potato; scoop out inside to make 6 shells, discarding tops. In bowl, mash together the scooped out potato, 3 tablespoons butter or margarine, ¾ teaspoon salt, and dash pepper. Add enough milk (about ¾ cup) to make fluffy consistency. Spoon back into potato shells.

Place on serving plate; dash each with paprika. Cook, uncovered, at **HIGH** for 4 minutes or till hot, giving dish a half turn once. Makes 6 servings.

Note: If made ahead and refrigerated, cook, uncovered, at **HIGH** for 8 minutes giving dish a half turn once. Or, wrap and freeze leftover potatoes. To serve, unwrap and heat at **HIGH** 5 minutes for 1 potato or 7 minutes for 2 potatoes, giving dish a half turn once.

BROCCOLI WITH CHEESE SAUCE

Total cooking time: 19 minutes 30 seconds

15	0:30	3	1				

- 2 10-ounce packages frozen broccoli spears
- 2 tablespoons butter or margarine
- 2 tablespoons all-purpose flour
- 1 cup milk
- ½ cup (2 ounces) shredded sharp process American cheese
- ½ cup (2 ounces) shredded process Swiss cheese
- ¼ teaspoon dried dillweed
- 1 3-ounce can sliced mushrooms, drained

Place broccoli in serving bowl with 2 tablespoons water. Cook, covered, at **HIGH** for 15 minutes, rearranging twice; set aside. In 4-cup glass measure, melt butter at **HIGH** for 30 to 45 seconds. Stir in flour. Add milk. Cook, uncovered, at **HIGH** for 3 to 4 minutes, stirring thoroughly every 30 seconds. Stir in cheeses and dillweed. Fold in mushrooms. Cook at **MEDIUM HIGH (7)** for 1 minute longer. Drain broccoli; spoon cheese sauce over. Makes 6 to 8 servings.

S'more Pudding

TIMETABLE

1. Make salad, potatoes, and pudding; refrigerate.
2. Cook broccoli; cover.
3. Set table while broccoli cooks.
4. Make cheese sauce; cover.
5. Cook meat loaf; cover.
6. Reheat potatoes; reheat broccoli.
7. Unmold salad on serving plate.
8. Arrange meat loaf, potatoes, and broccoli on platter.

MENU

Spicy Meat Loaf (recipe on page 17)

Twice Baked Potatoes (recipe on page 19)

Broccoli with Cheese Sauce (recipe on page 19)

Apple-mandarin Salad Mold (recipe on page 15)

S'more Pudding

Coffee   Milk

THE ABC'S OF MICROWAVE COOKING *(continued)*

Step-by-step to microwave menu planning

1. *Select complementary foods from the basic four food groups.* This is your key to serving nutritious meals. In addition, choose foods with different colors and textures. Complement spicy foods with more bland flavors. Create imaginative garnishes for extra eye appeal. And try to introduce one new recipe each week.

2. *Arrange your cooking schedule to dovetail times.* You will find Timetables with each menu in this book. It's our way of helping you adjust your thinking to microwave. After a few meals you will be planning your own micro menus like a master chef! Be sure to think through your menu carefully. Remember, if you are in a hurry, fix the food that cooks the longest in the microwave oven. Meanwhile, you can cook the rest of the meal conventionally. Use your microwave to complement the rest of your appliances.

3. *Make as many foods as possible ahead.* It's so easy to reheat foods in the microwave. Therefore it's possible to cook many foods early in the day, then cover and refrigerate. Reheat just before serving time. You'll want to look at the Reheating Chart on page 174. This will give you a good idea how long to reheat different foods. If the specific food you are reheating isn't listed, just look at the time for a similar food.

4. *Set the table.* Do it early! Microwave cooking goes so fast you may find dinner ready before the table is set.

5. *Finish cooking the meal.* Many foods such as meat and vegetables will hold heat well if tightly covered after cooking. In this menu, cover the cooked meat loaf tightly with foil to keep it hot while you reheat the vegetables just before serving.

Microwave cooking—it's your lifestyle

Lifestyle means the way you live, doing your own thing. You'll find microwave cooking complements any lifestyle. It's exciting, fast, economical. And it offers something for everyone. For old-time favorites, turn to our family chapter. It's chock-full of all-American choices like burgers, brownies, corn on the cob, barbecued ribs, and homemade ice cream.

For that extra special shindig, we'll show you how to throw a superb dinner party—complete with menu and timetable. Then we know there are times when you're only cooking for one or two—and there's a chapter tailor made for those occasions, too. Or if you need to give your busy schedule a lift, look at our chapter on meals that beat the clock. Here you'll find fast menus for those hectic days when cooking's a chore.

COOKIE CRUMB CRUST

Total cooking time: 1 minute

1							

In bowl, melt 6 tablespoons butter or margarine at **HIGH** for 1 minute. Stir in 1½ cups fine vanilla wafer, chocolate wafer, *or* gingersnap crumbs. Mix well and press into 9-inch pie plate. Chill before filling.

S'MORE PUDDING

Total cooking time: 8 minutes

8							

  2 3¾-ounce packages *regular* vanilla pudding mix
  3 cups milk
  1 cup dairy sour cream
  ¼ cup graham cracker crumbs
      Marshmallows
      Chocolate syrup

In 1½-quart bowl, combine pudding mixes and milk. Cook, uncovered, at **HIGH** for 8 to 9 minutes, stirring 3 times. Cool. Fold in sour cream. Spoon into 6 to 8 sherbet dishes. Sprinkle with graham cracker crumbs. Chill. If desired, top with a marshmallow and drizzle with chocolate syrup. Makes 6 to 8 servings.

QUICK CHOCOLATE PIE

Total cooking time: 6 minutes

6							

  1 9-inch gingersnap cookie crust
  1 3¾-ounce package *regular* chocolate pudding mix
  2 cups milk

        • • •

  1 3¾-ounce package *instant* vanilla pudding mix
  1 cup milk
  1 cup dairy sour cream
  2 tablespoons milk

Prepare gingersnap cookie crust (left). In 4-cup glass measure, combine chocolate pudding mix and the 2 cups milk. Cook, uncovered, at **HIGH** for 6 to 7 minutes, till mixture thickens and bubbles, stirring after 3 minutes, then after each minute. Cover surface with waxed paper or plastic wrap; cool.

Prepare vanilla pudding mix according to package directions, using the 1 cup milk and the 1 cup sour cream in place of the 2 cups milk called for. Stir *1 cup* of vanilla pudding into the cooled chocolate pudding till blended. Spread chocolate mixture evenly in crumb crust. Add 2 tablespoons milk to remaining vanilla pudding, beating till smooth. Spread over chocolate layer. Chill 3 to 4 hours or till filling is set.

HANDY COOK'S GUIDE

Use these color-keyed charts for easy reference:
Reheating foods (white) page 174
Cake mixes (yellow) page 175
Packaged convenience foods (purple) page 176
Frozen convenience foods (orange) page 169
How to cook vegetables (green) page 179
Defrosting meat and more (blue) page 184
Microwave roasting (red) page 187
Blanching vegetables (green) page 168

Beef chuck is cut into ½-inch cubes for Deviled Beef Stew (recipe on page 61)

DEFROSTING

Beef roasts, steaks, stew meat, and ground meat may all be thawed in about 30 minutes or less in your microwave oven. Large beef roasts that have been thawed in the microwave oven may cook more evenly when roasted conventionally. Thawing in the microwave oven is so quick and easy you will want to keep it in mind for those last minute menu changes. For complete directions on thawing in the microwave oven see page 184.

FROZEN BASIC BEEF BASES

For time-saving recipes keep in mind the various frozen beef bases that let you cook today and serve many delicious dishes up to 2 months later. Basic Meatballs on page 161 make a comeback Oriental-style, in stew, sandwiches, and with spaghetti. Basic Ground Beef on page 163 goes into casseroles and sandwiches, while Basic Beef Cubes on page 164 give a fast start to stew, soup, casseroles, and sandwiches.

BASIC MICROWAVE COOKING: BEEF

MEAT LOAF

Shape 1½ pounds ground beef thoroughly mixed with 2 eggs, ¾ cup liquid, ⅔ cup dry bread crumbs, and seasonings into a loaf, ring, or 6 individual loaves. Cook, covered with waxed paper, at **MEDIUM HIGH (7)** giving the dish a half turn once for the following approximate times:

    loaf shape: 20 to 22 minutes
    ring shape: 12 to 14 minutes
    individual loaves: 10 minutes

For more even cooking, rearrange the individual loaves once during the cooking time. If one corner of the loaf starts to overbrown, cover just that portion with a small piece of foil secured with wooden picks. Let the meat loaf stand 5 to 10 minutes before serving.

MEATBALLS

Form ground beef mixed with seasonings, egg, liquid, and bread crumbs into 1-inch balls. Place 18 balls in 9-inch pie plate. Cook, uncovered, at **MEDIUM (5)** for 8 minutes, turning meatballs over and rearranging twice.

HAMBURGERS

Shape 1 pound of ground beef into 4 patties about 4 inches in diameter. Place in 8×8×2-inch baking dish. Cook, covered with waxed paper, at **HIGH** for 4 to 5 minutes, giving dish half turn once. Or use ½ pound of ground beef, shape into 2 patties and cook, covered, at **HIGH** for 2½ to 3 minutes, giving dish a half turn once. See page 160 for more burger ideas.

BROWNING GROUND BEEF

It's handy to brown ground beef with chopped onion, green pepper, or other vegetables for use in sandwiches, chili, and casseroles. In large bowl, combine 2 pounds ground beef and 2½ cups of chopped vegetables. Cook, uncovered, at **HIGH** for 9 minutes, stirring 4 times. Drain off excess fat and continue with your favorite recipe. Or cook 1 pound ground beef and ½ cup chopped vegetables at **HIGH** for 5 minutes, stirring 3 times.

LEFTOVER GROUND BEEF

Create tasty dishes from leftover ground beef—see the ideas in the tip box on page 57.

CHILI

Crumble 1 pound ground beef into 2-quart casserole. Add chopped onion and green pepper. Cook at **HIGH** for 5 minutes, stirring 3 times. Drain off excess fat. Add one 16-ounce can kidney beans, drained, one 8-ounce can tomato sauce, and one 16-ounce can tomatoes, cut up. Season with salt, oregano, basil, chili powder, and bay leaf to taste. Cook, covered, at **MEDIUM HIGH (7)** for 15 minutes.

MEAT SAUCE FOR SPAGHETTI

Crumble 1 pound ground beef into 3-quart casserole. Add chopped onion and green pepper. Cook at **HIGH** for 5 minutes, stirring 3 times. Drain off excess fat. Stir in two 20-ounce jars Italian cooking sauce, 1 clove garlic, minced, 1 tablespoon sugar, and ½ teaspoon chili powder. Cook, covered, at **MEDIUM HIGH (7)** for 12 to 15 minutes.

BEEF STEW

For even cooking, cut meat into uniform ½-inch cubes. This means cutting the stew meat into much smaller pieces than for conventional cooking. In 3-quart casserole, combine 2 pounds stew meat, 1¾ cups liquid, and seasonings. Add thinly sliced carrots and onions—large pieces may not cook evenly. Cook, covered, at **MEDIUM (5)** for 1¼ to 1½ hours or till meat is tender. The meat may still have a slightly "bouncy" texture—it will not "fall apart" as it would in conventional cooking.

BEEF CHUCK (POT) ROAST

Pot roasts seem more tender if they are browned first in hot oil on top of range. However, if time is short you can eliminate this step. Add ½ cup water, broth, or wine to a 4-pound chuck roast. Cover with waxed paper and cook at **MEDIUM (5)** for 1¼ to 1½ hours, giving baking dish a half turn once. If part of the roast starts to overbrown, cover that area with a small piece of foil secured with wooden picks. The meat may have the same "chewy-tender" texture when cooked as described for the beef stew above.

ROLLED RUMP ROAST

Brown 2-pound boneless rump roast in hot oil on top of range. Or if time is short, eliminate browning. Place in 3-quart casserole with ½ cup water, broth, or wine. Cook, covered, at **MEDIUM (5)** for 1½ hours, turning roast over once. Roast may have the same "chewy-tender" texture when cooked as described for the stew above.

CORNED BEEF BRISKET

Place 3-pound corned beef brisket in 4-quart casserole. Add water to cover (about 7 cups). Cover with waxed paper. Cook at **MEDIUM (5)** for 1½ hours or till tender, turning brisket over once. Slice meat across the grain.

BEEF RIB ROASTS

If you need to cook a roast in a hurry, refer to the roasting instructions on page 187. Large tender cuts of beef such as rib roasts may give inconsistent results with microwave cooking. Generally it is better to cook rib roasts in a conventional oven.

STIR-FRY BEEF STRIPS

Cut 1 pound boneless beef sirloin steak into strips ¼ inch wide and 2 inches long (partially frozen meat is easier to cut). Allow meat to thaw completely. Melt 2 tablespoons butter or margarine in 8×8×2-inch baking dish at **HIGH** for 30 seconds. Add meat and seasonings. Cook, uncovered, at **HIGH** for 6 minutes or till meat is desired doneness, stirring 3 times.

STEAKS

For best results, cook steaks according to the directions for the Meal Browner browning dish.

REHEATING BEEF

To reheat sliced beef roast, hamburgers, casseroles, chili, spaghetti sauce, or stew see the reheating chart on page 174.

Slices of canned ham for Burgundy-berried Ham (recipe on page 146) heat more evenly than a whole ham.

DEFROSTING
Pork roasts, chops, and ribs can be thawed in about 30 minutes or less in your microwave oven. Roasts that are thawed in the microwave oven may cook more evenly in the conventional oven. For complete thawing instructions, see the chart on page 185.

REHEATING
To reheat roasts and chops see page 174.

LEFTOVER HAM
Here are some great ways to use up ham: Ham-vegetable Bake (recipe on page 61), Jiffy Cassoulet (recipe on page 60), Barbecued Ham (recipe on page 123), Tijuana Chef's Bowl (recipe on page 145), and Frozen Cheesy Ham Casseroles (recipe on page 147).

VERSATILE FROZEN PORK BASE
See a wide variety of recipes on page 159.

BASIC MICROWAVE COOKING: PORK

THICK HAM SLICE
Place 2-pound fully cooked ham slice (1 inch thick) in baking dish. Cover with waxed paper. Cook at **MEDIUM HIGH (7)** for 7 minutes. Turn ham slice over. Pour on desired glaze. Cook, covered, at **MEDIUM HIGH (7)** for 7 minutes or till hot.

CANNED HAM AND BONELESS FORMED HAM
Canned ham will heat more evenly if cut into ¼-inch slices. Place slices from a 3-pound ham in baking dish. Pour on desired glaze. Cook, covered with waxed paper, at **MEDIUM HIGH (7)** for 12 minutes or till heated through, giving dish a half turn once. To cook a whole 3- to 5-pound canned ham, the meat must be tied securely to help prevent the different muscles from separating during heating. Consequently this ham is often less attractive than ham heated conventionally. If quick cooking is necessary, follow the directions on page 188.

HAM LOAF
Thoroughly combine ¾ pound ground cooked ham, ½ pound ground fresh pork, 1 egg, ¾ cup soft bread crumbs, ¼ cup milk, and seasonings. Shape into a 6-inch ring in 8×8×2-inch baking dish. Cook, covered with waxed paper, at **HIGH** for 10 to 13 minutes or till done, giving dish a half turn once.

HAM KABOBS
Cut ¾ pound fully cooked ham in 1-inch cubes. Alternate ham, pineapple chunks, and canned sweet potato pieces on 4 bamboo skewers. Brush with desired glaze. Cook, uncovered, at **MEDIUM HIGH (7)** for 6 minutes, turning skewers over and brushing with glaze once.

HAM BONE SOUP
In 3-quart casserole, combine a meaty ham bone with 5 cups liquid and chopped onion, celery, green pepper, and one 10-ounce package of frozen mixed vegetables. Add seasonings. Cook, covered, at **HIGH** for 15 minutes or till boiling. Cook, covered, at **MEDIUM (5)** for 35 minutes or till tender. Cut meat from bone and return to soup.

SMOKED PORK CHOPS
Spread 4 smoked pork chops (1 pound) with prepared mustard, brown sugar, and catsup. Cook, covered, at **MEDIUM HIGH (7)** for 10 minutes or till hot.

CANADIAN-STYLE BACON
Cook ¼- or ⅛-inch thick slices of Canadian-style bacon, loosely covered with waxed paper, at **HIGH** according to the time in chart, giving dish a half turn once.

¼-inch-thick slices: number of slices	minutes at **HIGH**	⅛-inch-thick slices: number of slices	minutes at **HIGH**
2	1½	2	½
4	2½	4	1
6	3	6	1½
8	4	8	2

BACON
Arrange up to 4 slices bacon on paper towel on paper plate. Top with a paper towel. Cook to desired crispness at **HIGH** for approximately 1 minute per slice. To cook more than 4 slices, see page 48. Cooking times will vary depending on thickness of bacon and the brand.

HOT DOGS
Place hot dogs in buns and wrap each sandwich separately in a paper napkin. Heat at **HIGH** for time in chart.

Number of hot dogs	Time at **HIGH**
1	30 seconds
2	50 seconds
3	1 minute 20 seconds
4	1 minute 30 seconds
5	1 minute 50 seconds
6	2 minutes

SAUSAGE
Although sausage may be cooked in the microwave oven, it remains pale in appearance. For best results, cook brown and serve sausage links or sausage patties according to the instructions for the Meal Browner browning dish.

VIENNA SAUSAGES
Place sausages from one 5-ounce can on paper plate. Cook, uncovered, at **MEDIUM HIGH (7)** for 45 seconds or till sausages are hot.

LUNCHEON MEAT
Slice one 12-ounce can luncheon meat. Place in small baking dish. Cook, covered, at **HIGH** for 3 to 5 minutes.

PORK CHOPS
Place 6 pork chops (about 2 pounds) in baking dish. Season and top with desired sauce. Cook, covered, at **MEDIUM HIGH (7)** for 30 minutes or till tender, rearranging chops once for more even cooking.

PORK STEW
Cut 1 pound boneless pork into *½-inch cubes*—small cubes are necessary for even cooking. In 3-quart casserole, combine pork, 2 cups liquid, seasonings, and thinly sliced carrots and potatoes. Cook, covered, at **HIGH** for 10 to 15 minutes or till boiling. Cook, covered, at **MEDIUM (5)** for 30 to 45 minutes or till tender.

PORK ROASTS
Bone-in and boneless pork loin roasts are quite successfully cooked in the microwave oven—see page 187.

PORK RIBS
Cut 4 pounds loin back ribs in serving size pieces. Arrange ribs in baking dish. Cook, covered, at **MEDIUM HIGH (7)** for 20 minutes, rearranging ribs once. Drain. Spoon barbecue sauce over ribs. Cook, uncovered, at **MEDIUM HIGH (7)** for 25 minutes or till done, rearranging ribs and spooning sauce over once.

Stir the cooked outside edges of Down on the Farm Breakfast (recipe on page 47) toward the uncooked center.

SCRAMBLED EGGS

Use a cereal bowl or 10-ounce custard cup to scramble 1 or 2 eggs; for 4 eggs, use a 1-quart bowl. Combine eggs, milk, and salt and pepper to taste; beat with fork. Add butter or margarine. Cook, uncovered, at **MEDIUM HIGH (7)** according to time in chart or till done to your liking. Stir the cooked egg at the edges toward the uncooked egg in the center of the dish at equal intervals during cooking. For fast fix-ups, see the tip box on page 124.

number of eggs	milk	butter	minutes at MEDIUM HIGH (7)	stir
1	1 tbsp.	1 tsp.	¾ to 1¼	once
2	2 tbsp.	2 tsp.	1¾ to 2¼	once
4	¼ cup	4 tsp.	3 to 3½	twice
6	⅓ cup	2 tbsp.	4½ to 5½	twice

BASIC MICROWAVE COOKING: FISH AND EGGS

HARD COOKED OR SOFT COOKED EGGS
Do not cook eggs in the shell in the microwave oven because they may burst. Slice whole eggs before reheating to avoid a steam build up and possible bursting of the egg.

POACHED EGGS
To poach eggs see the instructions on page 48.

EGG SUBSTITUTE
To cook egg substitute see the instructions on page 48.

FRIED EGGS
To fry eggs in the microwave oven follow the instructions included with your browning dish.

DEFROSTING FISH
To thaw fish see the directions on page 186.

BREADED FISH
For best results, follow the directions included with your browning dish.

BAKED SMALL WHOLE FISH
Place 1½-pound pan dressed whole fish in melted butter in baking dish. Cook, covered, at **MEDIUM HIGH (7)** for 8 minutes, giving dish half turn once. Turn fish over. Cook, covered, at **MEDIUM HIGH (7)** for 8 minutes or till fish flakes with a fork, giving dish half turn once.

FISH FILLETS
Place 1 pound fillets with 1 cup desired sauce in baking dish. Cook, covered, at **HIGH** for 6 minutes or till fish flakes easily with a fork. Cook 2 pounds fillets with 1½ cups sauce, covered, at **HIGH** for 10 minutes. For basic fish fix-ups, see the tip box on page 69.

POACHED SALMON STEAKS
Place 4 salmon steaks (about 1 pound 6 ounces) in shallow baking dish with 1 cup water. Cook, covered, at **MEDIUM HIGH (7)** for 8 minutes or till fish flakes easily.

SALMON LOAF OR PATTIES
Combine one 16-ounce can salmon, drained and flaked, with ¼ cup milk, 2 beaten eggs, 1½ cups soft bread crumbs, and desired seasonings. Shape into 7½×4-inch loaf. Place in 8×8×2-inch baking dish. Cook, covered, at **MEDIUM HIGH (7)** for 10 minutes or till center is set. Or shape mixture into 4 patties. Sprinkle with yellow cornmeal. Coat patties with melted butter in baking dish. Cook, covered, at **HIGH** for 4 minutes. Turn and cook, covered, at **HIGH** for 3 minutes or till set.

SCALLOPS
Place 1 pound scallops in baking dish, cutting up any large pieces. Add a butter sauce and season. Cook, covered, at **HIGH** for 4 minutes or till tender.

LOBSTER TAILS
Split two 8-ounce lobster tails through the top shell, cutting to but not through the softer undershell. Spread tails open so meat is on top. Place in baking dish. Cook, covered, at **MEDIUM HIGH (7)** for 11 minutes, giving dish a quarter turn every 3 minutes and brushing with seasoned butter sauce.

BASIC MICROWAVE COOKING: VEAL AND LAMB

LAMB STEW
Cut 2 pounds boneless lamb in *½-inch cubes*—small cubes are necessary for even cooking. In 3-quart casserole, combine lamb, 2 cups liquid, seasonings, and cubed vegetables. Cook, covered, at **MEDIUM (5)** for 30 to 45 minutes or till tender, stirring twice.

LAMB SHANKS
In 4-quart casserole, combine 6 lamb shanks, halved crosswise (about 4 pounds), 1¼ cups liquid, and seasonings. Cook, covered, at **HIGH** for 5 minutes. Cook, covered, at **MEDIUM (5)** for 1 hour or till tender.

LAMB SHOULDER CHOPS
Slash fat edge of 2 chops at 1-inch intervals. Place in baking dish with 1 cup liquid and seasonings. Cook, covered, at **MEDIUM (5)** for 20 to 22 minutes, turning chops over after 10 minutes. Or cook 1 chop with ½ cup liquid, covered, at **MEDIUM (5)** for 10 minutes, turning over after 5 minutes cooking time.

LEG OF LAMB
Leg of lamb may be cooked in the microwave oven with quite consistent results—see page 187.

LAMB LOIN CHOPS
For best results cook loin lamb chops according to the directions for the Meal Browner browning dish.

VEAL STEW
Cut 8 ounces boneless veal in *½-inch cubes*—small cubes are necessary for even cooking. In 2-quart casserole, combine veal, 1½ cups liquid, seasonings, and cubed vegetables. Cook, covered, at **MEDIUM HIGH (7)** for 15 to 20 minutes or till tender.

VEAL STEAK
Pound 2 veal steaks (about 10 ounces) to 6×5-inch pieces. Dip in beaten egg, then in seasoned dry bread crumbs. Melt 2 tablespoons butter or margarine in 8×8×2-inch baking dish at **HIGH** for 30 seconds. Add veal. Cook, uncovered, at **HIGH** for 4 minutes or till veal is tender, turning after 3 minutes.

RABBIT
Arrange one 2- to 2½-pound dressed rabbit, cut up, in baking dish. Add 1 cup liquid and seasonings. Cook, covered, at **MEDIUM HIGH (7)** for 25 to 30 minutes or till rabbit is tender.

When making Indian Chicken (recipe on page 63) arrange the meaty portion toward the outside of the dish

DEFROSTING POULTRY
Whole chicken, chicken pieces, duckling, Cornish hens, turkey roasts, and whole turkeys may all be thawed in the microwave oven—see page 185. Large whole poultry items such as turkey may cook more evenly in a conventional oven after thawing in the microwave oven.

REHEATING
For reheating directions see page 174.

LEFTOVER CHICKEN AND TURKEY
Save leftover morsels to make Tijuana Chef's Bowl (recipe on page 145), Saucy Chicken Dinner (recipe on page 147), plus Creamy Chicken-ghetti Bake, Sweet-sour Turkey, Hearty Turkey Chowder, Turkey Divan, and Chippy Chicken Casserole (all recipes on pages 64 and 65).

FROZEN CHICKEN BASE
For recipes using handy Chicken Base see page 165.

BASIC MICROWAVE COOKING: POULTRY

CHICKEN PIECES
Place chicken pieces from one 2½-pound broiler-fryer with meaty side to outside of 12×7½×2-inch baking dish. Spoon sauce over as desired. Cover with waxed paper and cook at **MEDIUM HIGH (7)** for 25 minutes or till tender, rearranging pieces once.

CHICKEN BREASTS
Bone, skin, and halve 2 medium chicken breasts lengthwise. Place in 10×6×1½-inch baking dish with sauce as desired. Cook, covered with waxed paper, at **MEDIUM HIGH (7)** for 20 minutes or till tender, giving dish a half turn once. Or roll 6 halved chicken breasts up jelly-roll style with seasonings. Add sauce. Cook, covered, in 12×7½×2-inch baking dish at **MEDIUM HIGH (7)** for 20 minutes or till done, rearranging rolls and giving dish a half turn once.

CHICKEN WINGS OR DRUMSTICKS
Place 12 chicken wings or drumsticks (2½ pounds) tips down in 12×7½×2-inch baking dish. Spoon on sauce as desired. Cook, covered with waxed paper, at **MEDIUM HIGH (7)** for 30 minutes or till tender, rearranging pieces once.

CHICKEN WITH SEASONED COATING MIX
Shake and coat pieces from one 2½-pound broiler-fryer according to directions on coating mix package. Arrange in baking dish. Cook, covered loosely with waxed paper, at **MEDIUM HIGH (7)** for 20 to 25 minutes.

FRIED CHICKEN
While it is not possible to deep fry chicken in the microwave oven, using a browning dish to cook chicken will give a crisper coating. Use the directions included with your browning dish.

ROAST CHICKEN
If you plan to cube the chicken and not serve it as a roast, you can save time by using the all microwave cooking method. A better way to cook whole chickens, when appearance is important, is with a combination microwave and conventional cooking method. Both methods are given on pages 188 and 189.

CHICKEN LIVERS
Cut 10 chicken livers (about 8 ounces) in half. Melt 2 tablespoons butter or margarine in 10×6×1½-inch baking dish at **HIGH** for 30 seconds. Coat livers with butter. Cook, uncovered, at **MEDIUM (5)** for 6 minutes or till done, turning and rearranging once.

CREAMED CHICKEN
In 1½-quart casserole, melt 4 tablespoons butter or margarine at **HIGH** for 45 seconds. Blend in ⅓ cup all-purpose flour and ½ teaspoon salt. Stir in 1 cup chicken broth and 1 cup milk. Cook, uncovered, at **HIGH** for 1 minute. Stir. Cook at **HIGH** for 4 minutes, stirring after each minute or till mixture thickens and bubbles. Stir in 2 cups cubed cooked chicken, one 3-ounce can sliced mushrooms, drained, and ¼ cup chopped pimiento. Cook, covered, at **HIGH** 2 minutes or till heated through.

ROAST TURKEY
Turkeys may be cooked using an all microwave method if you need to save time or are going to use cubed turkey meat. A better way to cook turkeys, when appearance is important, is with a combination microwave and conventional method. The appearance of the all microwave turkey is not as attractive and the bird usually will be unevenly cooked. Both methods of cooking turkeys are given on pages 189 and 190.

FROZEN TURKEY BREAST
Thaw a 4-pound frozen turkey breast according to the chart on page 186. Place, breast down, in 8×8×2-inch baking dish. Cook, uncovered, at **HIGH** for 30 minutes, turning dish twice. Turn breast up; cook at **MEDIUM (5)** for 30 to 35 minutes or till done.

FROZEN TURKEY ROAST
Remove metal closure from end of 3-pound package of turkey roast. Leave roast in plastic wrapping (or remove from foil pan). Place in 12×7½×2-inch baking dish. Cook, uncovered, at **MEDIUM LOW (3)** for 15 minutes. Turn turkey roast over and cook, uncovered, at **MEDIUM LOW (3)** for 15 minutes more. Let stand 10 minutes to complete thawing. To cook, place thawed roast, skin side up, on microwave roasting rack or inverted saucers in 12×7½×2-inch baking dish. Cook, uncovered, at **HIGH** for 36 to 38 minutes or till done (till meat thermometer registers 180° F—do not use a conventional meat thermometer in the microwave oven or a microwave meat thermometer in a conventional oven), giving dish a half turn once. Let stand 15 minutes before serving.

FROZEN TURKEY BREAST FILLETS WITH CHEESE
Unwrap two (5 ounces each) frozen turkey breast fillets with cheese. Place in 1½-quart casserole. In bowl, combine one 10¾-ounce can condensed cream of mushroom soup and ⅓ cup wine or water. Stir in one 3-ounce can sliced mushrooms, drained. Pour sauce over turkey. Cook, covered, at **MEDIUM (5)** for 40 minutes or till tender, giving dish a half turn once.

ROAST CORNISH HENS
Cornish hens have a small compact shape and they cook quite successfully in the microwave oven. For complete roasting instructions see page 189.

ROAST DOMESTIC DUCKLING
Duckling has a bonier structure than most poultry and seems to cook quite evenly in the microwave oven. For complete roasting instructions see page 189.

PHEASANT
It's best to cook pheasant pieces with a sauce to prevent drying out during cooking. Place one 3-pound pheasant, cut up, in 13×9×2-inch baking dish. Pour 1½ cups desired sauce over pheasant (a soup-based sauce is easy). Cook, covered with waxed paper, at **MEDIUM (5)** for 30 minutes. Rearrange pieces and spoon sauce over. Cook, covered, at **MEDIUM HIGH (7)** for 20 minutes or till pheasant is tender. Pass pan juices with pheasant.

Fresh artichokes and corn on the cob are wrapped in waxed paper for cooking.

FRESH VEGETABLES

The flavor and texture of fresh vegetables cooked in the microwave oven is superb! Give fresh artichokes and corn on the cob a quick rinse in cold water, then wrap in waxed paper to cook—no pans to clean. Other fresh vegetables can be cooked at **HIGH** in covered casseroles—heat-proof serving dishes are ideal. Complete cooking instructions for fresh vegetables start on page 179. To blanch vegetables for freezing see page 168.

FROZEN VEGETABLES

To cook frozen vegetables in cooking pouches, simply cut a couple of slits in the top side of the pouch to let the steam escape during cooking. Other frozen vegetables can be cooked right in the carton. Just loosen the wrapping and cook as is. (Remove foil seasoning packets to prevent arcing.) Or cook in a covered casserole. Cooking times for frozen vegetables start on page 179. For frozen vegetables with sauce cubes or casseroles see page 170.

BASIC MICROWAVE COOKING: VEGETABLES & SALADS

CANNED VEGETABLES
To heat canned vegetables, pour undrained vegetables from can into bowl. Cook, covered with waxed paper, at **HIGH.** Heat an 8-ounce can for 2 minutes, 12-ounce can for 2½ to 3 minutes, and a 16-ounce can 3½ minutes, stirring once during the cooking time.

VEGETABLE SAUCES
Dress up plain vegetables with Easy Cream Cheese Sauce (recipe on page 72), Parsley Butter Topper (recipe on page 73), Almond Cheese Vegetable Sauce (recipe on page 149), and White Sauce with variations (recipe on page 37). Or use easy sauce mixes—see tip box on page 151.

VEGETABLE RELISHES
Corn relish, cranberry sauce, and sauerkraut relish are just three of the relishes on page 73.

BAKED POTATOES
In just 20 minutes at **HIGH,** 8 baked potatoes are ready to serve. See page 182 for cooking times for from 1 to 8 potatoes. For a special treat, serve one of the baked potato toppers from the tip box on page 113.

MASHED POTATOES
In 1½-quart casserole, combine 4 cups peeled cubed potatoes, ⅛ teaspoon salt, and water to cover. Cook, covered, at **HIGH** for 12 to 14 minutes or till tender; drain. Mash with butter or margarine and a little milk. Season with salt and pepper to taste.

INSTANT MASHED POTATOES
To make instant mashed potatoes see page 177.

SCALLOPED POTATOES
Classic scalloped potatoes layered with flour, butter, and milk do not work well in the microwave. Instead you'll enjoy serving Creamy Potato Bake on page 72. To prepare dry scalloped potatoes mix see page 177.

FROZEN FRENCH FRIES
Frozen French fries will not be crisp or brown when cooked in the microwave oven. To heat for use in casseroles, place on paper-towel-lined plate and cook, uncovered, at **HIGH** for 6 minutes for a 16-ounce package.

RICE
Regular rice takes as long to cook in the microwave oven as it does conventionally on top of the range. It hydrates much less evenly in the microwave resulting in some hard kernels. The precooked rice mixes work well—see page 177. To cook frozen rice see page 170.

PASTA
Pasta takes as long to cook in the microwave oven as it does conventionally on top of the range. It tends to hydrate unevenly in the microwave oven thus causing some hard spots. If you wish to try to cook pasta in the microwave oven, use a *very large* casserole and cook for about the same amount of time as on top of range.

MOLDED GELATIN SALAD
For directions and recipe suggestions see page 15.

WILTED LETTUCE SALAD
Use a heat-proof salad bowl to cook bacon, make sauce, and toss the salad—see the recipe on page 63.

BASIC MICROWAVE COOKING: BEVERAGES, SOUPS, AND SAUCES

HOT DRINKS INSTANTLY
Glass measuring cups are handy containers to heat water for hot drinks. One cup of water will boil at **HIGH** in about 2½ minutes, 2 cups in 4 minutes. Or heat the water right in heat-proof mugs. As a rule of thumb, figure on about 1 minute per mug at **HIGH.** After heating the water, add instant coffee, tea, or other hot drink mix.

COCOA
For easy ways to make cocoa see the tip box on page 48.

FANCY COFFEES AND BEVERAGES
The tip box on page 99 has delicious coffee fix-ups. See pages 99 to 101 for tasty hot drink recipes.

CANNED AND PACKAGED SOUPS
Canned and packaged soups are easy to make right in heat-proof mugs or glass measuring cups. See the tip box on page 53. Also try the Souper Vegetable Fix-ups featuring frozen vegetables and canned soups on page 52.

HOMEMADE SOUPS
Large quantities of homemade soups are best cooked conventionally. However, for a small amount of soup the microwave is ideal—see the tip box on page 129 for making "spontaneous soups".

SAUCE MIXES
The envelopes of dry sauce mixes are ideal to make in the microwave oven—cook in a glass measuring cup with only an occasional stir. For complete directions see the tip box on page 151.

HOMEMADE SAUCES
Made-from-scratch sauces add a highlight to vegetables, meats, fish, and poultry. See the recipes on page 149.

WHITE SAUCE AND VARIATIONS
Whether you make plain white sauce or a variation, there are two ways to make it in the microwave—from scratch and with a handy mix. See page 37 for details.

Fill paper bake cups set in custard cups just half full with Corny Bacon Muffin batter (recipe on page 141).

MUFFINS

Muffin batter rises more in the microwave oven—be sure to fill cups only *half full* to prevent overflowing during baking. Muffins cook quickly, will not brown, and may appear moist on surface. Cornmeal, whole wheat, or spice muffins are the most attractive. See page 141 for recipes.

BISCUITS

See directions for the Meal Browner browning dish.

QUICK BREADS

Fill baking dishes only *half full* with batter to allow room for batter to rise. Fruit toppings, brown sugar, and glazes will give a more attractive appearance. Cook at **MEDIUM (5)** until almost done, then a few minutes at **HIGH** to dry the surface. Test for doneness with a wooden pick. The bread may be done even though a few wet spots may still appear on the surface. Remove from microwave oven and cool on rack.

BASIC MICROWAVE COOKING: BREADS AND DESSERTS

YEAST BREADS
It's quick and easy to use the **LOW (1)** setting for rising dough. See page 75 for Bread Rising Basics. Generally, yeast breads baked in the microwave have a more compact texture and a pale appearance—so it's best to bake them in the conventional oven.

WARMING BREADS
Warm breads on a paper towel or a paper napkin to prevent the bottoms from getting soggy. Rolls may be warmed right in the napkin-lined serving basket, providing there is no metal trim. For instructions on warming bread, rolls, sweet rolls, and doughnuts see the chart on page 36. To heat frozen breads see page 171. Do not heat rolls until piping hot—they will become tough and very hard.

PANCAKES
See directions included with your browning dish. Cooked frozen pancakes may be reheated. Cook 3 pancakes on paper towel at **HIGH** 45 seconds.

WAFFLES
Reheat frozen waffles the same as pancakes above.

FRENCH TOAST
See directions included with your browning dish.

POPOVERS
Because of their egg-leavened structure, popovers do not work in the microwave oven.

PASTRY
Pastry is tender and flaky when cooked in the microwave oven, but not brown. Tart shells and crumb crust work well. See page 117 for pastry or tart shells and page 21 for crumb crust.

CAKES AND CUPCAKES
See quick breads on opposite page. Cakes will bake more evenly if a small glass is placed in the center of the baking dish. For complete cake mix directions see page 175. For cupcakes, see the tip box on page 133.

COOKIES
Bar cookies may be baked successfully in the microwave oven. Most drop cookies are better baked conventionally. Use the microwave oven for simple preparation of many candies and unbaked cookies—see pages 88-91.

FRUIT COMPOTES
Bake 2 cups fruit with ⅓ cup liquid at **HIGH** 4 minutes.

PUDDING
In 4-cup glass measure, combine one 3- to 4-ounce package regular pudding mix and milk as package directs. Cook, uncovered, at **HIGH** for 6 minutes, stirring every 2 minutes, till thickened and bubbly.

BAKING APPLES
In baking dish, bake 4 apples with liquid and spices at **HIGH** for 6 to 10 minutes or till tender.

BASIC MICROWAVE COOKING: APPETIZERS AND SANDWICHES

HOT DIPS
Use a heat-proof bowl to warm your favorite hot dip. Allow about 2½ minutes per cup at **MEDIUM (5)**.

REHEATING APPETIZERS
Make your favorite appetizers ahead of time, then refrigerate on heat-proof serving dishes. At serving time, whisk them into the microwave oven and cook a minute or two at **MEDIUM HIGH (7)** till hot.

STUFFED MUSHROOMS
Use 12 large mushroom caps. Stuff with your favorite filling. Place in 10×6×1½-inch baking dish or heat-proof platter. Cook, covered, at **MEDIUM (5)** for 4 to 6 minutes or till hot.

SEASONED NUTS
In heat-proof serving dish melt 1 tablespoon butter or margarine with desired seasonings at **HIGH** for 30 seconds. Add 8 ounces shelled nuts. Heat at **HIGH** for 7 minutes or till hot, stirring 3 times.

EASY APPETIZER KABOBS
See the quick recipes in the tip box on page 143.

WARMING SANDWICHES
Place sandwich on paper napkin or paper towel in the microwave oven—this prevents the bottom slice of bread from becoming soggy. Heat at **HIGH** for 15 to 20 seconds or till just warm. Keep this in mind especially for melting a slice of cheese on sandwiches. *Do not* heat too long—the bread will get tough and eventually very hard.

GRILLED SANDWICHES
See directions included with your browning dish.

SLOPPY JOES
In 1½-quart casserole, crumble 1 pound ground beef. Add chopped vegetables and seasonings. Cook, uncovered, at **HIGH** for 5 minutes, stirring 3 times. Drain off excess fat. Stir in one 10¾-ounce can condensed tomato soup and dash Worcestershire sauce. Cook, covered, at **HIGH** for 3 minutes or till hot. Serve in hamburger buns.

HOT DOGS PLUS
Heat hot dogs according to the tip box on page 87. Top with warmed canned chili, German potato salad, sauerkraut, or jalapeno bean dip; then pass bowls of shredded cheese, chopped onions, and crushed corn or potato chips.

MICRO TIPS

QUICKIES TO HEAT AND POUR

One container (coffee cup, pitcher, bowl, or measure) is all you need to prepare and serve these foods.

INSTANT COFFEE OR TEA: Fill your coffee cup with 6 to 8 ounces of cool tap water. Heat, uncovered, at **HIGH** for 1½ minutes, till steaming hot. Stir in the coffee powder, instant tea, or tea bag. Steep tea, as usual.

HOT BOUILLON: Bring an uncovered mug of cool tap water to boiling at **HIGH** for 2½ minutes. Stir in instant bouillon granules to dissolve.

ICED TEA FOR A CROWD: Fill a 2-quart serving pitcher (don't use a delicate crystal pitcher) with 3½ cups tap water. Heat, uncovered, at **HIGH** for 7 to 8 minutes, till steaming. Add 8 to 12 tea bags or about 3 tablespoons loose tea in a tea ball. Let stand to steep for 5 minutes. Remove bags or loose tea. Add 1 quart cold water. Serve over ice cubes in tall glasses; pass sugar and lemon wedges. Makes 2 quarts. Keep prepared tea at room temperature to prevent it from clouding.

QUICK MALTED MILK: Fill an 8- to 10-ounce glass tumbler about ¾ full of ice cream, spooned from the carton. Heat, uncovered, at **MEDIUM LOW (3)** for 30 to 40 seconds. Add 3 teaspoons malted milk powder and 3 teaspoons chocolate syrup. Fill glass with milk and stir.

QUICK MILKSHAKE: Same except omit malt powder.

HOT BUTTERED WINE: Pour 6 ounces hearty burgundy into a coffee cup or mug. Heat room temperature wine, uncovered, at **HIGH** for 1 to 1¼ minutes. (Heat refrigerator temperature wine 1½ to 1¾ minutes.) Top with a pat of butter and serve. If you wish, sprinkle the wine before heating with a dash or two of pumpkin pie spice or cinnamon, cloves, and nutmeg.

PANCAKE SYRUP: Pour 1 cup of room temperature syrup into serving pitcher. Warm at **HIGH** for 1½ minutes.

FRUIT-FLAVORED GELATIN: Mix and chill it in just one bowl. First, heat the 1 cup water in a bowl, uncovered, at **HIGH** for 2½ minutes. Stir in the gelatin till dissolved; add 1 cup cold water. Chill.

HOT CHOCOLATE SUNDAES: Remove lid and warm ice cream topping in the jar. Place a 12-ounce jar of room temperature topping in the microwave oven; heat, uncovered, at **HIGH** for 1 minute. Stir and serve it over ice cream. Chill remaining topping; reheat in the microwave, uncovered, for a shorter time to make it pour easily.

BOILING WATER: Use the chart below for bringing cool tap water to boiling. Be sure to choose a container twice the volume of the water to avoid spilling.

Amount Water	Time At **HIGH**
¼ cup	40 seconds
½ cup	1 minute 15 seconds
¾ cup	1 minute 45 seconds
1 cup	2 minutes 30 seconds
1½ cups	3 minutes 30 seconds
2 cups	4 minutes 15 seconds
2½ cups	6 minutes
3 cups	7 minutes 30 seconds

SNACKS IN A SNAP

CHEESE TOPPED CRACKERS: Cut process American cheese slices into 1-inch squares. Place one square on each cracker; arrange on a serving plate. Warm, uncovered, at **HIGH** just till the cheese melts, turning plate once. For 6 crackers, heat 10 to 15 seconds; for 12 crackers, heat 25 to 30 seconds.

NACHOS: Place whole tortilla chips on a serving plate. Top each with a generous ½ teaspoon jalapeno bean dip. Cut process American cheese slices into 1-inch squares; place one atop each and add a bit of green chili pepper if you wish. Cook, uncovered, at **HIGH**, turning plate once. Cook 10 seconds longer if the Nachos are chilled.

Amount	Time At **HIGH**
6 Nachos	25 to 30 seconds
12 Nachos	40 to 45 seconds

CRACKER FIX-UPS: Spread cracker squares generously with butter or margarine. Sprinkle with your choice of seeds or seasonings: caraway on rye crackers; dill, sesame, or poppy seed on saltines. Arrange 12 on a serving plate; heat, uncovered, at **HIGH** for 2 minutes.

DRY ROASTED NUT MIX: In a serving bowl, combine 1 cup *each* dry roasted pecans, peanuts, and cashews; add ⅛ teaspoon celery salt and a dash of garlic powder. Heat, uncovered, at **HIGH** for 2 to 2½ minutes, stirring mixture after about 1 minute. Makes 3 cups.

HOT MIXED NUTS: Place 1 cup of dry roasted mixed nuts or any salted nuts in a serving dish. Heat, uncovered, at **HIGH** for 1 minute 15 seconds.

BAGELS WITH CREAM CHEESE: Split a bagel and place on a serving plate; put a slice or two of cold cream cheese on each half of the bagel. Heat, uncovered, at **HIGH** for 30 seconds. The cream cheese is softened and easier to spread on the bagel, and it's warmed too.

PEPPERONI JERKY: Place about 12 slices presliced pepperoni on a paper plate between 2 sheets of paper toweling. Heat at **MEDIUM (5)** for 50 to 60 seconds. Cool.

FRESHENING STALE SNACK CHIPS: Place about 2 cups snack chips (corn chips, potato chips, or whatever) in a shallow baking dish. Heat, uncovered, at **HIGH** for 1 minute. Let stand 1 to 2 minutes before serving.

MINT FROSTED CUPCAKES: Unwrap a chocolate-covered candy mint patty and place it on an unfrosted baked and cooled cupcake. Heat, uncovered, at **HIGH**. Spread the softened mint around like frosting. For more than 2 cupcakes, place on a paper plate and give a half turn during warming.

Number	Time At **HIGH**
1 cupcake	20 seconds
2 cupcakes	35 seconds
4 cupcakes	55 seconds
6 cupcakes	1 minute 15 seconds

MELTING WORKS LIKE MAGIC

Recipes often call for *melted* chocolate or *softened* butter.

MELTING UNSWEETENED CHOCOLATE: Place a 1-ounce square of chocolate in a small custard cup; heat, uncovered, at **HIGH** for 1¾ minutes.

MELTING SEMISWEET CHOCOLATE PIECES: Place 6 ounces chocolate pieces in a large custard cup. Heat, uncovered, at **HIGH** for 1½ minutes. Stir.

MELTING CARAMELS: Place unwrapped caramels from a 14-ounce package in a deep 1-quart bowl. Warm, uncovered, at **HIGH** for 2½ minutes, stirring often after 1 minute.

CARAMELED APPLES: Insert sticks into 6 apples; dip in hot melted caramel (above) to coat. Place on buttered waxed paper to cool. If desired, sprinkle the paper first with toasted coconut or chopped nuts.

SOFTENING CHEESE SPREAD: Place an 8-ounce room temperature jar of cheese spread in the microwave oven. Heat, uncovered, at **LOW (1)** for 4 to 5 minutes. For a 5-ounce jar, heat, uncovered, at **LOW (1)** for 2 to 3 minutes.

SOFTENING BUTTER: Warm 1 stick of chilled butter, uncovered, at **LOW (1)** for 2 minutes. Warm 3 minutes if frozen.

SOFTENING CREAM CHEESE: Place unwrapped block of cheese in a bowl; heat, uncovered, at **LOW (1)** for 3 to 3½ minutes for 3-ounce size, 4½ to 5 minutes for 8-ounce.

MELTING MARSHMALLOW CREME: Spoon half of a 7-ounce jar marshmallow creme into a small bowl. Heat, uncovered, at **HIGH** for 35 to 40 seconds, stirring to blend.

SOFTENING ICE CREAM: Place 1 quart hard-frozen ice cream in a microwave oven; heat at **LOW (1)** for 1 minute to soften enough to scoop and serve with ease.

MARSHMALLOW-CEREAL SQUARES: In large bowl, melt 4 tablespoons butter or margarine at **HIGH** for 30 to 45 seconds. Add 30 large marshmallows. Warm, uncovered, at **MEDIUM HIGH (7)** for 1 minute. Stir in 5 cups crisp rice cereal, stirring to coat. Press into buttered 13×9×2-inch baking dish; cool and cut in squares.

TOASTING IS A BREEZE

Here's how to toast nuts, seeds, and coconut.

BLANCHING ALMONDS: In 2-cup glass measure, bring 1 cup of water to boiling at **HIGH** for 2½ minutes. Add unblanched nuts; cook, uncovered, at **HIGH** for 30 seconds. Drain and slip the skin from the nuts.

TOASTING COCONUT: Spread ½ cup flaked coconut in a pie plate. Cook, uncovered, at **HIGH** 3 to 4 minutes, till golden, stirring every 30 seconds after 1½ minutes.

TOASTING NUTS: Spread ½ cup nuts in pie plate. Cook, uncovered, at **HIGH** for 6 to 6½ minutes, till golden, stirring after 3 minutes, then after each minute.

TOASTING SESAME SEEDS: Spread ¼ cup seeds in pie plate. Cook, uncovered, at **HIGH** for 3½ to 4½ minutes till golden, stirring after 2 minutes, then after each minute.

MORE MICRO TIPS

HOT BREADS IN A FLASH

Place breads and rolls on a paper napkin on a plate to absorb moisture. For 3 or more items, give plate a half turn once. Overheating will cause breads to toughen.

Food	Amount	Time At **HIGH** From Room Temp.	Time At **HIGH** From Frozen
Bread, loaf	¼	15 seconds	30 seconds
(unsliced)	½	20 seconds	1 minute
	1	30 seconds	2¼ minutes
Bread, slices	2	10 seconds	20 seconds
	4	20 seconds	40 seconds
	6	30 seconds	1 minute
Large rolls or Hamburger buns	2	20 seconds	30 seconds
	4	30 seconds	50 seconds
	6	40 seconds	1¼ minutes
Medium rolls or Hot dog buns	2	20 seconds	25 seconds
	4	30 seconds	35 seconds
	6	40 seconds	45 seconds
Doughnuts	2	15 seconds	35 seconds
	4	25 seconds	1 minute
	6	35 seconds	1½ minutes
Sweet rolls	2	20 seconds	35 seconds
	4	30 seconds	1 minute
	6	40 seconds	1¾ minutes

FREEZER QUICKIES

Stock up on freezer containers that you can put in the microwave oven, as well, because you'll find plenty of ways to pair these two appliances.

COOKIE DOUGH: Next time, double the batch of cookie dough. Bake half the cookies the usual way, then freeze the remaining dough. You'll be able to thaw the frozen dough in a jiffy using your microwave oven.

Timing is likely to differ from recipe to recipe, so use this chocolate-chip-cookie-dough timing as a guide (based on ½ cup shortening, 1 cup flour, and 1 cup semisweet chocolate pieces). Heat frozen dough, uncovered, at **MEDIUM LOW (3)** for 1 minute; let stand a few minutes at room temperature before shaping into cookies to bake.

CAKE BATTER: Leftover cake batter can be frozen if you don't intend to bake it right away. Half the batter from a 2-layer-size mix can be frozen in a 3-cup freezer container. Thaw, uncovered, at **MEDIUM LOW (3)** for 5 minutes. Stir to blend, then bake as desired.

TORTILLAS: Open a 12-ounce package of frozen tortillas; place the opened package on a paper plate. Cook at **MEDIUM LOW (3)** for 4½ to 5 minutes, separating the tortillas after 4 minutes.

TWO CRUST PIES: When fruit is plentiful, prepare and freeze your favorite berry, cherry, apple, or peach pies. Treat the apples and peaches first with some ascorbic acid color keeper to prevent darkening. Prepare the pie as usual but don't slit the top crust. Use a 9-inch glass pie plate; cover with a paper plate. Wrap, seal, and freeze for up to two months.

To bake a frozen pie, unwrap and place the pie in the microwave oven. Cut slits in the top crust to vent. Heat, uncovered, at **HIGH** for 10 minutes to defrost. Then transfer the pie plate to a baking sheet; place in a preheated *conventional* oven at 450°F for 20 minutes.

GROUND BEEF: You can thaw and cook frozen ground beef in the same container for a casserole. One pound of hamburger can be defrosted in a baking dish. Cook, uncovered, at **HIGH** in 5 minutes. Break up meat; cook at **HIGH** 3 to 5 minutes more. Drain before using.

WAFFLES AND FRENCH TOAST: Can be cooked and frozen, too. Stack them with sheets of waxed paper between so they separate easily. To warm 3 small frozen waffles, place on a paper towel; cook at **HIGH** about 45 seconds.

WHITE SAUCE: TWO WAYS

Whether you make white sauce from scratch or from the handy homemade mix, you'll use it often. You can use it ladled over vegetables or as a base for mustard sauce or cheese sauce, as well. The stirring is very important during cooking to prevent lumps from forming.

WHITE SAUCE: In a 2-cup glass measure, melt 2 tablespoons butter or margarine at **HIGH** for 30 seconds. Blend in 2 tablespoons all-purpose flour; stir in 1 cup milk all at once. Cook, uncovered, at **HIGH** for 1 minute. Stir mixture and continue cooking 1½ minutes more at **HIGH**, stirring every 30 seconds. Makes about 1 cup.

HOMEMADE WHITE SAUCE MIX: In a mixing bowl, thoroughly combine 1⅓ cups nonfat dry milk powder, 1 cup all-purpose flour, and 1 teaspoon salt. With a pastry blender, cut in ½ cup butter or margarine till the mixture resembles small peas. Refrigerate this mixture in a tightly covered container and use as needed. Makes enough for 6 cups medium white sauce.

To make 1 cup sauce: In a 2-cup glass measure, combine ½ cup *Homemade White Sauce Mix* and 1 cup cold water. Cook, uncovered, at **HIGH** for 2 to 2¼ minutes, stirring every 30 seconds, till the mixture is thickened and bubbly. Makes 1 cup sauce.

MUSTARD SAUCE: To 1 cup hot white sauce, above, add 1½ to 2 tablespoons prepared mustard. Stir.

CHEDDAR CHEESE SAUCE: To 1 cup hot white sauce, above, add 1 cup shredded sharp natural cheddar cheese. Stir till the cheese melts.

BLUE CHEESE SAUCE: To 1 cup hot white sauce, above, add ¼ cup dairy sour cream and ¼ cup crumbled blue cheese. Stir the mixture till blended.

DOUBLE DUTY GARNISHES

Clever garnishes help make food appealing to the eye as well as disguising the unbrowned look common to foods cooked in a microwave oven.

MEATS can be sprinkled with brown gravy mix or bottled brown-and-season seasoning, but remember to cut down on salt in the recipe as some is contained in the browner. Snipped parsley, chives, and paprika are especially good for chicken and seafood dishes.

DESSERTS can be dressed up with a dash of toasted coconut, coarsely crushed cookies, or graham cracker crumbs. Pastry with a sprinkle of cinnamon sugar looks as tasty as oven-browned crusts.

PLATTER GARNISHES of fresh and canned fruits, or fresh vegetables do wonders to make foods more interesting. Try adding cucumber wheels, lemon twists, or cranberry-filled peaches to the meat platter; or perhaps deviled eggs or skewers with apple and orange wedges.

POTPOURRI

Some shortcuts are just too good to forget—the kind of tips that one good cook tells another. Once you read these, you'll think of several more yourself.

PEELING TOMATOES AND PEACHES is easier than ever. Simply bring a cup of water to boiling in a 2-cup glass measure or bowl, at **HIGH** for 2½ to 3 minutes. Spear the fruit on a fork and submerge it in the hot water, counting to twelve at the same time. Hold the fruit under cold tap water, and peel with ease.

DAY OLD ROLLS: They'll seem fresh as ever when warmed in the microwave. The chart on page 36 is your guide—but be careful not to overheat them or they'll become tough. Brush French bread slices with garlic butter and warm in the microwave for a few seconds—marvelous!

SYRUP SUBSTITUTE: Out of pancake syrup? Heat a pitcher of dark corn syrup instead. Or, prepare imitation maple-flavor-base using package directions.

KEEP-WARM SETTING: You can hold a casserole or batch of soup at serving temperature in the microwave. Use the **LOW (1)** setting for a 1½- to 4-quart casserole or tureen to keep the food warm .

EXTRA SCRAMBLED EGGS: A smart cook scrambles an extra egg or two at breakfast time then refrigerates the leftovers. A few seconds at **MEDIUM HIGH (7)** and the eggs are warmed up to make a hot sandwich for lunch.

ONIONS: A great many recipes start with cooking onions or celery in butter till tender. In the microwave oven, it's so easy to do. Combine the chopped vegetables with the unmelted butter in a casserole and cook, uncovered, at **HIGH** for 2 to 3 minutes. Stir it once about halfway through to coat all vegetables.

LOW CALORIE COOKING: Instead of cooking the vegetables in butter, do them in a tablespoon or two of water. You can cook many foods without fat—fish and chicken are good examples. Or, replace a rich milk-butter-flour sauce with a broth-cornstarch mixture.

BABY FOOD: To warm a baby bottle, remove the nipple and the cover; warm an 8-ounce bottle of milk at **HIGH** for 30 to 60 seconds. Baby food can be warmed in the microwave, too. Spoon the contents from a small jar into a dish. Heat for 30 to 45 seconds at **HIGH**.

WARM COOKIES: Although baking cookies in the microwave isn't always successful, the appliance is great for warming cookies that are already baked. Warm 2 cookies on a napkin, uncovered, at **HIGH** for 25 to 30 seconds; 2 frozen cookies at **HIGH** for 35 to 45 seconds.

SEPARATE COLD BACON: Remove refrigerator-cold bacon from the carton or outer wrap. Place the entire 12 to 16 ounces in the microwave oven at **MEDIUM LOW (3)** for 45 to 60 seconds and the slices will separate easily.

MORE MICRO TIPS

INDOOR-OUTDOOR BARBECUES

Indoor-outdoor barbecues team the speed of microwave cooking with that unbeatable flavor of meat cooked on an outdoor grill. Great idea for chicken, ribs, burgers—see page 146 for details.

FANCY COFFEES

Our exotic international coffees make splashy desserts that are a snap to prepare for guests. Garnish and serve with a flourish. Details on page 99.

CUBED CHICKEN

When a recipe calls for cooked chicken, think of your microwave oven. In twelve minutes or less, a pound of chicken is all cooked. Turn to the tip box on page 64.

QUICK CUPCAKES

Cupcakes make a quick snack or last-minute dessert. You may even want to keep a pitcher of cake mix batter on hand in the refrigerator (it will keep up to 1 week). Swirl tops with canned frosting. See page 133.

SPEEDY COCOA

Whether you prefer cocoa from a mix or from scratch, it's easy to make right in heat-proof mugs—no pans to wash on a busy morning. The kids will have fun watching marshmallows puff up on top, too. See page 48.

FLAMING DESSERTS

Serve a flaming dessert for a real show-stopper. On page 116 you'll find a trio of these dazzling finales— all featuring fresh fruits at their finest.

TASTY OMELETS

Turn everyday scrambled eggs into an omelet with some fancy fillings, easy toppings, and impressive garnishes—great for late-night snacks or early brunch. See page 124.

FROZEN FRUITS

Keep frozen fruits on hand for fast salad and dessert combinations. With the help of a microwave oven, a solid block of frozen fruit is just minutes away from use. See page 82 for details.

FISH FIX-UPS

Make a lowly block of frozen fish into a fast cooking Basic Buttered Fish, then add Sauce Amadine, Sauce Orient, or Sauce Devilish. It's all so easy you'll want to use the recipes on page 69 often.

BURGER BONUS

Let your microwave oven help you make creative use of pesky leftovers. Take extra burgers and bring them back in one of the many innovative ways you'll find on page 57.

NO-FUSS HOT DOGS

Hot dogs are as American as the Fourth of July and baseball—and your microwave oven is the new star. Imagine cooking 6 hot dogs right in the buns in just 2 minutes! Better keep mustard and relish handy—see page 87.

FREEZER TIPS

Your freezer and microwave oven make a rare pair. One dish meals go from freezer to table in about one-fourth the time of conventional-type cooking. This modern convenience opens up a whole new world of menu possibilities—see page 157.

MORE MICRO TIPS

BAKED POTATO TOPPERS

There's no need to think about baked potatoes an hour before serving time or to juggle broiler and oven meals. Your microwave oven makes baked potatoes at a moments notice. For some fancy fix-ups to go atop, see page 113.

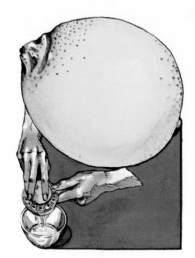

ZESTY BUTTER

You'll want to keep zesty Lemon Pepper Butter on hand in the refrigerator. It's great on steaks, fish, artichokes, or French bread. See the recipe ideas on page 104.

TV DINNERS

Bring back everyday leftovers for a return performance as make-your-own TV dinners. Simply arrange on sturdy partitioned paper plates, then wrap in moisture-vaporproof material and freeze. See our helpful ideas on page 134.

EASY KABOBS

Keep in mind the bite-sized nibbles on page 143 for a speedy appetizer or snack. You can choose from our Zesty Shrimp, Smoky Chokes, Sweet-sour Bites, Irish Kabobs, and Cocktail Franks. All are scrumptious!

SAUCE MIXES

Store packaged sauce and gravy mixes on your emergency shelf—you can make them in easy-to-use glass measuring cups in a matter of minutes. See page 151 for complete details.

HEATING SOUP

It's a dish-saver to warm canned or packaged soup right in heat-proof serving bowls. Or use a large glass measuring cup for easy pouring. All the directions are on page 53. Or if you'd rather make your own soups, see page 129.

HOW TO CONVERT YOUR FAVORITE RECIPES

As your experience with the microwave oven grows, you'll want to try doing some of your own recipes the microwave way. Many conventional recipes—oven and rangetop—can be changed with little effort; some may require a bit more experimentation. Follow our easy 1-2-3 method to convert recipes in your own "test kitchen".

Look in this cookbook for a recipe that's similar to yours. The index lists all recipes by title and by subject, and includes charts, as well.

Use the ingredients called for in your recipe and combine them in the usual way. Cubed meat and chopped vegetables cook more evenly when cut into uniform-size pieces. The liquid may need to be reduced a little because microwaves cook more rapidly with less evaporation. Spices and herbs may taste stronger for the same reason. Soak dehydrated onions before using so they have time to soften. Compare the conventional range or oven setting [high, medium (5), low (1)] with those on the microwave oven; use the microwave recipe settings as a guide.

Compare the cooking utensils in your recipe with those suggested for the microwave oven. Often you can use the same casserole or baking dish. Instead of a metal saucepan, choose an oven-proof glass or ceramic bowl or casserole. Use waxed paper or a casserole lid for a cover. For liquids that may boil, choose a bowl or measure that allows space for the liquid to bubble. Since baked goods rise higher in the microwave oven than when baked conventionally, fill the baking dish for a cake or quick bread just half full. Refrigerate any remaining batter and use it to bake cupcakes (in custard cups).

Adjust the cooking time, using the microwave recipe as a guide. Remember that although a cup of water boils in 2½ to 3 minutes, a half-dozen rolls take only seconds to heat in the microwave. The food's starting temperature, shape, composition, and volume are all factors that vary the cooking time. Reread the ABC's chapter . . . it explains these principles. Recipes in this book are a guide to help you estimate cooking time. Check the food during the estimated cooking time; allow for standing time.

CONVERTING A SAMPLE RECIPE

For example, let's convert a chicken recipe that calls for a 2½- to 3-pound broiler-fryer, cut up. Normally, you might brown the chicken pieces first in some butter, pour on canned tomato sauce, canned mushrooms, and a dash of Italian herbs; cover tightly, and simmer for 35 to 40 minutes, till the chicken is tender.

Step One: Several microwave recipes begin with a cut-up chicken. *Cranberry Barbecued Chicken* and *Ginger Orange Chicken* on page 64 illustrate the basics.

Step Two: Instead of a skillet, use a 12×7½×2-inch baking dish like the microwave recipes. Omit the browning step and arrange the chicken pieces in the baking dish. Combine the ingredients for the sauce—tomatoes, mushrooms, and herbs—and pour over the chicken. Cover the baking dish with waxed paper.

Step Three: Since the chicken in the two microwave recipes cooks 20 to 25 minutes, set your timer for 20 minutes. Cook at **MEDIUM HIGH (7),** as the microwave recipes indicate. After about 15 minutes, check the chicken; rearrange the pieces if those in the corners of the dish are cooking faster than those at the center. Cover and continue cooking for 5 minutes. Check again; remove the pieces that are done and give any remaining pieces another 3 to 5 minutes. Transfer all to a serving platter; pour on the sauce. Or, thicken it using the same method as for *Ginger Orange Chicken.*

UTENSIL CONVERSION

Become familiar with the volume of the baking dishes and casseroles that you use regularly. Knowing how much each holds can help you decide which to use. Allow for stirring room and space for the food to bubble or expand.

The volume may already be imprinted on the bottom of the dish. If not, you can measure the dish by filling it with water, a cup at a time; the total is the volume. Write the amount on masking tape with indelible marker and stick it to the underside of the dish.

Volume of some common baking dishes

Custard cup	6 ounces	¾ cup
8½×4½×2½-inch loaf dish	1⅛ quarts	5½ cups
8×1½-inch round baking dish	1½ quarts	6 cups
10×6×1½-inch baking dish	1½ quarts	6 cups
8×8×2-inch baking dish	2 quarts	8 cups
9×5×3-inch loaf dish	2 quarts	8 cups
12×7½×2-inch baking dish	2 quarts	8 cups
13×9×2-inch baking dish	3 quarts	12 cups

EVERYDAY FAMILY FAVORITES

Look what your microwave oven can cook—ever popular
Tacos and Butterscotch Marble Cake (recipes next page)!
And that's not all. In this chapter, you'll find
recipes for chicken, ribs, burgers, corn on the cob,
and homemade ice cream—traditional Americana cooked
a new-fangled way. Your family never had it so good!

MICRO MENU PLANNER

MAIN DISHES

SNACKS & CANDIES

DESSERTS

SOUPS & SANDWICHES

VEGETABLES/SALADS/SAUCES

BREADS

TACOS

For an extra special treat, pass a bowlful of guacamole to spoon atop these tasty tacos—

Total cooking time: 5 minutes

5							

  1 pound ground beef
  ½ cup chopped onion
  1 clove garlic, minced
  ¾ teaspoon salt
  1 teaspoon chili powder
    Onion rings
      • • •
 12 fried and shaped taco shells
  2 tomatoes, chopped and drained
  3 cups finely shredded lettuce
  2 cups (8 ounces) shredded natural cheddar cheese
    Canned Mexican hot sauce *or* enchilada sauce *or* taco sauce

Crumble beef into 1½-quart casserole; add chopped onion, garlic, salt, and chili powder. Cook, uncovered, at **HIGH** for 5 minutes, stirring three times. Drain off excess fat. Garnish with onion rings. To serve, spoon meat mixture into taco shells; top with tomato, lettuce, and cheese. Pass sauce. Makes 12 tacos, 6 servings.

If desired, meat-filled shells can be heated, uncovered, at **HIGH** for 1 minute. Use a straight-sided dish to keep them upright (13×9×2-inch baking dish for 12 tacos). Then fill with remaining ingredients to serve.

BUTTERSCOTCH MARBLE CAKE

Delicious topped with ice cream and butterscotch sauce—

Total cooking time: 14 minutes 30 seconds

12	2:30						

  1 package 2-layer-size white cake mix (no pudding in the mix)
  1 3¾- or 4-ounce package *instant* butterscotch pudding mix
  1 cup water
  ½ cup cooking oil
  4 eggs
  ½ cup chocolate syrup
    Powdered sugar

In large mixer bowl, combine cake mix, pudding mix, water, and oil. Beat on medium speed of electric mixer 2 minutes, till smooth. Add eggs, beating after each addition. Divide ⅔ of mixture between 2 waxed-paper-lined 9×5×3-inch glass loaf dishes. Mix remaining ⅓ of batter with the chocolate syrup and pour evenly over batter in dishes. Stir to marble. Bake, one at a time, uncovered, at **MEDIUM (5)** for 12 minutes, giving dish quarter turns every 4 minutes, then on **HIGH** for 2½ minutes. Cool 10 minutes; remove from pans. Cool thoroughly on rack. Sprinkle top of cakes lightly with powdered sugar.

Honeyed Fruit and Ham Kabobs

TIMETABLE

1. Make orange juice: If it is frozen, remove top of container. Cook 1 minute at **MEDIUM LOW (3).** Empty into measuring cup. Cook at **HIGH** till thawed (1½ minutes for 6-ounce can, 3 minutes for 12-ounce can), stirring once. Add water and chill before serving.
2. Prepare kabobs; cover to keep warm.
3. Heat sweet rolls.
4. Make Malted Hot Chocolate or cocoa.

MENU
Orange Juice

Honeyed Fruit and Ham Kabobs

Assorted Sweet Rolls

Coffee   Cocoa (page 48)

Malted Hot Chocolate

JOIN THE BETTER BREAKFAST CLUB

HONEYED FRUIT AND HAM KABOBS

Total cooking time: 6 minutes 30 seconds

0:30	3	3						

    1 tablespoon butter or margarine
    1 tablespoon lemon juice
    2 tablespoons honey
      Dash ground cloves
    ¾ pound fully-cooked ham, cut in 1-inch cubes
    4 pineapple slices, halved
    2 medium bananas, quartered crosswise

In a 1-cup glass measure, melt butter at **HIGH** for 30 to 40 seconds. Stir in lemon juice, honey, and cloves. Alternate ham, pineapple, and banana on four 8½-inch bamboo skewers. Place in 12×7½×2-inch baking dish. Brush with honey sauce. Heat, uncovered, at **MEDIUM HIGH (7)** for 3 minutes. Turn skewers over; brush with remaining honey sauce. Give dish a half turn and cook at **MEDIUM HIGH (7)** for 3 minutes or till hot. Makes 4 servings.

SHORTCUT BANANA BREAD

Total cooking time: 14 minutes

12	2							

    2 cups packaged biscuit mix
    ½ cup packed brown sugar
    3 tablespoons all-purpose flour
    2 teaspoons instant coffee powder or crystals
    ¼ cup milk
    1 beaten egg
    ⅔ cup mashed banana (1 large)
    ½ cup snipped dates
    ⅓ cup chopped walnuts
      Powdered sugar

In bowl, combine biscuit mix, brown sugar, and flour. Dissolve coffee powder in milk; combine with egg and banana. Add all at once to dry ingredients. Stir till blended. Stir in dates and nuts. Turn into 9×5×3-inch loaf dish that has been greased and the bottom lined with waxed paper. Cook, uncovered, at **MEDIUM (5)** for 12 minutes, giving dish half turn after 6 minutes. Increase to **HIGH** and cook 2 minutes more, or till pick comes out clean. Let stand 10 minutes; remove from dish to cool completely. Sprinkle with powdered sugar.

WARMING SWEET ROLLS

Place rolls or doughnuts on paper napkin and heat at **HIGH** according to time in chart.

	number to be heated		
	2	4	6
frozen rolls	35 sec.	1 min.	1 min. 45 sec.
thawed rolls	20 sec.	30 sec.	40 sec.
frozen doughnuts	35 sec.	1 min.	1 min. 30 sec.
thawed doughnuts	15 sec.	25 sec.	35 sec.

DOWN ON THE FARM BREAKFAST

Total cooking time: 13 minutes 30 seconds

4	4	5:30						

    1 9-ounce carton frozen French fried potatoes
    ¼ cup chopped green pepper
    ¼ cup chopped onion
    2 tablespoons cooking oil
    1½ cups cubed cooked ham
    4 beaten eggs
    ¼ cup milk

Heat frozen potatoes in original package at **HIGH** for 4 to 5 minutes to thaw; chop potatoes. In 8-inch round baking dish, combine green pepper, onion, and oil. Cook, uncovered, at **MEDIUM HIGH (7)** for 4 minutes. Stir in potatoes and ham. Combine eggs, milk, and dash salt; pour over ham mixture. Cook, uncovered, at **MEDIUM HIGH (7)** for 5½ minutes, stirring every 2 minutes, moving set portion of eggs from outside to center. Let stand a few minutes before serving. Makes 4 servings.

STICKY BUN RING

Total cooking time: 5 minutes 15 seconds

0:45	4:30							

    1 tablespoon butter or margarine
    ⅓ cup caramel ice cream topping
    3 tablespoons chopped pecans
    1½ cups packaged biscuit mix
    ½ cup milk
    2 teaspoons sugar
    ⅛ teaspoon ground cinnamon

Place butter in 8-inch round baking dish. Cook, uncovered, at **HIGH** for 45 seconds. Stir in caramel topping and nuts. Push mixture away from center of dish and set a custard cup, right side up, in center. Combine biscuit mix and milk, stirring just till blended. Drop in 16 teaspoonfuls onto caramel mixture. Combine sugar and cinnamon; sprinkle atop. Bake, uncovered, at **HIGH** for 4½ minutes, till no longer doughy at center, giving dish half turn once. Let stand 5 minutes in dish; invert. Serve warm.

MALTED HOT CHOCOLATE

Total cooking time: 5 minutes

5								

    ¾ cup milk
    1 tablespoon instant natural malted milk powder
    1 pint chocolate ice cream
      Marshmallow creme

In 4-cup glass measure, combine milk and malted milk powder; mix well. Add ice cream in spoonfuls. Cook, uncovered, at **HIGH** for 5 to 6 minutes or till hot. Ladle into mugs; top with marshmallow creme. Makes 4 servings.

FLUFFY SCRAMBLED EGGS

To cook 1 or 2 eggs, use a cereal bowl or 10-ounce custard cup. To cook 4 to 6 eggs, use a 1-quart bowl. In bowl, combine eggs, milk, and salt and pepper to taste; beat with fork. Add butter or margarine. Cook, uncovered, at **MEDIUM HIGH (7)** according to time in chart, stirring as indicated at equal intervals. Stir before serving.

number of eggs	milk	butter	minutes at MEDIUM HIGH (7)	stir
1	1 tbsp.	1 tsp.	¾ to 1¼	once
2	2 tbsp.	2 tsp.	1¾ to 2¼	once
4	¼ cup	4 tsp.	3 to 3½	twice
6	⅓ cup	2 tbsp.	4½ to 5½	twice

POACHED EGGS

Combine 1 cup hot water and ½ teaspoon vinegar in a 1-quart casserole. Cook, uncovered, at **HIGH** for 2 to 3 minutes, till boiling. Gently break eggs into water; push to center of dish. Cover with waxed paper and cook at **HIGH**.

number of eggs	minutes at HIGH	let stand (minutes)
1	1	1½ to 2
2	1¼	2
4	2	2

EGG SUBSTITUTE

Thaw using directions on page 169. Shake well and measure amount desired. Add ½ teaspoon oil or margarine for each "egg," if desired. Cook in 10-ounce custard cup, uncovered, at **MEDIUM HIGH (7)**, stirring at equal intervals. Season. Let stand a few seconds before serving.

number of egg substitutes	minutes at MEDIUM HIGH (7)	stir
1	1	twice
2	1½	twice

CANADIAN-STYLE BACON

Place ¼- or ⅛-inch thick slices of Canadian-style bacon on dinner plate, platter, or in baking dish. Cover loosely with waxed paper and cook at **HIGH** till hot, rotating dish once.

¼-inch-thick slices: number of slices	minutes at HIGH	⅛-inch-thick slices: number of slices	minutes at HIGH
2	1½	2	½
4	2½	4	1
6	3	6	1½
8	4	8	2

BACON

Place 1 or 2 pieces of paper toweling in shallow baking dish. Arrange up to 4 slices of bacon on toweling; cover with a single layer of toweling to prevent spattering. Cook to desired crispness at **HIGH** for time in chart. (Up to 4 slices can be cooked on a paper plate with paper toweling.) For bacon with drippings: Omit toweling under the bacon; cover with single towel.

For 6 to 8 slices, place on microwave roasting rack in baking dish.

number of slices	minutes at HIGH
2	2 to 2¼
4	4 to 4¼
6	5½ to 5¾
8	6½ to 7

TEST KITCHEN TIPS

Top cocoa with a marshmallow during the last 15 to 30 seconds of heating time. Watch it puff and soften as heating continues.

Presweetened Cocoa Mix: For each serving, pour 6 to 8 ounces milk or water (follow package directions) into a mug. Heat, uncovered, at **HIGH** following chart below. Add 2 to 3 teaspoons presweetened instant cocoa powder to each; stir.

Unsweetened Cocoa Powder: For each serving, stir together 1½ tablespoons cocoa powder, 1½ tablespoons sugar, and a dash salt in serving mug. Add about 1 tablespoon milk and stir till smooth. Add enough milk to fill mugs, 6 to 8 ounces each. Heat, uncovered, at **HIGH** following chart below. Stir.

For 4 servings: In 1½-quart bowl or glass pitcher, combine ⅓ cup cocoa powder, ⅓ cup sugar, and a dash salt. Add about ⅓ cup milk and stir till smooth. Add 3⅔ cups milk to make 1 quart in all. Heat, uncovered, at **HIGH** for 5½ minutes. Stir.

Amount	Time
1 cup	2 minutes
2 cups	3 minutes
3 cups	4 minutes
4 cups	5 minutes

AMBER HARVEST COMPOTE

This picture-pretty compote can make a return performance for dessert at lunch or supper—

Total cooking time: 30 minutes

10	20						

  1 21-ounce can cherry pie filling
2½ cups water
  ¼ cup sugar
  1 12-ounce package dried pitted prunes
  ½ of 11-ounce package (1⅓ cups) dried apricots
  1 13½-ounce can pineapple chunks (undrained)

In 3-quart casserole, combine pie filling, water, and sugar; stir in fruit. Cook, covered, at **HIGH** for 10 minutes; stir. Cook at **MEDIUM HIGH (7)**, covered, for 20 minutes, stirring after 10 minutes. Let stand till warm, 45 minutes. Makes 8 to 10 servings.

SPICY MOLASSES BAKED APPLES

Total cooking time: 6 minutes

6							

  ⅓ cup water
  ¼ cup light molasses
  ¼ cup sugar
  2 tablespoons lemon juice
  ¼ teaspoon ground cinnamon
  ¼ teaspoon ground nutmeg
      • • •
  4 large baking apples

In bowl, combine water, molasses, sugar, lemon juice, and spices. Core apples and peel ⅓ of the way down. Place apples in 1½-quart casserole. Pour molasses mixture over apples. Cook, uncovered, at **HIGH** for 6 minutes or till almost tender, turning apples over and spooning sauce over once. Makes 4 servings.

  Note: Cook 2 apples in a 6½×3½×3-inch baking dish, uncovered, (with half the molasses mixture) at **HIGH** for 3 minutes, turning apples over once.

RUBY GLAZED GRAPEFRUIT

Total cooking time: 3 minutes 30 seconds

3:30							

  2 grapefruit
  ⅓ cup raspberry jam
  ½ teaspoon ground cinnamon

Halve grapefruit crosswise; loosen sections. Remove the white membrane from centers. Place grapefruit in serving dishes. Spread about 2 teaspoons jam over each half and sprinkle lightly with cinnamon. Cook, uncovered, at **HIGH** for 3½ minutes or until grapefruit are warm; rearranging once. Makes 4 servings.

ENERGY-PACKED GRANOLA

Total cooking time: 10 minutes

10							

2½ cups old-fashioned rolled oats
  1 cup flaked coconut
  ½ cup coarsely chopped almonds
  ½ cup shelled sunflower seeds
  ½ cup unsweetened wheat germ
  ½ cup honey
  ¼ cup cooking oil
  ½ cup dried apricots, chopped
  ½ cup raisins

In large bowl, combine oats, coconut, almonds, sunflower seeds, and wheat germ. Combine honey and oil; stir into oat mixture. Spread out in 13×9×2-inch baking dish. Cook, uncovered, at **HIGH** for 10 minutes, stirring 3 times. Stir in fruits. Remove to another pan to cool. Stir occasionally during cooling to prevent lumping. Store in tightly covered jars or plastic bags. Makes 6 cups.

CRUNCHY BREAKFAST BARS

Total cooking time: 3 minutes

3							

  1 6-ounce package (1 cup) semisweet chocolate pieces
  ¾ cup peanut butter
  4 cups Energy-packed Granola *or* 3 cups round oat cereal

Place chocolate in 2-quart bowl. Heat, uncovered, at **HIGH** for 3 to 4 minutes or till melted. Stir in peanut butter till smooth. Fold in granola. Turn into waxed-paper-lined 8×8×2-inch dish; chill. Store in refrigerator. Makes 36.

QUICK COOKING HOT CEREALS

For 1 or 2 servings, use individual bowls, for 4 servings use a 1-quart bowl. Combine water, cereal, and dash salt. Cook, uncovered, at **HIGH** till mixture thickens and boils, stirring 2 or 3 times. Let stand 1 minute. Stir again.

	Quick-cooking Oatmeal			
servings	water (cups)	cereal (cups)	minutes at **HIGH**	stir
1	¾	⅓	2 to 2½	twice
2 (use 2 bowls same as above)			3 to 3½	twice
4	3	1⅓	5½ to 6	twice

	Quick-cooking Farina			
servings	water (cups)	cereal	minutes at **HIGH**	stir
1	¾	2½ Tbsp.	2½	twice
2 (use 2 bowls same as above)			3 to 3½	twice
4	2¾	⅔ cup	6	twice

Chicken-asparagus Muffinwiches

TIMETABLE

1. Chill cranberry sauce and peach halves.
2. Make iced tea; chill.
3. Make Vanilla Cream Pudding Quintet—plain or in one of the 5 delicious flavors; chill.
4. Cube cranberry sauce; place in peach halves.
5. Prepare Chicken-asparagus Muffinwiches.
6. Set table while sandwiches cook.

MENU

Chicken-asparagus Muffinwiches

Peach Half with Cranberry Sauce Cubes

Vanilla Cream Pudding Quintet

Iced Tea   Milk

50

SPOTLIGHT ON LUNCH

CHICKEN-ASPARAGUS MUFFINWICHES

Total cooking time: 12 minutes 15 seconds

0:45	3	0:30	8				

  6 tablespoons butter or margarine
  2 tablespoons all-purpose flour
  2 packages hollandaise sauce mix
  1 teaspoon prepared mustard
    Dash pepper
1¾ cups milk
  2 cups diced cooked chicken
  1 10-ounce package frozen asparagus spears
  8 toaster corn muffins or cornmeal rounds, toasted

In 4-cup glass measure, melt butter at **HIGH** for 45 to 60 seconds. Blend in flour, dry sauce mix, mustard, and pepper. Stir in milk. Heat, uncovered, at **HIGH** for 3 to 4 minutes, stirring after 1½ minutes. Add chicken; heat at **HIGH** for 30 seconds. Cover tightly and set aside.

Cook asparagus in original carton at **HIGH** for about 8 minutes rearranging once. Drain well. To serve, top 4 cornmeal rounds with a little chicken mixture and the asparagus. Top with remaining rounds and more chicken mixture. Garnish with snipped parsley and a watercress sprig, if desired. Makes 4 servings.

VANILLA CREAM PUDDING QUINTET

Total cooking time: 6 minutes 30 seconds

3	3	0:30					

½ cup sugar
  2 tablespoons cornstarch
¼ teaspoon salt
1⅔ cups milk
• • •
  1 well-beaten egg
  2 tablespoons butter or margarine
  1 teaspoon vanilla

In 1½-quart bowl, combine the sugar, cornstarch, and salt. Gradually stir in the milk; mix well. Cook, uncovered, at **HIGH** for 3 minutes; stir. Cook at **HIGH** 3 minutes more, stirring after each minute. Gradually stir a small amount of the hot pudding into the beaten egg; return to hot mixture and mix well. Cook, uncovered, at **HIGH** 30 seconds more, stirring after each 15 seconds. Add butter and vanilla. Stir till butter melts. Cool and chill. Makes 4 servings.

Coconut Cream: Same as above except stir in ½ cup flaked coconut with the butter and vanilla.

Butterscotch Cream: Substitute brown sugar for the granulated sugar; increase butter to 3 tablespoons.

Chocolate Cream: Increase sugar to ⅔ cup. Add 1½ squares (1½ ounces) unsweetened chocolate with the milk.

Butterscotch Nut: Same as Butterscotch except add ⅓ cup chopped pecans.

Mocha: Same as chocolate except add 1 teaspoon instant coffee powder with the butter.

CORNY BURGER BAKE

Total cooking time: 13 minutes

3	8	2					

½ cup finely chopped green pepper
½ cup finely chopped onion
  2 tablespoons water
  1 slightly beaten egg
1½ cups soft bread crumbs (2 slices)
¼ cup mayonnaise or salad dressing
    Dash pepper
  1 12-ounce can corned beef, finely flaked
        • • •
  1 10¾-ounce can condensed cream of celery soup
  1 8½-ounce can mixed vegetables, drained
  1 teaspoon horseradish mustard
  2 tablespoons milk
        • • •
  3 slices sharp process American cheese, halved
      diagonally
  3 English muffins, split and toasted

In medium bowl, combine green pepper, onion, and water. Cook, uncovered, at **HIGH**, 3 minutes; drain. Stir in egg, crumbs, mayonnaise, and pepper. Stir in meat; mix well. Using about ⅓ cup mixture for each, shape into 6 patties; set aside.

In bowl, combine soup, vegetables, and horseradish mustard. Add milk, stirring till smooth. Spoon *half* the soup mixture over bottom of 12×7½×2-inch baking dish. Arrange patties over sauce. Spoon on remaining sauce.

Cook, covered, at **MEDIUM HIGH (7)** for 8 minutes or till heated through, giving dish half turn once. Place cheese triangle over each patty. Cook, uncovered, at **MEDIUM (5)** for 2 to 2½ minutes or till cheese melts. Serve over English muffins. Makes 6 servings.

TURKEY-APPLE OPEN FACERS

Total cooking time: 3 minutes 30 seconds

1	1:30	1					

  1 envelope sour cream sauce mix
  1 tablespoon milk
  1 teaspoon curry powder
12 thin slices turkey
  1 large unpared apple, cored and cut into 12 wedges
  3 English muffins, split, toasted, and buttered

In 2-cup glass measure, prepare sauce mix according to package directions except add 1 tablespoon additional milk and the curry powder. Set aside. Wrap turkey slices and apple wedges separately in waxed paper; place to one side in microwave oven. Cook at **HIGH** 1 minute. Add glass measure with sauce to oven. Cook at **HIGH** 1½ to 2 minutes stirring sauce once. Arrange 2 turkey slices on each muffin half; top with 2 apple wedges. Place on serving plate. Spoon sauce over each sandwich. Return to oven. Cook at **HIGH** for 1 minute. Makes 6 sandwiches.

HOT TUNA SALADWICHES

Serve with one of the delicious vegetable soup fix-ups below. Then let the kids help make Choco-nut Banana Sticks (page 53) for a snack later on—

Total cooking time: 3 minutes 30 seconds

3:30							

  1 6½- or 7-ounce can tuna, drained
  ½ cup (2 ounces) shredded process American cheese
  ½ cup mayonnaise or salad dressing
  ¼ cup chopped celery
  2 tablespoons sweet pickle relish
  1 tablespoon minced onion
  1 teaspoon lemon juice
  ¼ teaspoon salt
  3 hard-cooked eggs, chopped
  8 onion rolls, split and toasted

In 1-quart bowl, flake tuna. Stir in cheese, mayonnaise, celery, relish, onion, lemon juice, and salt; fold in hard-cooked eggs. Cook, uncovered, at **HIGH** for 3½ to 4 minutes, stirring twice. Serve hot tuna filling in warm toasted onion rolls. Makes 8 servings.

INSIDE-OUT PIGS IN A BLANKET

Total cooking time: 10 minutes

2	3	3	2				

  ¼ cup finely chopped onion
  1 tablespoon butter or margarine
  2 cups herb-seasoned stuffing mix
  ¾ cup water
  ¼ cup catsup
  1 tablespoon sweet pickle relish
  1 pound (8) large frankfurters
  3 slices (3 ounces) sharp process American cheese, cut in strips

In 1½-quart bowl, place onion and butter. Cook, uncovered, at **HIGH** for 2 minutes. Stir in stuffing mix, water, catsup, and relish; set aside. Split frankfurters lengthwise almost to opposite side. Place in 12×7½×2-inch baking dish. Cook, loosely covered, at **HIGH** for 3 to 4 minutes. Mound stuffing atop franks. Cook, uncovered, at **HIGH** for 3 minutes or till heated through. Top with cheese strips. Cook, uncovered, at **MEDIUM (5)** for 2 minutes, or till cheese melts. Makes 8 stuffed hot dogs.

Souper Vegetable Fix-ups

Directions: In 2-quart casserole or bowl, combine soup, water, and frozen vegetables. Cook, uncovered, at **HIGH** for 15 to 20 minutes, stirring 2 or 3 times. When soup boils, reduce to **MEDIUM (5)** and cook 3 to 5 minutes or till tender. Stir again before serving. Makes 5 to 6 cups of soup.

Recipe	Soup	Water	Vegetables
Tivoli Garden Soup	2 10¾-ounce cans condensed cream of mushroom soup	1 soup can	1 10-ounce package frozen Danish-style vegetables in sauce
Bavarian Bowl	2 10¾-ounce cans condensed cream of celery soup	2 soup cans	1 10-ounce package frozen Bavarian-style beans and noodles in sauce
Consomme Chinese	2 10½-ounce cans condensed beef consomme	1 soup can	1 10-ounce package frozen Chinese-style vegetables in sauce
Potage Normandy	2 10¾-ounce cans condensed cream of potato soup	2 soup cans	1 10-ounce package frozen Parisian-style vegetables in sauce
Baja Bowl	1 11¼-ounce can condensed chili beef soup plus 1 10½-ounce can *condensed* beef broth	1 soup can	1 10-ounce package frozen Italian-style vegetables in sauce
Oriental Bowl	2 10½-ounce cans condensed chicken rice soup	2 soup cans	1 10-ounce package frozen Japanese-style vegetables in sauce
Aloha Chicken Soup	2 10½-ounce cans condensed chicken and stars soup	2 soup cans	1 10-ounce package frozen Hawaiian-style vegetables with pineapple in sauce

TEST KITCHEN
TIPS

Convenient canned or packaged soup plus a salad, sandwich, or dessert makes lunch or light supper a breeze. Warm soups right in the serving bowls or in a large glass measuring cup for easy pouring.

Canned Condensed Soup (3 servings): In a 4-cup glass measure, combine one 10½-ounce can condensed soup and 1 soup can water or milk. Cook, uncovered, at **HIGH** for 6½ to 7½ minutes, stirring once or twice. Let stand 1 or 2 minutes. Or, mix and divide soup into 3 serving bowls. Heat the 3 bowls together at **HIGH** for 6½ to 7½ minutes.

Canned Ready-to-serve Soup (2 servings): Pour a 19-ounce can ready-to-serve soup into 2 bowls or mugs. Heat, loosely covered, at **HIGH** for 4 minutes. Stir before serving.

Canned Ready-to-serve Soup (1 serving): Pour a 10¾-ounce can ready-to-serve soup into a bowl. Cook, loosely covered, at **HIGH** for 2½ to 3 minutes. Stir before serving.

Packaged Dry Soup Mix (3 servings): In a 4-cup glass measure, combine one 2-ounce envelope dry soup mix and water as package directs. Heat, uncovered, at **HIGH** for 5 to 6 minutes, till boiling. Reduce setting to **MEDIUM (5)**. Heat, uncovered, 10 minutes more, stirring once or twice. Let stand 1 to 2 minutes.

Packaged Dry Soup Mix (1 serving): In serving bowl, heat ¾ cup water, uncovered, at **HIGH** for 1¾ to 2 minutes, till boiling. Stir in one envelope dry one-cup soup mix. Let stand 1 to 2 minutes.

Reheat Leftover Soup: A 1-cup portion of chilled leftover soup can be warmed at **HIGH** in 4 to 5 minutes.

CHOCO-NUT BANANA STICKS

Total cooking time: 1 minute 30 seconds

1:30								

Place one 5¾-ounce package (1 cup) milk chocolate pieces in 8-inch pie plate. Cook, uncovered, at **HIGH** for 1½ minutes or just till *almost* melted. *Do not overheat.* Halve 4 small bananas crosswise. Insert wooden sticks into cut ends of bananas. Roll in chocolate, then in 1 cup chopped peanuts. Place on waxed-paper-lined baking sheet and freeze till firm. If not eaten the same day, wrap in freezer wrap and freeze. Makes 8.

SPICY PINEAPPLE-APRICOT COMPOTE

Total cooking time: 5 minutes 30 seconds

5:30								

- 1 20-ounce can pineapple chunks
- 1 17-ounce can apricot halves
- 1 tablespoon cornstarch
- ¼ teaspoon ground allspice
- Dash salt
- 1 tablespoon lemon juice
- 1 cup lemon-flavored yogurt

Drain fruits reserving syrup. In 4-cup glass measure, combine cornstarch, allspice, and salt. Blend with a little of the fruit syrup till smooth. Add remaining syrup. Cook, uncovered, at **HIGH** for 5½ to 6 minutes, stirring after every 2 minutes. Stir in lemon juice. Add fruits. Chill. Serve in sauce dishes topped with spoonfuls of lemon yogurt. Makes 6 servings.

TURKEY GUMBO BUNWICHES

Total cooking time: 9 minutes

3	6							

- ¼ cup chopped onion
- 2 tablespoons butter or margarine
- 2 cups diced cooked turkey
- 1 10¾-ounce can condensed chicken gumbo soup
- ¼ cup extra-hot catsup
- 1 teaspoon Worcestershire sauce
- 1 teaspoon prepared mustard
- 8 hamburger buns, split and toasted

In 1½-quart bowl, combine onion and butter. Cook, uncovered, at **HIGH** for 3 minutes. Stir in turkey, soup, catsup, Worcestershire, and mustard; mix well. Cook, covered with waxed paper, at **MEDIUM HIGH (7)** for 6 minutes, stirring once. Serve on buns. Makes 8 servings.

GRANDMA'S THICK SPLIT PEA SOUP

Total cooking time: 1 hour

30	30							

- 1 quart boiling water
- 1 cup (½ pound) dried split peas
- 1 meaty ham bone (1 pound)
- ¾ cup sliced onion
- ½ teaspoon salt
- ¼ teaspoon pepper
- ⅛ teaspoon dried marjoram, crushed

In 5-quart casserole, pour boiling water over peas. Add ham bone, onion, salt, pepper, and marjoram. Cover tightly; cook at **MEDIUM (5)** for 30 minutes. Remove bone from soup; cut off meat and dice. Return ham to soup. Cook, covered, at **MEDIUM (5)** for 30 to 35 minutes, stirring once. (Thin with water, if desired.) Serves 4.

Favorite Hamburger Casserole and Crusty Bread Fix-up

TIMETABLE

1. Make Best-ever Granola Squares early in the day.
2. Prepare cole slaw and refrigerate.
3. Chill apricots.
4. Prepare Crusty Bread Fix-up except for final heating.
5. Prepare Favorite Hamburger Casserole.
6. Heat Crusty Bread Fix-up.
7. Chill or freeze leftover casserole (see reheating times at end of recipe).

MENU

Favorite Hamburger Casserole

Cole Slaw

Crusty Bread Fix-up

Chilled Canned Apricots

Best-ever Granola Squares

Coffee   Milk

HEARTY GROUND BEEF RECIPES

FAVORITE HAMBURGER CASSEROLE

Total cooking time: 18 minutes

5	3	7	2:30	0:30			

  1 **pound ground beef**
  ½ **cup chopped onion**
  ½ **teaspoon salt**
    Dash pepper
  1 **16-ounce can cut green beans, drained**
  1 **10¾-ounce can condensed tomato soup**
  4 **servings instant mashed potatoes**
  1 **beaten egg**
  ½ **cup (2 ounces) shredded process American cheese**

In 1½-quart casserole, crumble beef; add onion. Cook at **HIGH** for 5 minutes, stirring 3 times. Drain off excess fat. Add salt and pepper. Stir in beans and soup. Set aside. In mixer bowl, measure water and butter for potatoes as called for on package (omit milk). Cook, covered, at **HIGH** for 3 minutes or till boiling. Stir in instant potato. Add egg; season. Set aside.

Cook casserole, covered, at **MEDIUM HIGH (7)** for 7 to 8 minutes or till boiling, stirring once. Spoon potatoes in mounds atop casserole. Cook, covered, at **HIGH** for 2½ minutes or till potatoes are hot through. Top potatoes with cheese. Cook, uncovered, at **HIGH** till cheese melts, about 30 seconds. Makes 4 to 6 servings.

To reheat one serving of chilled casserole, cook, covered, at **MEDIUM HIGH (7)** for 5 to 6 minutes, giving dish 3 quarter turns. Individual servings may be frozen in 12-ounce casseroles. Thaw, covered, at **MEDIUM LOW (3)** for 10 minutes, giving dish 3 quarter turns. Cook, covered, at **MEDIUM HIGH (7)** for 4½ to 5 minutes, until mixture is heated through giving dish one half turn.

BEST-EVER GRANOLA SQUARES

Happiness is a warm cookie with a big glass of icy cold milk when you come home from school—

Total cooking time: 8 minutes

2	6						

  4½ **cups packaged granola (1 pound)** *or* **Energy-packed Granola (recipe on page 49)**
  ½ **cup packed brown sugar**
  ¼ **cup light corn syrup**
  2 **tablespoons butter or margarine**
  ⅓ **cup** *sweetened condensed* **milk**
  ½ **teaspoon vanilla**

Place granola in buttered 13×9×2-inch baking pan. Set aside. In 4-cup glass measure, combine brown sugar, corn syrup, and butter. Cook, uncovered, at **MEDIUM (5)** for 2 minutes, till mixture is combined and boils. Stir in condensed milk. Cook, uncovered, at **MEDIUM (5)** for 6 minutes, stirring vigorously once each minute. Stir in vanilla. Pour over granola, stirring to coat. Press evenly into the pan. Cool. Cut into squares. Makes 24 squares.

SPAGHETTI PIE

This top-rated recipe is pictured on our cover—

Total cooking time: 17 minutes

2	5	3	6	1			

  6 **ounces spaghetti**
  2 **tablespoons butter or margarine**
  ⅓ **cup grated Parmesan cheese**
  2 **well-beaten eggs**
  1 **pound ground beef** *or* **bulk pork sausage**
  ½ **cup chopped onion**
  ¼ **cup chopped green pepper**
  1 **8-ounce can (1 cup) tomatoes, cut up**
  1 **6-ounce can tomato paste**
  1 **teaspoon sugar**
  1 **teaspoon dried oregano, crushed**
  ½ **teaspoon garlic salt**
  1 **cup (8 ounces) cottage cheese**
  ½ **cup (2 ounces) shredded mozzarella cheese**

On top of range, cook spaghetti according to package directions; drain. Stir butter into hot spaghetti. Stir in Parmesan cheese and eggs. Form spaghetti mixture into a "crust" in a 10-inch pie plate. Cook on **HIGH**, uncovered, for 2 minutes. In 1½-quart bowl crumble ground beef or sausage. Add onion and green pepper. Cook, uncovered, at **HIGH** 5 minutes, stirring 3 times to break up meat. Drain off excess fat. Stir in *undrained* tomatoes, tomato paste, sugar, oregano, and garlic salt. Cook, covered, at **HIGH** till sauce is bubbly 3 to 3½ minutes, stirring once.

Spread cottage cheese over bottom of spaghetti "crust." Fill "pie" with tomato mixture. Cook, covered, at **HIGH** till heated through 6 to 7 minutes giving dish half turn after 3 minutes. Top with the mozzarella cheese. Cook at **HIGH** till cheese is melted, 1 minute more. Let stand 8 to 10 minutes before serving. Garnish with snipped parsley, if desired. Makes 6 servings.

CRUSTY BREAD FIX-UP

Total cooking time: 2 minutes

0:30	1:30						

  1 **1-pound French bread** *or* **round loaf**
  6 **tablespoons butter or margarine**
  1 **clove garlic, minced**
    Snipped parsley

Cut bread in ½-inch slices, cutting to but not through bottom crust. In custard cup, melt butter at **HIGH** for 30 to 45 seconds. Stir in garlic and parsley. Brush on loaf between slices. Place loaf in oven on paper toweling. Cook at **HIGH** for 1½ to 2 minutes or till heated through.

Cheesy-chive Loaf: In bowl, combine 2 tablespoons butter, ¼ cup sharp cheese spread, and 1 tablespoon snipped chives. Heat, uncovered, at **MEDIUM LOW (3)** for 1 to 2 minutes till just melted. Blend. Spread on cut slices of bread; heat as above.

ITALIAN MEAT LOAF

Total cooking time: 27 minutes

3	24						

½ cup finely chopped onion
¼ cup finely chopped green pepper
2 tablespoons water

• • •

1 cup medium cracker crumbs (24 crackers)
1 6-ounce can tomato paste
2 beaten eggs
½ teaspoon garlic salt
½ teaspoon salt
Dash pepper
1½ pounds ground beef

• • •

⅓ cup fine cracker crumbs (10 crackers)
1 cup cream-style cottage cheese
1 slightly beaten egg
1 3-ounce can chopped mushrooms, drained
1 tablespoon snipped parsley
½ teaspoon dried oregano, crushed

In medium mixing bowl, combine onion, green pepper, and 2 tablespoons water. Cook on **HIGH,** covered with waxed paper, till just tender, 3 minutes. Drain off water. To onion mixture, add the 1 cup cracker crumbs, tomato paste, 2 eggs, garlic salt, salt, and pepper; stir to blend. Add ground beef; mix well. Pat half the mixture into bottom of 8×8×2-inch baking dish.

Combine remaining ⅓ cup crumbs, the cottage cheese, 1 egg, mushrooms, parsley, and oregano. Blend with beater until somewhat smooth. Spread mixture evenly over meat. On a piece of waxed paper, pat remaining meat to 8×8 inches. Invert over cheese in dish; peel off paper. Cook, covered with waxed paper, at **MEDIUM HIGH (7)** 24 minutes, giving dish quarter turns after 8 and 16 minutes. Let stand, covered, 5 minutes before serving. Makes 8 servings.

TACO BURGER STACK-UPS

The kids will go for these sloppy Joes a la Mexicana—

Total cooking time: 9 minutes

5	4						

1 pound ground beef
1 16-ounce can (2 cups) tomatoes
1 envelope taco seasoning mix
6 hamburger buns, split and toasted
1 cup (4 ounces) shredded natural cheddar cheese
2 cups shredded lettuce

Crumble beef into bowl. Cook at **HIGH** for 5 minutes, stirring 3 times. Drain off fat. Drain tomatoes reserving ⅔ cup juice. Cut up tomatoes and add along with reserved juice and seasoning mix to beef. Cook at **HIGH** for 4 minutes, stirring once. Serve in buns topped with cheese and lettuce. Makes 6 servings.

RELISH BURGERS

To cook 2 burgers: Cook, covered, at HIGH for 2½ to 3 minutes, giving dish half turn once—

Total cooking time: 4 minutes

4							

1 tablespoon sugar
2 tablespoons cider vinegar
½ teaspoon salt
⅛ teaspoon pepper
½ cup chopped onion
½ cup chopped tomato
½ cup unpared cucumber, sliced paper thin

• • •

1 pound ground beef
¾ teaspoon salt
Dash pepper
2 tablespoons chopped sweet pickle
4 hamburger buns, split

Mix sugar, vinegar, the ½ teaspoon salt, and the ⅛ teaspoon pepper; add onion, tomato, and cucumber. Cover and refrigerate 1 to 2 hours; drain well.

Combine beef and remaining salt and pepper; shape into 4 patties, 4 inches in diameter. Place in an 8×8×2-inch baking dish. Cook, covered, at **HIGH** for 4 to 5 minutes, giving dish half turn once. Stir chopped pickle into onion mixture. Serve burgers in buns topped with the cucumber relish. Makes 4 servings.

PIZZA DOGBURGERS

How can you miss—hot dogs and burgers rolled into one—

Total cooking time: 6 minutes 30 seconds

4	1	1:30					

1 slightly beaten egg
¾ cup soft bread crumbs (1 slice)
¼ cup milk
½ teaspoon salt
½ pound bulk Italian sausage
½ pound ground beef
6 frankfurters
1 8-ounce can (1 cup) pizza sauce
6 frankfurter buns, split and toasted

Combine egg, crumbs, milk, and salt in bowl. Add sausage and beef; mix thoroughly. Divide into 6 portions. Shape meat around frankfurters, leaving ends open; roll each between waxed paper to make uniform thickness. Place in 12×7×2-inch baking dish, making sure rolls do not touch.

Cook, covered, at **HIGH** for 4 to 5 minutes giving dish half turn once. Brush with pizza sauce. Cook, covered, at **HIGH** for 1 to 2 minutes more. Brush with sauce again. Serve in buns. Pour remaining pizza sauce into small bowl. Heat at **HIGH** for 1 minute 30 seconds, till bubbly and hot. Pass with dogburgers. Makes 6 servings.

MEAT ROLL SPAGHETTI DINNER

Great way to serve packaged spaghetti dinner—

Total cooking time: 21 minutes

14	3	4					

  1 beaten egg
  2 tablespoons milk
  ¼ cup chopped onion
  ¼ cup soft bread crumbs
  ¼ teaspoon salt
  ⅛ teaspoon pepper
  1 pound ground beef
  1 8-ounce package Italian-style dinner mix with
      spaghetti and Parmesan cheese
  2 tablespoons chopped onion
  2 tablespoons chopped celery
  1 8-ounce can (1 cup) tomato sauce
  1 tablespoon brown sugar
  1 tablespoon vinegar

In bowl, combine egg, milk, the ¼ cup onion, crumbs, salt, and pepper. Add beef; mix well. Shape into 2 rolls about 6 inches long. Place in 10×6×1½-inch baking dish. Cook, covered, at **MEDIUM HIGH (7)** for 14 minutes, giving dish half turn after 7 minutes. Meanwhile, cook spaghetti from dinner mix conventionally; drain. Remove meat rolls; cover to keep warm. In medium bowl, cook 2 tablespoons onion and celery in ½ cup water, covered, at **HIGH** till tender, about 3 to 4 minutes. *Do not drain.* Stir in tomato sauce, herb-spice mix from Italian dinner, brown sugar, and vinegar. Cook at **HIGH** 4 to 5 minutes, till bubbly, stirring 2 or 3 times. Serve spaghetti and meat rolls with sauce. Pass Parmesan cheese from mix. Makes 4 servings.

CORNY PIZZA

Total cooking time: 14 minutes 30 seconds

6	3:30	5					

  1 8-ounce package corn muffin mix
  ½ pound ground beef
  2 tablespoons chopped green pepper
  ¼ teaspoon salt
  ¼ teaspoon chili powder
  1 8-ounce can (1 cup) pizza sauce
  1 cup shredded mozzarella cheese

Prepare muffin mix batter using package directions. Spread on ungreased 12-inch ovenproof glass pizza plate; place 2-inch-diameter glass in the center of the dish. Cook, uncovered, at **HIGH** for 6 minutes, till batter looks dry on top. Set aside. In 1-quart casserole, combine ground beef and green pepper; cook at **HIGH** for 3½ minutes till beef is done, stirring once. Drain off fat; stir in salt, chili powder, and dash pepper. Sprinkle beef mixture on corn bread on plate; spoon on pizza sauce. Sprinkle with cheese. Heat, uncovered, at **MEDIUM HIGH (7)** for 5 minutes, till hot. Makes 6 to 8 servings.

EASY CHILI BAKE

Total cooking time: 21 minutes 30 seconds

5	15	1:30					

  1 pound ground beef
  1 15-ounce can pinto beans, drained
  1 10-ounce can hot enchilada sauce
  1 8-ounce can tomato sauce
  1½ cups shredded sharp process American cheese
  1 tablespoon instant minced onion

• • •

  1 6-ounce package (4 cups) corn chips
  1 cup dairy sour cream

Crumble beef into 2-quart casserole. Cook at **HIGH** for 5 minutes, stirring 3 times. Drain off fat. Add beans, sauces, *1 cup* of the cheese, and onion. Reserve 1 cup chips. Crush remaining chips into casserole; mix well. Cook, covered, at **MEDIUM HIGH (7)** for 15 to 16 minutes, or till hot, stirring once. Top with sour cream and ½ cup cheese. Cook at **MEDIUM HIGH (7)** for 1½ minutes. Ring with reserved corn chips. Makes 6 to 8 servings.

TEST KITCHEN TIPS

Leftover burgers can make a return performance in any of the following delightful new guises:

Reheat one hamburger, without the bun, loosely covered, at **MEDIUM HIGH (7)** for 1 minute 15 seconds.

Disguise the hamburger patties with toppings like guacamole, a dollop of sour cream chip dip, or a heap of sauteed fresh mushroom slices.

Sauce the meat patties with quick hollandaise from a package or creamy onion gravy from canned condensed soup.

Serve hamburgers spread with liver paté on thick tomato slices with crisp crumbled bacon.

Crumble the cooked meat into a bowl of chili, spaghetti sauce, or taco sauce.

Stir burger pieces into a simmering cheese soup or Oriental vegetable stir-fry.

Beef up the cheese filling for manicotti shells or a rice filling for stuffed green peppers.

Sprinkle well-seasoned hamburger chunks on a pizza or into cornbread or waffle batter.

Barbecued Ribs and Glazed Squash Rings

TIMETABLE

1. Make Molded Fruit Salad early in the day.
2. Make Baked Custard; chill.
3. Cook Glazed Squash Rings except for glaze.
4. Cook Barbecued Ribs; cover to keep warm.
5. Set table while ribs cook.
6. Glaze squash rings.
7. Heat rolls (about 40 seconds at **HIGH**).

MENU

Barbecued Ribs
Glazed Squash Rings
Molded Fruit Salad (page 15)
Hard Rolls   Butter
Baked Custard
Coffee   Milk

TEMPTING PORK AND BEEF MENUS

BARBECUED RIBS

Be sure and try the Oriental version of this recipe, too—

Total cooking time: 55 minutes

10	10	10	15	10			

- 1 cup catsup
- 1 tablespoon Worcestershire sauce
- 2 or 3 dashes bottled hot pepper sauce
- 1 cup water
- ¼ cup vinegar
- 1 tablespoon sugar
- 1 teaspoon salt
- 1 teaspoon celery seed
- 4 pounds pork loin back ribs

In bowl, combine all ingredients except ribs. Cook, uncovered, at **MEDIUM (5)** for 10 minutes, stirring occasionally; set aside. Cut ribs in serving size pieces. Arrange in 13×9×2-inch baking dish, overlapping slightly.

Cook ribs, covered with waxed paper, at **MEDIUM HIGH (7)** for 10 minutes. Rearrange ribs; cook, covered, at **MEDIUM HIGH (7)** for 10 minutes more. Drain off juices and again rearrange ribs in dish. Pour barbecue sauce over ribs.

Cook, uncovered, at **MEDIUM HIGH (7)** for 15 minutes; baste and rearrange in baking dish. Cook, uncovered, at **MEDIUM HIGH (7)** for 10 minutes or till done. Remove ribs to platter; skim off fat and spoon sauce over ribs. Garnish with lemon slices, if desired. Makes 4 to 6 servings.

Oriental Spareribs: In bowl, combine ⅔ cup orange marmalade, ⅓ cup soy sauce, ¼ teaspoon garlic powder, ¼ teaspoon ground ginger, dash pepper, and ⅓ cup water; mix well. Substitute for barbecue sauce in *Barbecued Ribs* recipe above.

ZESTY BAKED PORK CHOPS

Total cooking time: 30 minutes

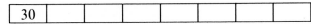

30							

- 6 pork chops (about 2 pounds)
  Salt
- 2 tablespoons brown sugar
- 2 teaspoons cornstarch
- ½ teaspoon dry Italian salad dressing mix
- ½ teaspoon dry mustard
- 1 10¾-ounce can condensed tomato soup
- 2 tablespoons vinegar
- 2 teaspoons Worcestershire sauce

Trim excess fat from pork chops. Season chops lightly with salt. Place chops in 12×7½×2-inch baking dish with bones toward center of dish. Blend brown sugar, cornstarch, salad dressing mix, and mustard. Blend in soup, vinegar, and Worcestershire sauce. Pour atop chops. Cook, covered, at **MEDIUM HIGH (7)** for 30 minutes, rearranging chops once. Makes 6 servings.

GLAZED SQUASH RINGS

Total cooking time: 13 minutes

8	1	4					

- 2 acorn squash
- 3 tablespoons butter or margarine
- ⅓ cup maple flavored syrup

Pierce whole squash 2 or 3 times with tines of fork. Place in 12×7½×2-inch baking dish. Cook at **HIGH** for 8 to 10 minutes or until soft to the touch, turning over and rearranging once. Cut in 1-inch slices; discard seeds and ends. Place squash in 12×7½×2-inch baking dish. Season with salt and pepper. Place butter in 1 cup measure; cook at **HIGH** for 1 minute. Add maple syrup to make ½ cup. Pour over squash. Cook, covered with waxed paper, at **HIGH** for 4 to 5 minutes, basting once. Makes 4 servings.

BAKED CUSTARD

Total cooking time: 13 minutes

3	10						

- 2 cups milk
- 3 beaten eggs
- ¼ cup sugar
- ½ teaspoon vanilla
  Ground nutmeg

Measure milk in 4-cup glass measure. Cook, uncovered, at **HIGH** for 3 to 4 minutes, till milk is very hot. Combine the beaten eggs, sugar, and vanilla in mixing bowl. Gradually add the hot milk to the egg mixture, stirring constantly. Pour into six 6-ounce custard cups. Sprinkle with nutmeg. Place cups in 12×7½×2-inch baking dish. Pour hot water into baking dish to depth of 1 inch.

Bake, uncovered, at **HIGH** for 10 minutes, till almost set, giving dish a half turn once. (A knife inserted halfway between center and outside edge will come out clean.) Cool on rack. Makes 6 servings.

CHOCOLATE MARSHMALLOW PARFAITS

Total cooking time: 2 minutes 30 seconds

2	0:30						

- 1 6-ounce package (1 cup) semisweet chocolate pieces
- ½ cup evaporated milk
- ½ of 7-ounce jar marshmallow creme
  Vanilla ice cream
  Toasted coconut

In 4-cup glass measure, combine chocolate pieces and evaporated milk. Cook, uncovered, at **HIGH** for 2 minutes, till chocolate melts, stirring twice to blend. Stir in marshmallow creme. Cook at **HIGH** for 30 seconds, till melted; stir to blend. Cool. Alternate layers of ice cream and chocolate sauce in parfait glasses; top with coconut. Makes 1⅔ cups sauce or 6 parfaits.

GLAZED CORNED BEEF AND PEACHES

Total cooking time: 1 hour 45 minutes

90	15							

   1 **3-pound ready-to-cook corned beef brisket**
   1 **29-ounce can peach halves**
  ¼ **cup packed brown sugar**
  ¼ **cup catsup**
   2 **tablespoons vinegar**
   2 **teaspoons prepared mustard**

Place corned beef brisket in 4-quart casserole. Add water to cover (7 cups) and seasonings from brisket package. Add 1 bay leaf. Cook, covered, at **MEDIUM (5)** for 1½ hours, till tender, turning brisket over once. Let cool in cooking liquid for 10 minutes.

   Slice meat across the grain. Arrange slices in 12×7½×2-inch baking dish. Drain peaches, reserving ¼ cup syrup. Arrange peaches around meat. Combine reserved syrup with brown sugar, catsup, vinegar, and mustard; pour over meat and peaches. Cook, covered, at **MEDIUM (5)** for 15 minutes. Spoon sauce over. Makes 8 to 10 servings.

JIFFY CASSOULET

Total cooking time: 16 minutes

3	13							

  ½ **pound bulk pork sausage**
   1 **medium onion, chopped (½ cup)**
   1 **clove garlic, minced**
  ½ **pound diced cooked ham (1½ cups)**
   2 **tablespoons snipped parsley**
   1 **bay leaf**
   2 **15½-ounce cans navy beans**
  ¼ **cup dry white wine**
     Dash ground cloves

In 2-quart bowl, combine sausage, onion, and garlic. Cook, uncovered, at **HIGH** for 3 minutes, stirring once. Drain off excess fat. Add ham, parsley, and bay leaf; mix well. Stir in *undrained* beans, ½ cup water, wine, and cloves. Cook, covered, at **MEDIUM HIGH (7)** for 13 to 14 minutes, stirring once. Remove bay leaf. Serve in bowls. Makes 6 servings.

HASH MEXICANA

Total cooking time: 13 minutes

3	10							

In 8×8×2-inch baking dish, combine 2 tablespoons butter or margarine and ⅓ cup chopped onion. Cook, uncovered, at **HIGH** for 3 minutes. Stir in 2 cups diced cooked roast beef, 2 cups finely diced cooked potatoes, one 12-ounce can whole kernel corn (drained), one 10¾-ounce can condensed tomato soup, and ¼ teaspoon chili powder. Cook, covered, at **MEDIUM HIGH (7)** for 10 minutes, stirring once. Makes 4 servings.

BEANTOWN RUMP ROAST

Total cooking time: 1 hour 25 minutes

45	15	25						

   2 **tablespoons all-purpose flour**
  ½ **teaspoon salt**
  ¼ **teaspoon paprika**
   2 **pound boneless beef rump roast**
   2 **tablespoons cooking oil**
   1 **11½-ounce can condensed bean and bacon soup**
  ½ **cup water**
   1 **teaspoon beef-flavor gravy base**
   1 **bay leaf**
   6 **to 8 carrots, cut in 1-inch pieces**
   8 **to 12 small onions, peeled**
   1 **green pepper, cut in pieces**

Combine flour, salt, paprika, and dash pepper. Coat roast thoroughly with flour mixture. In skillet on top of range, brown roast on all sides in hot oil. In 3-quart casserole, combine soup, water, gravy base, and bay leaf. Place roast in casserole, spooning sauce over.

   Cook, covered, at **MEDIUM (5)** for 45 minutes, spooning sauce over after 20 minutes. Turn roast over. Add carrots and onions to casserole dish. Cook, covered, at **MEDIUM (5)** for 15 minutes. Add green pepper and cook, covered, at **MEDIUM (5)** for 25 to 30 minutes more or till tender. Discard bay leaf. Arrange meat and vegetables on platter. Pass soup mixture for gravy. Makes 6 servings.

HERBED POT ROAST

Total cooking time: 1 hour 18 minutes

75	3							

   4 **pound beef chuck roast (1½-inches thick)**
   2 **tablespoons all-purpose flour**
   1 **tablespoon cooking oil**
   1 **teaspoon salt**
  ½ **teaspoon dried marjoram, crushed**
  ¼ **teaspoon dried basil, crushed**
  ¼ **teaspoon dried thyme, crushed**
  ¼ **teaspoon pepper**
  ½ **onion, sliced**
  ½ **cup dry red wine *or* beef broth**
     Herbed Gravy

Sprinkle roast lightly with flour; rub in. In skillet on top of range, brown in oil on both sides. Transfer to 2-quart (12×7½×2-inch) baking dish. Combine salt, herbs, and pepper; sprinkle on roast. Add onion and wine or broth. Cook, covered, at **MEDIUM (5)** for 1¼ to 1½ hours, giving dish half turn after 45 minutes.

   Serve with **Herbed Gravy:** Skim fat off meat juices. Measure 1½ cups meat juices in a 4-cup glass measure. In shaker, combine ½ cup cold water and ¼ cup flour; mix well. Stir into juices. Cook, uncovered, at **HIGH** 3 to 3½ minutes till mixture is thickened and bubbly, stirring once each minute. Makes 8 servings.

SOUTHERN-STYLE PORK CHOPS

Total cooking time: 31 minutes 30 seconds

15	15	1:30					

6 **pork chops**
2 **18-ounce cans vacuum-packed sweet potatoes**
2 **medium oranges**
½ **cup packed brown sugar**
⅛ **teaspoon salt**
   Dash ground cinnamon
   Dash ground nutmeg
2 **tablespoons cold water**
1 **tablespoon cornstarch**

Trim excess fat from chops. Place chops in 13×9×2-inch baking dish. Cook, covered, at **MEDIUM HIGH (7)** for 15 minutes, giving dish half turn once. Drain off pan juices and rearrange chops. Halve large potatoes; place potatoes over chops. Slice one of the oranges thinly and place over potatoes. Squeeze the other orange and add water to make ½ cup. Combine juice mixture, brown sugar, salt, and spices; pour atop potatoes.

Cook, covered, at **MEDIUM HIGH (7)** for 15 minutes, till chops are tender, giving dish a half turn once. Transfer meat, potatoes, and oranges to serving platter; keep warm. Combine water and cornstarch; stir into pan juices. Cook, uncovered, at **HIGH** for 1½ minutes, or till thickened and bubbly, stirring every 30 seconds. Drizzle over meat and potatoes. Makes 6 servings.

ZIPPY LIVER AND BACON

Total cooking time: 10 minutes

4	6		,				

6 **slices bacon**
1 **pound beef liver (½-inch thick), cut in 1½-inch strips**
1 **tablespoon catsup**
1 **tablespoon lemon juice**
2 **teaspoons Dijon-style mustard**
1 **teaspoon Worcestershire sauce**
¼ **teaspoon onion powder**
   Snipped parsley

In 12×7½×2-inch baking dish, place bacon on microwave roasting rack. Cook at **HIGH** for 4 to 5 minutes, turning dish once. Remove bacon and rack, reserving 2 tablespoons drippings in dish. Drain and crumble bacon; set aside.

Place liver strips in same dish; stir to coat with bacon fat. Cook, covered, at **MEDIUM (5)** for 6 minutes, stirring twice, till center of liver is just barely pink. Meanwhile, combine catsup, lemon juice, mustard, Worcestershire, and onion powder. Drain off juices from liver and discard. Add catsup mixture to liver, stirring gently to coat. Turn into serving dish; sprinkle with crumbled bacon and snipped fresh parsley. Makes 4 servings.

HAM-VEGETABLE BAKE

Total cooking time: 24 minutes 30 seconds

6	6	1	6	5	0:30		

1 **10-ounce package frozen mixed vegetables**
⅓ **cup water**
1 **6-ounce can sliced mushrooms**
2 **envelopes chicken noodle soup mix**
2 **cups water**
   • • •
6 **tablespoons butter or margarine**
½ **cup all-purpose flour**
1 **13-ounce can (1⅔ cups) evaporated milk**
4 **cups diced cooked ham**
   • • •
¼ **cup coarsely crushed rich round cracker crumbs (6 crackers) per casserole**

In small casserole or mixing bowl, combine frozen vegetables and ⅓ cup water. Cook, covered, at **HIGH** 6 minutes, stirring once. Do not drain. Set aside. Drain mushrooms, reserving liquid. In 4-cup glass measure, combine dry soup mix and 2 cups water; cook at **HIGH**, uncovered, 6 minutes, stirring twice. Let stand 5 minutes. Strain to separate broth from noodles, reserving both.

In large bowl, melt butter at **HIGH** for 1 minute. Blend in flour. Stir in reserved broth, mushroom liquid, and evaporated milk. Cook, uncovered, at **HIGH** till thickened and bubbly, 6 to 7 minutes, stirring every 2 minutes. Add cooked vegetables, mushrooms, ham, and noodles.

Turn the mixture into two 1½-quart casseroles. Cover tightly. Seal, label, and freeze. Or, cook one now and freeze one for later. Cook unfrozen casserole at **HIGH**, uncovered, for 5 to 6 minutes, stirring twice. Sprinkle with cracker crumbs; return to oven and heat, uncovered, at **HIGH** 30 seconds.

Cook frozen casserole, uncovered, at **MEDIUM LOW (3)** for 30 minutes, stirring after 20 minutes, then every 5 minutes. Turn to **HIGH** and cook 6 minutes, stirring once. Sprinkle with crumbs and cook at **HIGH**, uncovered, 30 seconds. Makes 2 casseroles, 6 to 8 servings each.

DEVILED BEEF STEW

Total cooking time: 1 hour 17 minutes

75	2						

2 **pounds beef stew meat, cut in ½-inch cubes**
1¾ **cups water**
3 **tablespoons prepared mustard**
1½ **teaspoons seasoned salt**
6 **small onions, quartered**
2 **cups diagonally sliced carrots**
3 **tablespoons cornstarch**

In 3-quart casserole, combine all ingredients except cornstarch. Cook at **MEDIUM (5)**, covered, for 1¼ to 1½ hours or till meat is tender. Stir ⅓ cup cold water into cornstarch; add to stew. Cook at **HIGH** for 2 minutes or till thickened and bubbly, stirring once. Makes 6 servings.

Indian Chicken

TIMETABLE

1. Prepare Cupcake Surprises.
2. Cook Indian Chicken except for glazing.
3. Set table while chicken cooks.
4. Cook rice conventionally.
5. Cook Wilted Lettuce Salad; serve at once.
6. Cook beans (page 179) while eating salad.
7. Glaze chicken and serve over rice.

MENU

Wilted Lettuce Salad
Indian Chicken
Fluffy Hot Cooked Rice
Buttered Green Beans
Whole Wheat Bread   Butter
Cupcake Surprises
Coffee   Milk

CHAMPION CHICKEN AND TURKEY DINNERS

INDIAN CHICKEN

Total cooking time: 28 minutes

5	20	3						

- 2 tablespoons cooking oil
- 2 tablespoons butter or margarine
- 2 medium onions, very thinly sliced and separated into rings (2 cups)
- 1 teaspoon salt
- ¼ teaspoon coarsely ground pepper
- ¼ teaspoon saffron, crushed
- ⅛ teaspoon cayenne pepper

• • •

- 2 whole chicken breasts, split
- 4 chicken thighs *or* 2 drumsticks and 2 thighs
- 1 tablespoon cornstarch
- 2 tablespoons cold water
- ½ cup raisins
- ¼ cup blanched whole almonds, toasted
- 2 teaspoons lemon juice

In 12×7½×2-inch baking dish, combine oil, butter, and onion. Cook, covered, at **HIGH** for 5 minutes, till onion is tender. Stir in salt, pepper, saffron, and cayenne pepper. Add chicken, turning to coat with butter sauce. Heat, covered, at **MEDIUM HIGH (7)** for 20 to 22 minutes or till chicken is done, giving dish half turn once.

Remove chicken to platter; cover to keep warm. Blend cornstarch with water. Stir into pan juices; add raisins and nuts. Cook, uncovered, at **HIGH** for 3 to 4 minutes, till thickened and bubbly, stirring after each minute. Stir in lemon juice. Spoon over chicken. Trim with parsley sprig, if desired. Makes 6 servings.

CUPCAKE SURPRISES

Total cooking time: 3 minutes 30 seconds

1:30	1:30	0:30						

- 1 3-ounce package cream cheese
- 2 tablespoons sugar
- 1 egg yolk
- ⅛ teaspoon salt
- ½ of 6-ounce package (½ cup) semi-sweet chocolate pieces
- 1 package 1-layer-size chocolate cake mix

Place cream cheese in small mixing bowl. Cook, uncovered, at **LOW (1)** for 1½ minutes. Stir in sugar, then egg yolk, and salt. Add chocolate pieces; set aside. Prepare chocolate cake mix using package directions. Fill 4 paper-lined 6-ounce custard cups half full (about 2½ tablespoons batter for each cupcake).

Drop one level tablespoon of the cheese mixture into each cupcake. Cook, uncovered, at **HIGH** for 1½ minutes; rearrange cups and bake at **HIGH** 30 to 40 seconds longer, or until surface is no longer moist. Cupcakes may be immediately removed from custard cups to cooling rack. Repeat with remaining batter and filling. Makes 12.

WILTED LETTUCE SALAD

Total cooking time: 12 minutes 30 seconds

6	3	2:30	1					

- 6 slices bacon
- ½ cup sliced green onion
- ¼ cup vinegar
- 1 tablespoon sugar
- 2 tablespoons water
- ½ teaspoon salt

• • •

- 4 cups leaf lettuce, torn in bite-size pieces
- 4 cups fresh spinach, torn in bite-size pieces
- 6 radishes, thinly sliced
- 2 hard-cooked eggs, chopped

Place bacon on microwave roasting rack in baking dish. Cook at **HIGH** for 6 minutes, giving dish half turn once. Remove bacon from dish, reserving 1½ tablespoons drippings. Crumble bacon; set aside. In large bowl, cook onion in reserved drippings, uncovered, at **HIGH** for 3 minutes. Add vinegar, sugar, water, and salt.

Cook, uncovered, at **HIGH** 2½ minutes or till boiling. Stir to dissolve sugar. Place lettuce and spinach in same bowl, tossing to coat well with dressing. Cook, uncovered, at **HIGH** 1 minute, tossing again after 30 seconds. Serve in salad bowl garnished with radishes, bacon, and hard-cooked egg. Makes 6 servings.

LO-CAL CHICKEN CACCIATORE

Total cooking time: 22 minutes

20	2							

- 2 medium chicken breasts, boned, skinned, and halved lengthwise
- ¾ cup sliced fresh mushrooms
- ½ of 8-ounce can (½ cup) tomatoes, cut up
- ½ cup chopped green pepper
- ¼ cup chopped onion
- 3 tablespoons dry red wine
- 1 clove garlic, minced
- ½ teaspoon dried oregano, crushed
- ¼ teaspoon salt
  Dash pepper

• • •

- 2 teaspoons cornstarch
- 2 tablespoons cold water

Place chicken breasts in 10×6×1½-inch baking dish. Combine mushrooms, tomatoes, green pepper, onion, wine, garlic, oregano, salt, and pepper; pour over chicken. Cook, covered, at **MEDIUM HIGH (7)** for 20 minutes, giving dish half turn after 10 minutes. Remove chicken to serving plate; cover to keep warm. Combine cornstarch and water; add to liquid in baking dish. Cook, uncovered, at **HIGH** for 2 to 3 minutes, stirring after each minute, till thickened and bubbly. Pass the sauce with chicken. Makes 4 servings (approximately 139 calories per serving).

CHIPPY CHICKEN CASSEROLE

Serve with broccoli spears, frozen cranberry salad, and tender spiced muffins with honey—

Total cooking time: 9 minutes

8	1							

    2 cups cubed cooked chicken *or* turkey
    2 cups sliced celery
    ⅓ cup toasted slivered almonds
    2 teaspoons grated onion
    ½ teaspoon salt
    ¾ cup mayonnaise or salad dressing
    2 tablespoons lemon juice
    ½ cup (2 ounces) shredded process American cheese
    1 cup crushed potato chips

Combine chicken, celery, almonds, onion, and salt. Blend mayonnaise and lemon juice together; stir into chicken mixture. Spread evenly in 8×1½-inch round baking dish. Cook, covered, at **HIGH** for 8 minutes, stirring after 4 minutes. Stir again and sprinkle with cheese. Cook at **HIGH** 1 minute more. Top with potato chips before serving. Makes 6 servings.

CRANBERRY BARBECUED CHICKEN

Delicious with corn on the cob and potato salad—

Total cooking time: 25 minutes

25								

    1 cup canned whole cranberry sauce
    ½ cup finely chopped onion
    ½ cup catsup
    ¼ cup finely chopped celery
    4 teaspoons cornstarch
    1 tablespoon brown sugar
    2 tablespoons lemon juice
    1 tablespoon prepared mustard
    1 tablespoon Worcestershire sauce
    1 tablespoon vinegar
        • • •
    1 2½- to 3-pound broiler-fryer, cut up

In 12×7½×2-inch baking dish, combine all ingredients except chicken. Place chicken pieces, skin side down, in dish. Turn skin side up to coat with sauce. Sprinkle with salt. Cover with waxed paper. Cook at **MEDIUM HIGH (7)** for 25 minutes, or till chicken is tender.

   Place chicken pieces on platter. Skim excess fat from sauce. Stir sauce and spoon some over chicken; pass remaining sauce. Makes 4 servings.

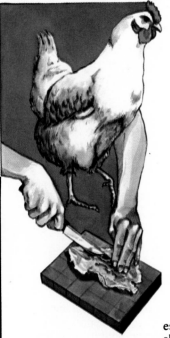

TEST KITCHEN TIPS

When a recipe calls for cooked chicken, turn to your microwave oven. In twelve minutes or less, a pound of chicken is ready, tender and juicy. Use this method for small servings of chicken for children or dieters, too. Flavor with a sprinkle of mixed herbs before cooking; add salt and pepper before serving.

   Start with 12 ounces of chicken breasts, skin and bones still intact. Place in a 2-quart casserole and add 1 tablespoon water. Cook, covered, at **HIGH** for 6 to 8 minutes, turning chicken over after 4 minutes. Cool and cube, if desired. Makes 1 cup cooked chicken.

   Cook 16 ounces chicken breasts for 9 to 12 minutes; expect 1½ cups cooked meat.

GINGER ORANGE CHICKEN

Accompany with fluffy rice, pea pods, fortune cookies—

Total cooking time: 23 minutes 30 seconds

20	3:30							

    1 2½-pound broiler-fryer, cut up
    1 teaspoon salt
    ¼ teaspoon paprika
    ⅓ cup (3 ounces) frozen orange juice concentrate,
        thawed
    ⅓ cup water
    2 tablespoons brown sugar
    2 tablespoons snipped parsley
    2 teaspoons soy sauce
    ½ teaspoon ground ginger
        • • •
    1 tablespoon cornstarch
    1 tablespoon cold water
      Hot cooked rice

Arrange chicken in 12×7½×2-inch baking dish. Sprinkle with salt and paprika. Combine orange concentrate, water, brown sugar, parsley, soy, and ginger; pour over chicken. Cook, covered, at **MEDIUM HIGH (7)** for 20 minutes, till tender. Remove chicken to platter. Cover; keep warm.

   Skim off fat from pan juices. Blend cornstarch and water. Add to pan juices. Cook at **HIGH** for 3½ minutes, till mixture thickens and bubbles, stirring after each minute. Spoon sauce over chicken before serving. Serve with rice, if desired. Makes 4 servings.

CREAMY CHICKEN-GHETTI BAKE

Tasty way to use up leftover spaghetti or noodles along with chicken or turkey. For variety substitute cream of chicken or celery soup for the mushroom—

Total cooking time: 23 minutes

3	2	2	16				

3 slices bacon, chopped
½ cup chopped onion
1 clove garlic, minced
• • •
3 tablespoons all-purpose flour
1 16-ounce can tomatoes, cut up
1 10¾-ounce can condensed cream of mushroom soup
1 cup (4 ounces) shredded process American cheese
2½ cups (4 ounces) cooked spaghetti
2 to 3 cups cubed cooked chicken *or* turkey
1 10-ounce package frozen peas, thawed
• • •
¼ cup grated Parmesan cheese

In 2½-quart casserole, combine bacon, onion, and garlic. Cook, covered, at **HIGH** for 3 minutes. Blend in flour. Add tomatoes and soup. Cook, uncovered, at **HIGH** for 2 minutes; stir. Cook at **HIGH** 2 minutes longer, till thickened and bubbly, stirring every 30 seconds.

Stir in American cheese till melted. Stir in spaghetti, chicken, and peas. Cook, uncovered, at **MEDIUM HIGH** (7) for 16 to 17 minutes, till heated through. Sprinkle with Parmesan cheese. Makes 8 servings.

TURKEY DIVAN

Serve with fresh fruit salad, biscuits, gingerbread—

Total cooking time: 21 minutes 30 seconds

10	0:30	1:30	4:30	5			

2 10-ounce packages frozen chopped broccoli
2 tablespoons butter or margarine
3 tablespoons all-purpose flour
½ teaspoon salt
2 cups milk
• • •
½ cup (2 ounces) shredded natural Swiss cheese
2 cups cooked turkey *or* chicken cut in strips
¼ cup grated Parmesan cheese

Place broccoli in 10×6×1½-inch baking dish. Cook, covered, at **HIGH** for 10 minutes, breaking up and stirring twice. Drain well. Cover and set aside.

In 4-cup glass measure, place butter. Cook, uncovered, at **HIGH** for 30 seconds. Blend in flour and salt. Add milk all at once. Cook, uncovered, at **HIGH** for 1½ minutes. Stir. Cook at **HIGH** for 4½ to 5 minutes, stirring after each minute. Stir in Swiss cheese till melted.

Place turkey over broccoli. Pour sauce atop. Sprinkle with Parmesan cheese. Cook, covered, at **MEDIUM HIGH** (7) for 5 to 8 minutes or till hot. Makes 6 servings.

SWEET-SOUR TURKEY

Cook the vegetables just till tender-crisp—

Total cooking time: 15 minutes

7	3	3	2				

1 cup diagonally sliced celery
1 cup julienne-cut carrots
½ cup chopped onion
3 tablespoons butter or margarine
1 13¼-ounce can pineapple tidbits (undrained)
1 cup chicken broth
• • •
2 tablespoons cornstarch
2 tablespoons brown sugar
¼ teaspoon salt
3 tablespoons lemon juice
2 tablespoons soy sauce
2 cups cubed cooked turkey *or* chicken
¼ cup toasted slivered almonds
Hot cooked rice

In 2-quart casserole, combine celery, carrots, onion, and butter. Cook, covered, at **HIGH** for 7 minutes or till tender, stirring twice. Add *undrained* pineapple and chicken broth. Combine cornstarch, brown sugar, salt, lemon juice, and soy sauce; stir into vegetable mixture.

Cook, uncovered, at **HIGH** 3 minutes, stirring once. Cook at **HIGH** 3 to 4 minutes more, stirring after each minute. Stir in turkey. Cook at **HIGH** 2 minutes or till mixture is heated through. Sprinkle with almonds. Serve over fluffy hot cooked rice. Makes 4 servings.

HEARTY TURKEY CHOWDER

Total cooking time: 35 minutes

20	15						

1 10-ounce package frozen baby lima beans
½ cup chopped onion
½ cup sliced celery
¼ teaspoon salt
1 cup water
• • •
1 10¾-ounce can condensed cream of chicken soup
1 16-ounce can tomatoes, cut up
2 cups loose-pack frozen hash browns
1½ cups chopped cooked turkey *or* chicken
¼ teaspoon poultry seasoning
¼ teaspoon garlic salt
½ cup (2 ounces) shredded natural cheddar cheese

In 3-quart bowl, combine lima beans, onion, celery, salt, and water. Cook, covered, at **HIGH** for 20 minutes, or till beans are tender, stirring twice. Stir in soup, tomatoes, hash browns, turkey, poultry seasoning, and garlic salt. Cook, uncovered, at **MEDIUM** (5) for 15 minutes, stirring once or twice. To serve, ladle into bowls and sprinkle cheese atop. Makes 8 servings.

Thrifty Thermidor

TIMETABLE

1. Prepare Easy Mint Candy Topping.
2. Make Garden Batter Bread.
3. Prepare salads (brush apple with lemon juice); chill.
4. Prepare Thrifty Thermidor; cut lemon wedges.
5. Cook peas conventionally on top of range.
6. Set table while thermidor and peas cook.
7. Thaw frozen cake for dessert (page 171).

MENU

Thrifty Thermidor   Lemon wedges
Buttered Peas
Grapefruit and Apple Wedge Salad
Garden Batter Bread (page 77)   Butter
Easy Mint Candy Topping on Cake Squares
Coffee   Milk

MEATLESS MEALS

THRIFTY THERMIDOR

Total cooking time: 22 minutes

7	5	2:30	1:30	4	2			

 1 pound fresh or frozen cod fillets
 2 cups water
 1 small onion, quartered
   Lemon slice
   • • •
 1 10¾-ounce can condensed cream of shrimp soup
 3 tablespoons all-purpose flour
 ¼ cup milk
 ¼ cup dry white wine *or* milk
 ¼ cup (1 ounce) shredded mozzarella cheese
 2 tablespoons snipped parsley
   • • •
 2 tablespoons grated Parmesan cheese
 ½ teaspoon paprika

For frozen fish: Place on paper towel in original carton. Cook at **MEDIUM LOW (3)** for 7 minutes, turning over once. Remove from carton. In 1½-quart casserole, combine water, onion, and lemon slice. Cook at **HIGH** till water boils, 5 minutes. Add fish; cook, covered, at **HIGH** for 2½ to 3 minutes. Drain and cube fish, removing skin and bones if necessary. Set fish aside.

In same casserole combine shrimp soup and flour. Gradually stir in milk and wine. Cook, uncovered, at **HIGH** for 1½ minutes. Stir. Continue cooking at **HIGH** for 4 to 4½ minutes, stirring after each minute. Stir in mozzarella cheese and parsley. Fold in fish. Spoon into 4 large baking shells or individual bakers.

Place in 13×9×2-inch baking dish. Cook, uncovered, at **HIGH** for 2 minutes. Combine Parmesan cheese and paprika. Sprinkle atop shells. Garnish with pimiento strips and parsley sprigs, then pass fresh lemon wedges if desired. Makes 4 servings.

EASY MINT CANDY TOPPING

Total cooking time: 6 minutes

6								

 1 3- or 3¼-ounce package *regular* vanilla pudding mix
 1½ cups milk
 ½ cup chocolate-covered cream-filled mint patties, cut up (8 patties)
   • • •
 1 2-ounce envelope dessert topping mix

In 4-cup glass measure, combine pudding mix and milk. Add mint patties. Cook, uncovered, at **HIGH** for 6 minutes, stirring every 2 minutes. Cover surface of pudding with clear plastic wrap; cool. Prepare topping mix according to package directions; fold in pudding. Cover; chill.

Serve as sauce over cake squares, angel food cake, ice cream, or as filling for cream puffs, or use as a pudding in parfait glasses. Use immediately or store in refrigerator up to 4 or 5 days. Makes 3 cups.

TWO-WAY SALMON LOAF

Total cooking time: 12 minutes

2	10							

 ¼ cup chopped onion
 2 tablespoons butter or margarine
 ¼ cup milk
 2 beaten eggs
 1½ cups soft bread crumbs (2 slices)
 2 tablespoons snipped parsley
 2 teaspoons lemon juice
 ½ teaspoon salt
   • • •
 1 16-ounce can salmon, drained, flaked, and bones removed
 1 8- or 10-ounce package frozen peas with cream sauce

In small bowl, combine onion and butter. Cook, uncovered, at **HIGH** for 2 to 3 minutes, till onion is tender. Combine with milk, eggs, bread crumbs, parsley, lemon juice, and salt. Add salmon; mix well. Shape into 7½×4-inch loaf. Place in 8×8×2-inch baking dish. Cook, covered, at **MEDIUM HIGH (7)** for 10 minutes, till center is set. Cover and keep warm. Cook frozen peas in cream sauce in pouch or bowl according to directions on page 170. Serve with sliced loaf. Makes 4 servings.

For patties: Shape salmon mixture into 4 patties. Using about ¼ cup yellow corn meal, sprinkle both sides of patties to coat. Place 2 tablespoons butter in 8×8×2-inch baking dish. Cook at **HIGH** 45 seconds. Add patties, turning once to coat with butter; cook, covered, at **HIGH** for 4 minutes; turn and cook, covered, at **HIGH** 3 minutes. Serve with creamed peas. Makes 4 servings.

SALMON-RAREBIT BAKE

Reheat a 1-cup individual casserole at HIGH 2½ minutes—

Total cooking time: 24 minutes 30 seconds

5	1:30	4	6	8				

 1 10-ounce package frozen Welsh rarebit
 2 tablespoons all-purpose flour
 1¼ cups milk
   • • •
 1 16-ounce can salmon, drained, boned, and broken in large pieces
 ½ of 10-ounce package (1 cup) frozen peas
 1 16-ounce package frozen fried potato nuggets

Remove frozen rarebit from foil pan; place in 2-quart casserole. Cook, covered, at **HIGH** for 5 minutes, stirring once. Blend flour and milk in a shaker. Stir into rarebit. Cook, uncovered, at **HIGH** for 1½ minutes. Stir. Cook at **HIGH** for 4 to 4½ minutes, stirring after each minute, till thickened and bubbly.

Fold in salmon, peas, and *half* of the potato nuggets. Cook, covered, at **MEDIUM HIGH (7)** for 6 minutes. Stir. Top with remaining potato nuggets. Cook, uncovered, at **MEDIUM HIGH (7)** for 8 minutes. Makes 6 servings.

TUNA CAN-COCTION

Total cooking time: 6 minutes

6								

- 1 4-ounce can shoestring potatoes
- 1 10¾-ounce can condensed cream of mushroom soup
- 1 6½- or 7-ounce can tuna, drained
- ⅓ cup milk
- 1 3-ounce can sliced mushrooms, drained
- ¼ cup chopped pimiento

Reserve 1 cup shoestring potatoes. Combine the remaining potatoes with soup, tuna, milk, mushrooms, and pimiento in 1½-quart casserole. Cook, covered, at **HIGH** for 6 minutes till hot, stirring once. Top with reserved shoestring potatoes. Makes 4 servings.

SHALLOT BUTTERED SALMON STEAKS

Total cooking time: 12 minutes

8	2	2					

- 4 fresh or frozen salmon steaks (1 pound 6 ounces)
- 1 cup water

• • •

- 3 tablespoons chopped shallots
- 1 tablespoon butter or margarine
- ⅛ teaspoon dried rosemary, crushed
- 1 tablespoon cornstarch
- ¾ cup chicken broth
- 1 teaspoon lemon juice

Thaw salmon steaks, if frozen (see page 186). Place in 10×6×1½-inch baking dish. Pour water around fish and cook, covered, at **MEDIUM HIGH (7)** for 8 minutes, till fish flakes with a fork. Drain and place on serving dish; cover and keep warm.

In 2-cup glass measure, combine shallots and butter. Heat, uncovered, at **HIGH** for 2 minutes, till tender, stirring once. Add rosemary, cornstarch, and chicken broth. Heat, uncovered, at **HIGH** for 2 to 2½ minutes, till mixture is thickened and bubbly, stirring after each minute. Stir in lemon juice. Spoon sauce over fish to serve. Makes 4 servings.

BAKED RED SNAPPER

Total cooking time: 16 minutes 30 seconds

0:30	8	8					

Melt 2 tablespoons butter in 13×9×2-inch baking dish on **HIGH** 30 to 45 seconds; tilt dish to coat. Sprinkle one 1½-pound pan-dressed whole red snapper cavity with salt and pepper; drizzle with lemon juice. Place fish in dish. Cook, covered, at **MEDIUM HIGH (7)** for 8 minutes, giving dish half turn once. Carefully turn fish over with large spatulas. Cook at **MEDIUM HIGH (7)** for 8 minutes till fish flakes with fork, giving dish half turn once. Makes 4 servings.

TUNA-MAC CASSEROLE

Serve with parslied buttered carrots, crisp coleslaw and cinnamon baked apples with cream—

Total cooking time: 23 minutes

1	2	5	15					

- 4 tablespoons butter or margarine
- ¼ cup all-purpose flour
- 3 cups milk

• • •

- 2 cups (8 ounces) shredded sharp process American cheese
- 1 9¼-ounce can tuna, drained
- 3 or 4 tart green summer apples, cored, pared, and diced (1 pound)
- 1 7-ounce package (2 cups) macaroni, cooked and drained

Place butter in 2-quart casserole. Cook, uncovered, at **HIGH** for 1 minute. Blend in flour. Stir in milk. Cook, uncovered, at **HIGH** for 2 minutes. Stir. Cook, uncovered, at **HIGH** for 5 to 6 minutes, stirring after each minute. Stir in cheese till melted. Stir in tuna, apples, and macaroni. Cook, covered, at **MEDIUM HIGH (7)** for 15 minutes, stirring once. Makes 8 servings.

CHILI MANICOTTI

Total cooking time: 28 minutes 30 seconds

4	24	0:30					

- 1 beaten egg
- 1½ cups cream-style cottage cheese, drained
- 1 cup (4 ounces) shredded sharp process American cheese
- 1 small pickled jalapeño pepper, seeded and finely chopped (2 teaspoons)

• • •

- 8 manicotti shells, cooked in *unsalted* water and drained

• • •

- 2 11¼-ounce cans condensed chili beef soup
- ¾ cup water
- ¼ teaspoon garlic powder
- ¼ teaspoon onion powder

Combine egg, the cottage cheese, ½ cup of the American cheese, and the chopped pepper; mix well. Spoon about ¼ cup cheese mixture into each manicotti shell. Set aside. In 4-cup glass measure, combine soup, water, garlic powder, and onion powder. Heat, uncovered, at **HIGH** for 4 minutes, stirring once.

Pour *half* the sauce into a 12×7½×2-inch baking dish. Top with stuffed manicotti; pour remaining sauce over all, being sure all pasta is coated. Cook, covered, at **MEDIUM (5)** for 24 minutes, giving dish a half turn once. Sprinkle with remaining ½ cup of cheese; cook, uncovered, at **MEDIUM (5)** for 30 seconds. Let stand, covered, 5 minutes to set up. Makes 4 servings.

TEST KITCHEN TIPS

Make A Frozen Fish Your Dish. Fillets such as sole, perch, halibut, haddock, snapper, or flounder frozen in one-pound packages can be used in this versatile three-way recipe. Serve with a crisp lettuce and tomato salad, broccoli spears and fresh fruit for a savory low-calorie meal.

Basic Buttered Fish: Thaw two 1-pound packages frozen fish fillets according to directions on page 186. Let stand 5 minutes. In 13×9×2-inch baking dish, melt 3 tablespoons butter or margarine at **HIGH** for 30 to 45 seconds. Stir in *one* of the sauces below (Sauce Amandine, Sauce Orient, or Sauce Devilish), as desired.

Place each piece fish in butter mixture, turning to coat both sides. Sprinkle with salt. Cook, covered, at **MEDIUM HIGH (7)** for 9 to 10 minutes, till fish flakes easily, rearranging pieces and rotating dish twice. Spoon sauce over to serve. Makes 6 servings.

Sauce Amandine: Stir 2 tablespoons lemon juice, 2 to 3 teaspoons snipped parsley, and dash *each* salt and pepper into butter in baking dish; cook as directed. Before serving, remove fish and stir ¼ cup toasted sliced almonds into baking dish. Serve almond-butter sauce over fish.

Sauce Orient: Stir 3 tablespoons soy sauce, 2 tablespoons thawed frozen orange or pineapple juice concentrate, and dash *each* garlic salt and pepper into butter in baking dish. Cook as directed. Before serving, sprinkle fish with ¼ teaspoon grated orange peel.

Sauce Devilish: Stir ¼ cup chili sauce, 1 teaspoon prepared mustard, ½ teaspoon prepared horseradish (optional), ½ teaspoon Worcestershire sauce, and dash salt into butter in baking dish. Cook as directed.

If three servings suits your family better, use just one 1-pound package fish. Use 2 tablespoons butter and *half* the sauce recipe. Cook at **MEDIUM HIGH (7)** for 6 to 7 minutes.

Garnish with a flourish to give that extra eye appeal. Lemon, lime, or orange cartwheels can be slit halfway across, then made into jaunty twists. Or give them the cogwheel notching treatment and serve on endive. Lemon or lime halves with sawtooth edges also make pretty plate trims.

MACARONI AND CHEESE DELUXE

Garnish with tomato slices and green pepper rings—

Total cooking time: 12 minutes 30 seconds

2	10	0:30						

¼ cup finely chopped onion
¼ cup finely chopped green pepper
2 tablespoons water
• • •
1 7-ounce package (2 cups) macaroni, cooked and drained
2 cups (8 ounces) shredded natural cheddar cheese
1 10¾-ounce can condensed cream of mushroom soup
1 6-ounce can sliced mushrooms, drained
¾ cup milk
¼ cup chopped pimiento
1½ cups rich round cheese cracker crumbs (36 crackers)
1 tablespoon butter or margarine

In 2-quart casserole, combine onion, green pepper, and water. Cook at **HIGH** 2 minutes. Add macaroni, cheese, soup, mushrooms, milk, pimiento, and *1 cup* of the cracker crumbs. Cook, covered, at **MEDIUM HIGH (7)** for 10 to 12 minutes, stirring once. In 1-cup glass measure, melt butter at **HIGH** for 30 seconds; stir in remaining ½ cup crumbs. Sprinkle over top of casserole. Makes 8 servings.

CREAMY NOODLE CASSEROLE

Total cooking time: 18 minutes

3	15							

½ cup finely chopped onion
1 clove garlic, minced
2 tablespoons butter or margarine
3 cups (4 ounces) green spinach noodles, cooked and drained
8 hard-cooked eggs, chopped
• • •
2 cups (16 ounces) small-curd cream-style cottage cheese
⅓ cup grated Parmesan cheese
1 teaspoon Worcestershire sauce
½ teaspoon salt
Dash bottled hot pepper sauce
• • •
½ cup dairy sour cream
Poppy seed

In 2-quart casserole, combine onion, garlic, and butter. Cook, uncovered, at **HIGH** for 3 minutes, stirring once. Add noodles and hard-cooked eggs to onion mixture. In blender container, combine cottage cheese, Parmesan, Worcestershire, salt, and pepper sauce. Cover and blend till smooth. Fold into noodle mixture. Cook, covered, at **MEDIUM HIGH (7)** for 15 minutes, stirring twice. Stir in sour cream; sprinkle top with poppy seeds. Pass additional Parmesan cheese. Garnish with additional hard-cooked egg wedges, if desired. Makes 6 servings.

Hot Three Bean Salad and Corn on the Cob with Sauces

TIMETABLE

1. Prepare Choco-marble Brownies early in the day.
2. Fix frozen lemonade; chill.
3. Prepare relish for burgers; chill.
4. Cook French fries in conventional oven or fryer.
5. Meanwhile, prepare Hot Three Bean Salad; cover to keep warm.
6. Prepare burgers and serve with relish.

MENU

Relish Burgers (page 56)

French Fried Potatoes

Hot Three Bean Salad

Choco-marble Brownies (page 83)

Lemonade

VITAMIN-PACKED VEGETABLES AND RELISHES

HOT THREE BEAN SALAD

Total cooking time: 10 minutes

3	2	5					

    4 slices bacon
   ⅓ cup sugar
    1 tablespoon cornstarch
   ½ teaspoon salt
   ½ teaspoon chili powder
     Several dashes bottled hot pepper sauce
     Dash pepper
   ¼ cup vinegar
   ¼ cup water
    1 16-ounce can green beans, drained
    1 16-ounce can kidney beans, drained and rinsed
    1 16-ounce can garbanzo beans, drained

In 1½-quart casserole, cook bacon, covered with paper toweling, at **HIGH** for 3 minutes, till crisp. Reserve 2 tablespoons drippings in casserole; crumble bacon pieces and set aside. To casserole, add sugar, cornstarch, salt, chili powder, pepper sauce, and pepper. Stir in vinegar and water; cook, uncovered, at **HIGH** for 2 minutes, till thickened and bubbly, stirring once.

Add beans and *half* the bacon; stir to mix. Cook at **HIGH**, uncovered, for 5 minutes, till hot, stirring twice. Sprinkle with remaining bacon. Makes 6 servings.

CREAMY HOT POTATO SALAD

Total cooking time: 29 minutes

12	5:30	2	3:30	6			

    5 medium potatoes, peeled and cubed (4 cups)
   ⅛ teaspoon salt
    6 slices bacon
    2 tablespoons chopped onion
    2 tablespoons cornstarch
   ½ teaspoon salt
   ½ of 14-ounce can (⅔ cup) *sweetened condensed* milk
   ⅔ cup water
   ½ cup vinegar

In 1½-quart casserole, combine potatoes, ⅛ teaspoon salt, and enough water to cover. Cover and cook at **HIGH** for 12 to 14 minutes or till tender; drain. Set potatoes aside. In 12×7½×2-inch baking dish, place bacon on microwave roasting rack. Cook at **HIGH** for 5½ to 6 minutes or till crisp, removing crisp pieces as done. Remove bacon and rack, reserving 1 tablespoon drippings in dish.

Crumble bacon. Add onion to drippings in dish. Cook, uncovered, at **HIGH** for 2 minutes. Pour onion and drippings into 4-cup measure. Blend in cornstarch and ½ teaspoon salt. Add milk and water; mix well. Cook at **HIGH** for 3½ minutes, till thickened and bubbly, stirring thoroughly after each minute. Stir in vinegar and bacon. Pour hot dressing over potatoes in the casserole. Cook, uncovered, at **MEDIUM (5)** for 6 to 8 minutes, stirring once. Serve warm. Makes 6 servings.

CORN ON THE COB WITH SAUCES

Total cooking time: 9 minutes

8	1						

    6 ears fresh corn on the cob, husks removed (2½ pounds)
     • • •
    1 4-ounce carton whipped cream cheese with chives
    4 tablespoons butter or margarine, softened
   ¼ teaspoon salt
     Dash pepper
     • • •
    4 tablespoons butter or margarine
    1 cup catsup
    2 tablespoons vinegar
    2 teaspoons dry mustard
    1 teaspoon salt
   ¼ teaspoon dried basil, crushed
   ¼ teaspoon onion powder
    2 teaspoons Worcestershire sauce

Place corn in 12×7½×2-inch baking dish. Heat, covered, at **HIGH** till tender, 8 to 9 minutes. Serve with *Cheese Sauce* or spread with *Barbecue Sauce* and cook, covered, at **HIGH** 1 minute. Pass remaining sauce.

Cheese Sauce: Blend together whipped cream cheese, the first 4 tablespoons butter, salt, and pepper.

Barbecue Sauce: Melt the remaining 4 tablespoons butter in 4-cup glass measure at **HIGH** for 45 seconds. Add remaining ingredients. Heat at **HIGH**, uncovered, till boiling, 3 to 4 minutes. Spread on corn; heat as above. Reheat and pass remaining sauce.

SQUASH-STUFFING CASSEROLE

Total cooking time: 32 minutes 45 seconds

0:45	17	15					

    2 tablespoons butter or margarine
    1 cup herb-seasoned stuffing mix
     • • •
    2 pounds chopped yellow summer or zucchini squash (7 cups)
    1 cup shredded carrot
   ¼ cup chopped onion
   ¼ cup water
   ¼ teaspoon salt
    1 10¾-ounce can condensed cream of chicken soup
    1 cup dairy sour cream

Place butter in small bowl; cook, uncovered, at **HIGH** for 45 seconds. Toss with stuffing mix; set aside. In large mixing bowl, combine squash, carrot, onion, water, and salt. Cook, covered, at **HIGH** for 17 minutes, till crisp-tender, stirring every three minutes. Drain well.

Combine soup and sour cream. Fold in vegetables. Turn into 12×7½×2-inch baking dish. Cook, uncovered, at **MEDIUM (5)** for 15 minutes, till hot, stirring once. Sprinkle with stuffing mixture. Makes 6 to 8 servings.

SCALLOPED BROCCOLI CASSEROLE

Total cooking time: 13 minutes 30 seconds

7	0:30	6							

- 1 10-ounce package frozen chopped broccoli
- ¼ cup finely chopped onion
- 2 tablespoons butter or margarine
- 1 16-ounce can cream-style corn
- 1 beaten egg
- ½ cup coarse saltine cracker crumbs (12 crackers)
- ½ teaspoon salt

Place broccoli and onion in 1½-quart bowl. Cook, covered, at **HIGH** for 7 to 8 minutes, stirring once; drain and set vegetables aside. Place butter in same bowl. Cook, uncovered, at **HIGH** for 30 seconds.

Stir in corn, egg, crumbs, salt, and dash pepper. Fold in broccoli. Turn into 1-quart casserole. Cook, covered, at **MEDIUM HIGH (7)** for 6 minutes, giving dish half turn once. Makes 6 servings.

CREAMY POTATO BAKE

Total cooking time: 18 minutes

10	8								

- 4 cups thinly sliced pared potatoes (4 medium)
- ¼ cup chopped onion
- ¼ teaspoon salt
- ½ cup water
- 1 10¾-ounce can condensed golden mushroom soup
- ¼ cup milk

Place potatoes, onion, salt, and water in 1½-quart casserole. Cook, covered, at **HIGH** for 10 to 12 minutes or till barely tender; stirring gently once. Drain well. Combine soup and milk; add to potatoes. Cook, uncovered, at **HIGH** for 8 to 10 minutes or till mixture bubbles, stirring twice. Makes 6 servings.

ZESTY BAKED BEANS

Total cooking time: 17 minutes

4	3	10							

- 4 slices bacon
- ½ cup chopped onion
- 2 16-ounce cans pork and beans in tomato sauce
- 2 tablespoons brown sugar
- 1 tablespoon Worcestershire sauce
- 1 teaspoon prepared mustard

Place bacon in 1½-quart casserole. Cover with paper toweling. Cook at **HIGH** for 4 minutes. Remove towels and bacon, reserving all the drippings in casserole dish. Crumble bacon and set aside. Cook onion in bacon drippings at **HIGH** for 3 minutes. Stir in remaining ingredients. Cook, uncovered, at **HIGH** for 10 minutes, stirring twice. Top with crumbled bacon. Makes 6 servings.

HOT FRENCHY TOMATOES

Total cooking time: 5 minutes 20 seconds

0:20	5								

- 6 medium tomatoes
- 1 tablespoon sugar
- 1 teaspoon instant minced onion
- ¼ teaspoon dry mustard
- ¼ cup cooking oil
- 4 teaspoons vinegar
- ½ teaspoon Worcestershire sauce

• • •

- 1 tablespoon butter or margarine
- ½ cup medium cracker crumbs (14 crackers)

Cut thin slice from top of tomatoes; hollow out slightly, removing seeds. Combine sugar, onion, ¼ teaspoon salt, mustard, oil, vinegar, and Worcestershire; spoon into tomatoes. In small bowl, melt butter at **HIGH** for 20 seconds. Mix crumbs and butter; spoon atop. Place in 12×7½×2-inch baking dish. Cook, uncovered, at **HIGH** for 5 to 6 minutes, rearranging once. Makes 6 servings.

GINGER GLAZED CARROTS

Total cooking time: 10 minutes

8	1	1							

- 7 or 8 medium carrots
- 1 tablespoon sugar
- 1 teaspoon cornstarch
- ¼ teaspoon salt
- ½ teaspoon ground ginger
- ⅓ cup orange juice
- 1 tablespoon butter or margarine

Slice carrots diagonally about ½ inch thick (3 cups). Combine with 2 tablespoons water in 1½-quart casserole. Cook, covered, at **HIGH** for 8 to 9 minutes, stirring once. In 1-cup glass measure, combine sugar, cornstarch, salt, and ginger. Add orange juice. Cook, uncovered, at **HIGH** for 1 minute, stirring once. Stir in butter till melted. Drain carrots. Pour orange sauce over, tossing to coat evenly. Cook, uncovered, at **HIGH** for 1 minute. Makes 6 servings.

EASY CREAM CHEESE SAUCE

Total cooking time: 4 minutes

1:30	2	0:30							

In 2-cup glass measure, combine one 3-ounce package cream cheese and ⅓ cup milk. Cook at **LOW (1)** for 1½ minutes. Add ⅛ teaspoon salt, ⅛ teaspoon dry mustard, and dash cayenne pepper; stir till smooth. Cook, uncovered, at **MEDIUM (5)** for 2 minutes, stirring every 30 seconds or till hot. Beat in 1 egg and 1 tablespoon lemon juice; cook, uncovered, at **MEDIUM (5)** for 30 seconds. Serve over broccoli, asparagus, or cauliflower. Makes ⅔ cup.

OLD-FASHIONED CORN RELISH

Total cooking time: 14 minutes

6	5	3						

- 1 10-ounce package frozen corn
- 2 tablespoons water
- ½ cup sugar
- 1 tablespoon cornstarch
- ½ cup vinegar
- ⅓ cup cold water
- 2 tablespoons finely chopped celery
- 2 tablespoons finely chopped green pepper
- 2 tablespoons chopped pimiento
- 1 tablespoon finely chopped onion
- 1 teaspoon ground turmeric
- ½ teaspoon dry mustard

In 1-quart casserole, combine corn and 2 tablespoons water. Cook, covered, at **HIGH** for 6 to 7 minutes, stirring once. Drain in colander. In same casserole, mix sugar and cornstarch; stir in vinegar and ⅓ cup water.

Add corn, celery, pepper, pimiento, onion, and seasonings. Cook, uncovered, at **HIGH** for 5 minutes, till mixture is thickened and bubbly, stirring after each minute. Cook, covered, at **HIGH** 3 minutes more. Cool; chill thoroughly. Stir before serving. Makes 2 cups.

ZIPPY SAUERKRAUT RELISH

Total cooking time: 4 minutes

2	2							

- ½ cup sugar
- ½ cup vinegar
- 1 16-ounce can sauerkraut, drained
- ½ cup diced celery
- ½ cup diced green pepper
- ¼ cup diced onion
- 3 tablespoons chopped pimiento

In 1½-quart casserole, combine sugar and vinegar. Heat, uncovered, at **HIGH** for 2 minutes, till dissolved. Stir in remaining ingredients; heat, uncovered, at **HIGH** for 2 minutes, till warm. Cool; chill. Makes 3 cups.

PARSLEY-BUTTER TOPPER

Total cooking time 2 minutes

2								

- ½ cup butter or margarine
- 2 tablespoons finely snipped parsley
- 1 teaspoon snipped chives
- ½ teaspoon lemon juice

Place butter in 1½-quart bowl. Heat at **LOW (1)** for 2 to 2½ minutes, or till butter is soft. Blend in remaining ingredients. Serve with broccoli, asparagus, carrots, green beans, or potatoes. Chill remaining topper. Makes ½ cup.

CARROT RELISH SALAD

Total cooking time: 12 minutes

12								

- 2 pounds fresh carrots, sliced in ¼-inch rounds (4½ cups)
- ½ cup water
- 2 medium onions, thinly sliced and separated into rings
- 1 medium green pepper, cut in thin strips

• • •

- 1 10¾-ounce can condensed tomato soup
- ¾ cup vinegar
- ⅔ cup sugar
- ½ cup cooking oil
- 1 teaspoon Worcestershire sauce
- 1 teaspoon prepared mustard
- ½ teaspoon salt

In 2-quart casserole, combine carrots and water. Cook, covered, at **HIGH** for 12 to 14 minutes, stirring once. Drain. Stir in onion and green pepper; stir together remaining ingredients and pour over. Cover; marinate in refrigerator several hours or overnight. Drain, reserving marinade. Serve on lettuce. Refrigerate leftover vegetables in marinade. Makes 5 cups.

PICKLED ONION RINGS

Total cooking time: 5 minutes

5								

- 1 cup vinegar
- ⅓ cup sugar
- 6 inches stick cinnamon, broken
- ½ teaspoon salt
- ½ teaspoon whole cloves
- 2 medium sweet onions, thinly sliced and separated into rings (2 cups)

In 1-quart casserole or bowl, combine 1 cup water, vinegar, sugar, cinnamon, salt, and cloves. Heat, covered, at **MEDIUM (5)** for 5 minutes. Pour hot mixture over onions. Cover; chill at least 4 hours. Drain before serving. Makes about 2 cups relish.

CRANBERRY SAUCE

Total cooking time: 22 minutes

8	5	9						

- 2 cups sugar
- 2 cups water
- 1 pound (4 cups) fresh or frozen cranberries

In 3-quart casserole, combine sugar and water. Cook, uncovered, at **HIGH** for 8 to 9 minutes, till boiling, stirring once. Boil at **HIGH** for 5 minutes more. Add cranberries; cook, loosely covered, at **HIGH** for 9 to 10 minutes, stirring once. Serve chilled. Makes 4 cups.

MICRO-RISE YEAST BREADS

BREAD RISING BASICS

Use this microwave method for all the recipes on pages 75 through 79 except the frozen doughs. Adapt the rising method for your own favorite breads, using these directions as a general timing guide—

Prepare the dough as usual, following the recipe. Use a greased non-metal mixing bowl for rising the dough; choose glass baking dishes and loaf dishes instead of metal.

Fill a 4-cup glass measure with 3 cups of tap water. Heat, uncovered, at **HIGH** for 7 to 8 minutes, till the water is boiling. Reduce oven setting to **LOW (1)**. Move the measure to a corner of the oven; place the container of dough in the oven next to the water. Heat at **LOW (1)** according to the time indicated in the recipe. (Generally, a bowl of unshaped dough takes 15 minutes at **LOW (1)** to rise. A plate of rolls or one or two loaves of shaped dough takes 6 to 8 minutes at **LOW (1)** to rise.)

Punch the unshaped dough down and shape it into loaves or rolls. Let rise again, then bake *conventionally* in a preheated oven.

We do not recommend baking breads in the microwave oven; the crust would be unbrowned and the product generally unsatisfactory.

HONEY WHOLE WHEAT BREAD

    2 **packages active dry yeast**
    3 **cups whole wheat flour**
   ⅓ **cup honey**
    1 **tablespoon salt**
   ¼ **cup shortening**
  2¼ **cups water**
  2¾ **to 3 cups all-purpose flour**

In large mixer bowl, combine yeast and the whole wheat flour. In 4-cup glass measure, combine honey, salt, shortening, and water. Heat, uncovered, at **HIGH** for 2 minutes, till warm and shortening begins to melt (115°–120°F). Add to dry mixture in mixer bowl. Beat at low speed on electric mixer for 30 seconds, scraping bowl constantly. Beat 3 minutes at high speed. By hand, stir in enough all-purpose flour to make a moderately stiff dough. Turn onto floured surface; knead till smooth and elastic, 8 to 10 minutes. Place in greased bowl; turn once to grease surface.

Fill a 4-cup glass measure with 3 cups water; heat, uncovered, at **HIGH** for 7 to 8 minutes, till boiling. Place bowl of dough in microwave oven with water. Heat, uncovered, at **LOW (1)** for 15 minutes.

Punch down; divide in half. Shape each into a smooth ball. Cover and let rest 10 minutes. Shape each into a loaf; place in 2 greased 8½×4½×2½-inch loaf dishes. Brush tops lightly with a little melted butter; sprinkle top with whole wheat flour. Heat 3 cups water in 4-cup glass measure at **HIGH** for 7 to 8 minutes, till boiling. Place loaf dishes in oven with water; heat, uncovered, at **LOW (1)** for 7 minutes.

Bake in *conventional oven* at 375°F for 40 to 45 minutes. Cool on rack. Makes 2 loaves.

HERB LOAVES

  6 **to 6¼ cups all-purpose flour**
  2 **packages active dry yeast**
  1 **tablespoon dried celery flakes, crushed**
  1 **teaspoon dried thyme, crushed**
  1 **tablespoon dried parsley flakes, crushed**
 ¼ **cup sugar**
  2 **tablespoons shortening**
  2 **teaspoons onion salt**

In large mixer bowl, combine 2½ *cups* of the flour and the yeast. In 4-cup glass measure, combine herbs, 2¼ cups water, sugar, shortening, and onion salt. Heat, uncovered, at **HIGH** for 1 minute 45 seconds or till warm (115°–120°F). Add to dry mixture. Beat at low speed on electric mixer for ½ minute. Beat at high speed 3 minutes. Stir in enough remaining flour to make moderately stiff dough. Knead on floured surface till smooth, 5 to 8 minutes. Place in greased bowl; turn once to grease surface.

Fill a 4-cup glass measure with 3 cups water. Heat, uncovered, at **HIGH** for 7 to 8 minutes, till boiling. Place bowl of dough, covered with waxed paper, in microwave with the measure of water. Heat at **LOW (1)** for about 15 minutes till bread has risen. Punch down; cover and let rest 10 minutes. Divide in half; shape each into a loaf. Place in 2 well-greased 8½×4½×2½-inch loaf dishes. Let rise using same method as before (boil water; place in oven with the 2 loaves covered with waxed paper; heat at **LOW (1)** till risen, 6 minutes).

Bake in *conventional oven* at 375°F for 30 to 35 minutes. Makes 2 loaves.

YOUR OWN FROZEN BREAD DOUGH

  6 **to 6¼ cups all-purpose flour**
  2 **packages active dry yeast**
 ¼ **cup sugar**
  2 **tablespoons shortening**

In large mixer bowl, combine 2½ *cups* of the flour and the yeast. In 4-cup glass measure, combine 2¼ cups water, sugar, shortening, and 2 teaspoons salt. Heat, uncovered, at **HIGH** for 1 minute 45 seconds or till warm (115°–120°F). Add to dry mixture. Beat at low speed on electric mixer for ½ minute. Beat at high speed 3 minutes. Stir in enough remaining flour to make moderately stiff dough. Turn out and knead on floured surface till smooth, 5 to 8 minutes. Cover and let rest 10 minutes. Shape into 2 loaves 7 inches long. Place on cookie sheet in freezer till frozen. Wrap, label, and freeze. Will store up to 4 weeks.

To prepare one loaf for serving: Remove one loaf from freezer; place rounded side down in a well-greased 8½×4½×2½-inch loaf dish. Fill a 4-cup glass measure with 3 cups water; heat at **HIGH** for 7 to 8 minutes, till boiling. Place loaf dish in oven with water. Heat, uncovered, at **HIGH** for 30 seconds; let stand 20 minutes. Repeat heating and standing. Turn loaf over in dish. Repeat heating and standing three or four more times, till dough is about double. Bake in *conventional oven* at 375°F for 30 to 35 minutes. Makes 1 loaf.

SWEET ROLLS AND SPECIAL BREADS

REFRIGERATOR SWEET ROLL DOUGH

    3½ to 4 cups all-purpose flour
    1 package active dry yeast
              • • •
    1 cup milk
    ⅓ cup granulated sugar
    ⅓ cup shortening
    ½ teaspoon salt
    2 eggs

In large mixer bowl, combine *2 cups* of the flour and the yeast. In 4-cup glass measure, combine milk, sugar, shortening, and salt. Heat, uncovered, at **HIGH** for 1½ to 1¾ minutes, just till mixture is warm and shortening starts to melt (115°–120°F).

Add to dry mixture in bowl; add eggs. Beat at low speed on electric mixer for 30 seconds, scraping bowl constantly. Beat 3 minutes at high speed. By hand, stir in enough of the remaining all-purpose flour to make moderately stiff dough.

Turn out on lightly floured surface; knead till smooth and elastic, 5 to 8 minutes. Shape in a ball. Place in greased bowl; turn once to grease surface. Cover and refrigerate 2 hours or up to 5 days.

Shape into *Super Fast Breakfast Rolls, Cinnamon* or *Orange Rolls,* or *Morning Sun Coffee Cake.* Let rise and bake as directed. Frost with *Powdered Sugar Icing,* if desired. Makes 24 rolls or 2 coffee cakes.

POWDERED SUGAR ICING

    ½ cup sifted powdered sugar
    ¼ teaspoon vanilla
    2 to 3 teaspoons milk

In small bowl, combine powdered sugar and vanilla. Stir in enough of the milk to make drizzling consistency. Makes about 3 tablespoons icing.

SWEET ROLL TIPS

Cutting a filled sweet roll dough, such as *Cinnamon or Orange Rolls,* is especially easy when it's done with thread. Use ordinary sewing weight or heavy-duty white thread. Cut off a long enough piece of thread so you can work comfortably. Place thread under the rolled dough where you want the cut to be, and pull it up around the sides. Then crisscross the thread across the top of the roll, and pull quickly as though tying a knot.

A sharp knife can also be used to cut roll dough. But with a knife, it's more difficult to keep from denting the rolls as they are cut.

When icing sweet rolls or coffee cake, start with slightly cooled bread. Place the bread on a wire rack with a sheet of waxed paper under the rack. The waxed paper catches the drips and makes cleanup easy.

Drizzle icing on the bread from a spoon, or use a spatula to spread on the icing. Be sure to add nuts, fruits, or other decorations quickly before icing sets.

SUPER FAST BREAKFAST ROLLS

Use ¼ of the chilled *Refrigerator Sweet Roll Dough.* Divide into 6 pieces. Roll each piece into a 12-inch rope. Form each into a loose coil on ungreased baking plate, tucking outside ends under.

Fill a 4-cup glass measure with 3 cups water. Heat at **HIGH** for 7 to 8 minutes, till boiling. Place plate of dough in oven with water and heat at **LOW (1)** for 7 minutes.

Bake in *conventional oven* at 375°F for 15 minutes. Cool slightly; spread with topping. Makes 6 rolls.

Toppings: Spread with *Powdered Sugar Icing* and sprinkle with raisins and cinnamon. Or, beat together 2 tablespoons honey and 1 tablespoon butter; spread on rolls and sprinkle with 1 tablespoon chopped toasted almonds.

CINNAMON OR ORANGE ROLLS

    ½ recipe *Refrigerator Sweet Roll Dough*
    2 tablespoons butter or margarine, softened
    2 tablespoons granulated sugar
    ½ teaspoon ground cinnamon *or* ¾ teaspoon grated
        orange peel
    Powdered Sugar Icing

Roll out chilled dough on floured surface to 12×8-inch rectangle. Spread with softened butter. Combine sugar and cinnamon (or orange peel); sprinkle mixture evenly over butter. Roll up, starting with the long side; seal seams. Slice into 12 rolls. Place each, cut side down, in greased 8×1½-inch round baking dish.

Fill a 4-cup glass measure with 3 cups water. Heat at **HIGH** for 7 to 8 minutes, till boiling. Place dish of dough in oven with water and heat at **LOW (1)** for 7 minutes.

Bake in *conventional oven* at 375°F for 20 to 25 minutes. Remove from dish; cool on rack. Drizzle with *Powdered Sugar Icing.* (For *Orange Rolls,* substitute 2 to 3 teaspoons orange juice for the milk used to make the icing drizzling consistency.) Makes 12 rolls.

MORNING SUN COFFEE CAKE

    ½ recipe *Refrigerator Sweet Roll Dough*
    ¼ cup currant jelly
    Powdered Sugar Icing

Roll out chilled dough on floured surface to 10-inch circle. With a doughnut cutter, cut in 12 doughnuts (you may need to reroll). Arrange doughnut holes in solid circle on 12-inch glass baking plate to form center. Stretch the doughnut rings to make slightly oval shape; arrange around the doughnut holes.

Fill a 4-cup glass measure with 3 cups water. Heat at **HIGH** for 7 to 8 minutes, till boiling. Place plate of dough in oven with the measure of water. Heat, uncovered, at **LOW (1)** for 7 to 8 minutes.

Bake in *conventional oven* at 375°F for 12 to 15 minutes. Cool on rack. Spoon currant jelly in centers of outer rings. Drizzle with *Powdered Sugar Icing.* Sprinkle center with yellow sugar crystals, if desired. Makes 1 coffee cake.

Super Fast Breakfast Rolls

Cinnamon or Orange Rolls

Morning Sun Coffee Cake

GARDEN BATTER BREAD

   1 cup coarsely grated carrot (2 medium)
   ¼ cup water
   • • •
   3 cups all-purpose flour
   2 packages active dry yeast
   2 teaspoons salt
   ¼ cup light molasses
   2 tablespoons cooking oil
   1 egg
   1¼ cups warm water (115°–120°F)
   ½ cup wheat germ
   ¼ cup snipped parsley

In small bowl, combine carrots and ¼ cup water. Heat, covered, at **HIGH** for 4 minutes. Drain; blot dry with paper toweling. Set aside.

In large mixer bowl, combine *2 cups* of the flour, the yeast, and salt. Add molasses, oil, egg, and 1¼ cups warm water. Beat with electric mixer on low speed for 30 seconds, scraping bowl constantly. Beat at high speed 3 minutes. By hand, stir in remaining flour, the wheat germ, parsley, and carrots. Turn dough into greased 2-quart casserole.

Fill a 4-cup glass measure with 3 cups water. Heat at **HIGH** for 7 to 8 minutes, till boiling. Place casserole of dough in oven with water. Heat, uncovered, at **LOW (1)** for 12 to 15 minutes, till bread has risen.

Bake in *conventional oven* at 350°F for 20 minutes; cover with foil and bake 30 to 40 minutes more. Makes 1 loaf.

HOT ROLL MIX

Prepare a 14-ounce package hot roll mix according to package directions. Cover dough in mixing bowl.

Fill a 4-cup glass measure with 3 cups water. Heat, uncovered, at **HIGH** for 7 to 8 minutes, till boiling. Place bowl of dough in oven with water. Heat at **LOW (1)** for 20 minutes, till doubled.

Shape into a loaf; place in 8½×4½×2½-inch loaf dish. Bring the measure of water to boiling again, 7 to 8 minutes at **HIGH.** Place loaf dish in oven with water; heat, covered, at **LOW (1)** for 5 to 6 minutes, till risen.

Bake in *conventional oven* at 350°F for 30 to 35 minutes, covering with foil after 20 minutes. Makes 1 loaf.

FROZEN BREAD DOUGH

Start with a one-pound loaf of commercially-frozen bread dough. Place in well-greased 8½×4½×2½-inch loaf dish. Fill a 4-cup glass measure with 3 cups water. Cook, uncovered, at **HIGH** for 7 to 8 minutes, till boiling. Place frozen dough in dish in oven with water. Heat, uncovered, at **HIGH** for 30 seconds. Let stand 20 minutes. Repeat heating and standing. Turn loaf over in dish.

Repeat heating 30 seconds and standing 20 minutes three or four more times, till dough is about doubled, just above the top of the baking dish.

Bake in *conventional oven* at 350°F for 30 to 35 minutes. Brush top with a little melted butter. Makes 1 loaf.

SWEET ROLLS AND SPECIAL BREADS *(continued)*

REFRIGERATOR YEAST ROLLS

See the photos, right, for roll shaping techniques—

>   1 package active dry yeast
> 3½ cups all-purpose flour
> 1¼ cups milk
>   ¼ cup sugar
>   ¼ cup shortening
>   1 teaspoon salt
>   1 egg

In large mixer bowl, combine yeast and *2 cups* of the flour. In 4-cup glass measure, combine milk, sugar, shortening, and salt. Heat, uncovered, at **HIGH** for 1½ to 2 minutes, till warm and shortening begins to melt (115°–120°F). Add to dry mixture in mixer bowl; add egg. Beat at low speed on electric mixer for 30 seconds, scraping bowl constantly. Beat 3 minutes at high speed. By hand, stir in enough remaining flour to make a soft dough. Place in greased bowl; turn once to grease surface. Cover; chill at least 2 hours or up to 5 days.

Shape ½ of chilled dough at a time into *Pan, Crescent,* or *Bowknot Rolls,* as directed below.

Fill a 4-cup glass measure with 3 cups water; heat, uncovered, at **HIGH** for 7 to 8 minutes, till boiling. Place shaped unrisen dough, uncovered, in oven with the water. Heat at **LOW (1)** for 7 to 9 minutes. Bake in *conventional oven* at 400°F for 12 to 15 minutes. Makes 16 to 24 rolls.

Pan Rolls

PAN ROLLS

Use ½ of the chilled *Refrigerator Yeast Roll* dough. Divide and shape it into 12 balls, rolling the edges under to make smooth tops. Place 3 balls, smooth side up, in center of greased 8×1½-inch round baking dish. Surround with 9 remaining balls. Let rise in the microwave oven and bake *conventionally* as directed. Makes 12.

CRESCENT ROLLS

Use ½ of the chilled *Refrigerator Yeast Roll* dough. Round it into a ball. On lightly floured surface, roll ball into a 12-inch circle. Brush surface with melted butter. Cut circle into 12 equal wedges. To shape rolls, begin at wide end of each wedge and roll toward the point. Place, point down, 2 to 3 inches apart on greased 12-inch glass baking plate. Let rise in the microwave oven and bake *conventionally* as directed. Makes 12 rolls.

Crescent Rolls

BOWKNOT ROLLS

Use ½ of the chilled *Refrigerator Yeast Roll* dough. Divide into 8 pieces. On a lightly floured surface, roll each piece of dough into a pencil-like strand, each about 9 inches long. Form a loose knot (pull strands gently before tying knots if they shrink). Place 2 to 3 inches apart on greased 12-inch glass baking plate. Let rise in microwave oven and bake *conventionally* as directed. Makes 8 rolls.

Bowknot Rolls

Basic Homemade Ice Cream

TIMETABLE

1. Make Homemade Ice Cream; let ripen.
2. Set table.
3. Make Creamy Hot Potato Salad.
4. Grill steak while potato salad cooks.
5. Slice tomatoes just before serving.
6. Slice peaches after dinner to serve with ice cream.

MENU

Charcoal Grilled Steak
Creamy Hot Potato Salad (page 71)
Sliced Tomatoes
Beer   Milk
Basic Homemade Ice Cream
Chocolate Sauce   Butterscotch Sauce
Sliced Fresh Peaches   Chopped Nuts

OLD-FASHIONED DESSERTS

BASIC HOMEMADE ICE CREAM

Total cooking time: 6 minutes

4	2						

- ¾ cup sugar
- 4 cups light cream
- ½ envelope (1½ teaspoons) unflavored gelatin
- 2 tablespoons cold water
- 1 slightly beaten egg
- 1 tablespoon vanilla

In 2-quart casserole or mixing bowl, combine sugar and *2 cups* of the cream. Sprinkle gelatin over water to soften; add to sugar mixture. Heat, uncovered, at **HIGH** for 4 minutes, till gelatin dissolves, stirring once. Slowly stir about *½ cup* of the hot mixture into the beaten egg; return all to hot mixture. Heat again at **HIGH** till mixture thickens slightly, about 2 minutes, stirring twice. Chill. Add remaining cream, the vanilla, and dash salt. Freeze in ice cream freezer according to manufacturer's directions. Makes 1½ quarts.

Chocolate Fleck Almond: Increase sugar to 1 cup. To sugar-gelatin mixture, add 3 squares (3 ounces) semi-sweet chocolate. Proceed as directed, adding 2 minutes to time while chocolate melts. To chilled mix, add ½ cup toasted slivered almonds.

For Strawberry: Decrease sugar to ½ cup. Crush 1 quart fresh strawberries with ¾ cup sugar; add to the chilled mix.

For Rum Raisin: Omit vanilla. Soak 1 cup chopped seedless raisins in 3 tablespoons rum for 2 hours at room temperature. Add to gelatin mixture before freezing.

BROWN BETTY CONTEMPORARY-STYLE

Total cooking time: 12 minutes

12							

- 8 cups sliced, pared tart apples
- ¾ cup apple juice
- ½ cup raisins
- ⅓ cup honey
- ¼ cup packed brown sugar
- 3 tablespoons all-purpose flour
- 1 teaspoon ground cinnamon

• • •

- ½ cup quick-cooking rolled oats
- ½ cup whole wheat flour
- ½ cup wheat germ
- ½ cup shelled sunflower seeds
- ¼ cup honey
- 4 tablespoons butter or margarine, melted

In 13×9×2-inch baking dish, combine apples, juice, raisins, the ⅓ cup honey, the brown sugar, flour, and cinnamon; mix well. Combine remaining ingredients; mix well and spread over apple mixture. Cook, uncovered, at **HIGH** for 12 to 15 minutes, giving dish half turn once, till apples are tender. Serve with vanilla ice cream, if desired. Makes 8 to 10 servings.

CHOCOLATE BROWNIES

Total cooking time: 11 minutes 30 seconds

2:30	7	2					

- 2 squares (2 ounces) unsweetened chocolate

• • •

- 4 tablespoons butter or margarine
- 1 cup sugar
- 2 egg yolks
- ¼ cup milk
- ½ teaspoon vanilla

• • •

- ⅔ cup all-purpose flour
- ½ teaspoon baking powder
- ½ teaspoon salt
- 2 stiff-beaten egg whites
- ¼ cup chopped walnuts

To melt chocolate: place 2 squares in 6-ounce custard cup. Cook at **HIGH** 2½ minutes. Set aside to cool. Cream together the butter and the 1 cup sugar till light and fluffy. Add egg yolks, milk, and vanilla; beat well. Stir in chocolate. Stir together flour, baking powder, and salt; add to creamed mixture and mix well.

Fold in the beaten egg whites and nuts. Spread in 8×8×2-inch baking dish. Cook, uncovered, at **MEDIUM (5)** for 7 minutes, giving dish half turn after 3 minutes. Cook at **HIGH** for 2 minutes. Frost if desired. Makes 24.

LEMON AND ICE CREAM PIE

Total cooking time: 7 minutes

0:30	3	0:30	1:30	1:30			

- 1 9-inch Graham Cracker Pie Crust
- 4 tablespoons butter or margarine
- ⅓ cup lemon juice
- ¾ cup sugar
- Dash salt
- 3 slightly beaten eggs
- 2 pints vanilla ice cream, softened

For Graham Cracker Pie Crust: heat 5 tablespoons butter or margarine in 9-inch pie plate at **HIGH** for 30 to 45 seconds. Stir in ¼ cup sugar and 1¼ cups graham cracker crumbs. Press mixture firmly over bottom and sides of pie plate. Cook at **MEDIUM HIGH (7)** for 3 minutes, giving dish one half turn. Cool.

In 4-cup glass measure, melt butter at **HIGH** for 30 to 45 seconds. Stir in lemon juice, sugar, and salt. Cook, uncovered, at **HIGH** for 1½ minutes, till sugar dissolves. Pour the hot mixture into beaten eggs; return all to measure. Cook, uncovered, at **HIGH** for 1½ minutes, till mixture thickens, stirring every 30 seconds. Chill.

Place 1 pint of the ice cream in graham cracker shell, spreading evenly. Spread *half* the chilled lemon sauce over ice cream. Freeze pie several hours or till firm. Repeat layers of remaining 1 pint of ice cream and lemon sauce and freeze again till firm.

3-WAY FRUIT COBBLER

Total cooking time: 4 minutes

4							

- 1 cup all-purpose flour
- 2 tablespoons sugar
- 1 teaspoon baking powder
- ¼ teaspoon salt
- 4 tablespoons butter or margarine

• • •

- ¼ cup milk
- 1 slightly beaten egg

• • •

- Rhubarb, cherry, *or* peach filling
- 2 teaspoons sugar
- ⅛ teaspoon ground cinnamon *or* pumpkin pie spice
- Light cream or ice cream

In bowl, mix together flour, 2 tablespoons sugar, baking powder, and salt. Cut in butter till crumbly. Combine milk and egg; add all at once to dry ingredients, stirring just to moisten. Set aside. In 2-quart casserole, prepare hot fruit filling (see recipes below and at right). Immediately spoon biscuit mixture atop fruit in 5 or 6 mounds around edges. Combine 2 teaspoons sugar and cinnamon; sprinkle atop dumplings. Cook, covered, at **HIGH** for 4 minutes or till biscuits are done. Serve warm with cream or ice cream. Makes 5 or 6 servings.

RHUBARB COBBLER FILLING

Total cooking time: 7 minutes

7							

- ¾ cup sugar
- 2 tablespoons cornstarch
- ⅛ teaspoon ground cinnamon
- 1 cup water
- 4 cups fresh rhubarb, cut in ½-inch pieces
- 1 tablespoon butter or margarine

In 2-quart casserole, combine sugar, cornstarch, and cinnamon. Stir in water. Add rhubarb and butter. Cook, covered, at **HIGH** for 7 minutes, stirring twice till fruit mixture is boiling hot. Continue directions for *Fruit Cobbler* recipe.

CHERRY COBBLER FILLING

Total cooking time: 5 minutes

5							

- 1 21-ounce can cherry pie filling
- ½ cup water
- 1 tablespoon lemon juice

In 2-quart casserole, combine pie filling, water, and lemon juice; heat, covered, at **HIGH** for 5 minutes, till mixture is boiling hot, stirring once. Continue directions in *Fruit Cobbler* recipe.

PEACH COBBLER FILLING

Total cooking time: 6 minutes

1	5						

- ⅓ cup packed brown sugar
- 1 tablespoon cornstarch
- ¼ teaspoon pumpkin pie spice
- ½ cup water
- 3 cups sliced fresh peaches (6 medium)
- 1 tablespoon butter or margarine

In 2-quart casserole, combine brown sugar, cornstarch, and pumpkin pie spice. Stir in water. Cook, uncovered, at **HIGH** for 1 minute, stirring after 30 seconds, till mixture is thickened and bubbly. Add peaches and butter; heat again, covered, at **HIGH** for 5 minutes, till fruit mixture is boiling hot. Continue directions for *Fruit Cobbler* recipe.

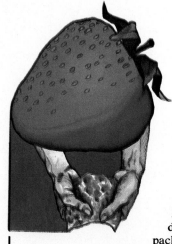

TEST KITCHEN TIPS

Frozen fruits make a command performance in such scrumptious desserts as blueberry-sauced dessert waffles, pound cake slices with strawberries and sour cream, and brandied peach sundaes. Use the convenient packages mentioned here or your own fruit frozen in bags or plastic cartons. All can be placed in the microwave oven to speed thawing. Defrost them till ice still remains in the center; then let the fruit stand a minute or two to thaw completely. Stir before serving.

Sweetened Fruit in Plastic Pouch (10 ounces): Place the unopened pouch in oven, in a bowl if desired. Cook at **MEDIUM LOW (3)** for 1 minute. Bend the pouch between your hands several times to separate fruit and distribute heat. Replace in oven; cook at **MEDIUM LOW (3)** for 2 to 3 minutes bending pouch twice.

Sweetened Fruit in Cartons with Metal Ends (10 ounces): Remove one of the metal ends. Place opened package in oven, open side up. Cook, uncovered, at **MEDIUM LOW (3)** for 1 minute. Remove from carton into bowl. Replace in oven; cook, uncovered, at **MEDIUM LOW (3)** for 2 to 2½ minutes, breaking fruit apart with a fork after 1 minute.

See page 171 and 186 for more on fruit defrosting.

PINEAPPLE UPSIDE DOWN CAKE

Make the cupcake variation for an after-school snack—

Total cooking time: 10 minutes 30 seconds

0:30	10						

   1 8¾-ounce can (1 cup) pineapple tidbits
   3 tablespoons butter or margarine
   ½ cup packed brown sugar
   4 maraschino cherries, halved
   1 package 1-layer-size yellow cake mix (no pudding in the mix)

Drain pineapple, reserving 1 tablespoon syrup. Melt butter in 8×8×2-inch baking dish, at **HIGH** for 30 seconds. Stir in reserved syrup and brown sugar. Arrange pineapple and cherries in dish. Prepare cake mix according to package directions. Carefully pour batter from outside in, over pineapple mixture in pan. Cook, uncovered, at **MEDIUM HIGH (7)** for 10 to 11 minutes, giving dish quarter turns every 3 minutes. Let stand 1 to 2 minutes before inverting cake onto serving plate. Serve warm with whipped topping. Makes 8 servings.

Or, prepare sugar mixture in small bowl; divide among 16 paper bake cups. Place 4 at a time in glass custard cups. Spoon 2 tablespoons batter into each. Arrange custard cups in oven (none in center); cook, uncovered, at **MEDIUM HIGH (7)** for 3 minutes. Repeat with remaining batter. Invert to serve. Makes 16 cupcakes.

PLYMOUTH CRANBERRY CAKE

Total cooking time: 16 minutes 30 seconds

10	5	1:30					

   1 16-ounce can whole cranberry sauce
   2 tablespoons butter or margarine
   1 package 1-layer-size yellow cake mix (no pudding in the mix)
   4 tablespoons butter or margarine
   ½ cup sifted powdered sugar
   ½ cup cold water
  1½ teaspoons cornstarch
   1 teaspoon vanilla
   ½ teaspoon vinegar

Break up cranberry sauce in buttered 8×8×2-inch baking dish, spreading evenly. Dot with the 2 tablespoons butter. Prepare cake mix according to package directions. Carefully pour over cranberry sauce in dish. Cook, uncovered, at **MEDIUM (5)** for 10 minutes, giving dish half turn after 5 minutes. Then, cook, uncovered, on **HIGH** for 5 minutes. Let stand 5 minutes; loosen edges and invert cake on serving plate.

Serve with *Butter Sauce:* In mixer bowl, cream the 4 tablespoons butter and powdered sugar till fluffy. In 2-cup measure, combine water and cornstarch. Cook, uncovered, at **HIGH** for 1½ minutes or till bubbly, stirring every 30 seconds. Stir in vanilla and vinegar. Gradually stir into butter mixture. Makes 6 to 8 servings.

CHOCO-MARBLE BROWNIES

The kids will really go for these chewy treats along with big glasses of milk at bedtime—

Total cooking time: 22 minutes

2	20						

   1 3-ounce package cream cheese
   ¼ cup sugar
   1 egg
   ½ teaspoon vanilla
       • • •
   1 15½-ounce package brownie mix
   ½ cup chopped walnuts

Place cream cheese in small mixing bowl. Cook at **LOW (1)** for 2 minutes or till softened. Stir in sugar; beat in egg and vanilla. Set aside. Prepare brownie mix according to package directions; stir in nuts. Place an inverted "shot glass" in center of greased 8×8×2-inch baking dish; spread chocolate mixture in dish.

Pour cheese mixture atop, swirling with narrow spatula to marble. Cook, uncovered, at **MEDIUM (5)** for 20 minutes or till toothpick comes out clean, giving dish quarter turns every 5 minutes. Cool; cut into squares. Makes 16.

DATE APPLE SQUARES

Total cooking time: 15 minutes

14	1						

   1 cup all-purpose flour
   ½ cup packed brown sugar
  1¼ teaspoons baking powder
   ½ teaspoon salt
   1 teaspoon ground cinnamon
   ¼ teaspoon ground allspice
       • • •
   1 slightly beaten egg
   ½ of 21-ounce can apple pie filling (about 1 cup)
   ¼ cup cooking oil
   ½ teaspoon vanilla
   ½ cup chopped dates
   ¼ cup chopped walnuts
       • • •
   ½ cup lemon or apple yogurt
   ½ of 4½-ounce carton (1 cup) frozen whipped dessert topping, thawed

In mixing bowl, stir together flour, brown sugar, baking powder, salt, and spices. Combine egg, pie filling, oil, and vanilla; stir into flour mixture and mix well. Stir in chopped dates and walnuts.

Place inverted "shot glass" in center of 8×8×2-inch baking dish. Spread batter evenly in dish. Cook, uncovered, at **MEDIUM (5)** for 14 minutes, giving dish half turn after 7 minutes. Cook at **HIGH** 1 minute. Cool. Combine lemon or apple yogurt and whipped dessert topping; spread over top of cake. Refrigerate any leftover squares. Makes 6 to 8 servings.

Chili Dogs

TIMETABLE

1. Make relishes; chill.
2. Set table or trays and crush corn chips.
3. Heat chili for chili dogs; cover.
4. Heat vegetable soup (see page 53); cover to keep warm.
5. Heat frankfurters and chili together.
6. Pour milk.

MENU

Vegetable Soup

Chili Dogs

Pickles   Carrot and Celery Sticks

Corn Chips

Ice Cream Bars

Milk

WHEN THE KIDS TAKE OVER

CHILI DOGS

Total cooking time: 6 minutes 30 seconds

3	2	1:30					

- 1 15-ounce can chili with beans
- 8 frankfurters
- 8 frankfurter buns, split and buttered
- ½ cup crushed corn chips

Place chili in small bowl. Cook, covered, at **HIGH** for 3 to 4 minutes; set aside. Place one frank in each bun; place four on a plate. Cook at **HIGH** for 2 minutes. Spoon about 2 tablespoons chili mixture on each frank and sprinkle each with about 1 tablespoon chips. Cook 1½ minutes at **HIGH** till hot. Repeat with remaining franks, chili, and chips. Makes 8 servings.

HOME RUN BURGERS

Total cooking time: 9 minutes

5	4						

- 1 pound ground beef
- ¼ cup chopped onion
- 1 tablespoon all-purpose flour
- ¼ teaspoon salt
- 1 10¾-ounce can condensed vegetable soup
- ½ teaspoon Worcestershire sauce
- ½ cup dairy sour cream
- 8 hamburger buns, split and toasted

In 1½-quart bowl or casserole, combine ground beef and onion. Cook, uncovered, at **HIGH** for 5 minutes, stirring 3 times. Drain off excess fat. Blend in flour and salt. Add soup and Worcestershire. Cook, uncovered, at **HIGH** for 4 minutes, stirring after every 2 minutes. Stir in sour cream. Serve in buns. Makes 8 or 9 servings.

DENVERWICHES

Total cooking time: 4 minutes 30 seconds

2	2:30						

- 6 hamburger buns, split and toasted
- 1 4½-ounce can corned beef spread
- ¼ cup chopped onion
- 2 tablespoons finely chopped green pepper
- 2 tablespoons butter or margarine
- 4 eggs
- ¼ cup milk
  Dash *each* salt and pepper

Spread bottom halves of buns with beef spread; set aside. In 1-quart casserole, combine onion, green pepper, and butter. Cook, uncovered, at **HIGH** for 2 minutes, till tender. Beat eggs, milk, salt, and pepper; add to onion mixture. Heat, uncovered, at **MEDIUM HIGH (7)** for 2½ to 3 minutes, stirring every 30 seconds, till eggs are done. Pile atop corned beef; cover with bun tops. Makes 6 servings.

PIZZA BURGERS

Total cooking time: 14 minutes

8	5	1						

- 1 slightly beaten egg
- ¼ cup fine dry bread crumbs
- ¼ cup finely chopped onion
- 1 8-ounce can (1 cup) pizza sauce
- ¾ teaspoon garlic salt
- 1½ pounds ground beef
- 1 cup shredded mozzarella cheese

In bowl, combine egg, crumbs, onion, *¼ cup* of the pizza sauce, and the garlic salt; mix well. Add beef; mix well. In 13×9×2-inch baking dish, shape into six 3½-inch circles, building up the edges to a ¾-inch rim. Cook, covered, at **HIGH** for 8 minutes. Spoon off pan drippings. Spoon remaining pizza sauce into burger cups. Cook, covered, at **HIGH** for 5 minutes. Sprinkle with cheese; cook at **HIGH** for 1 minute. Makes 6 servings.

BARBECUE BURGERS

Total cooking time: 10 minutes

5	5						

- 1 pound ground beef
- ¼ cup chopped onion
- ¼ cup chopped green pepper
- ½ teaspoon salt
- 1 8-ounce can tomato sauce
- 3 tablespoons vinegar
- 2 tablespoons brown sugar
- 1 teaspoon Worcestershire sauce
  Dash bottled hot pepper sauce
- 6 hamburger buns, split and toasted

In 2-quart casserole, combine beef, onion, green pepper, and salt. Cook, uncovered, at **HIGH** for 5 minutes, stirring 3 times to break up meat. Drain off excess fat. Stir in tomato sauce, vinegar, brown sugar, Worcestershire, and hot pepper sauce. Cook, covered, at **HIGH** for 5 minutes. Spoon onto buns. Makes 6 servings.

S'MORES

Total cooking time: 15 seconds

0:15							

- 2 graham crackers
- 4 squares milk chocolate candy bar
- 1 large marshmallow or 6 small marshmallows

Place one graham cracker on paper towel. Top with chocolate squares, then marshmallow. Heat, uncovered, at **HIGH** for 15 seconds. Top with second cracker. Let stand 1 minute before serving. Makes 1.

2 or 3 s'mores:	20 seconds
4 s'mores:	25 seconds

NUTS AND BOLTS

Vary the flavor by using different salad dressing mixes, cashews, or spoon-size shredded wheat or corn biscuits—

Total cooking time: 10 minutes 30 seconds

0:30	10						

- 6 tablespoons butter or margarine
- 1 envelope cheese Italian salad dressing mix
- 4 cups (4 ounces) round oat cereal
- 3 cups pretzel sticks
- 1 cup mixed salted nuts

In 3-quart mixing bowl, heat butter, uncovered, at **HIGH** for 30 to 45 seconds. Stir in dressing mix. Add cereal, pretzels, and nuts, tossing to coat evenly with butter mixture. Heat, uncovered, at **MEDIUM LOW (3)** for 10 minutes, till warmed, stirring occasionally. Cool; store in air-tight container. Makes 8 cups.

PEANUT BUTTERSCOTCH FUDGE

Total cooking time: 4 minutes

2:30	1:30						

- 2 6-ounce packages (2 cups) butterscotch pieces
- 1 14-ounce can *sweetened condensed* milk
- ½ cup creamy peanut butter
- 1 teaspoon vanilla
- Dash salt

In mixing bowl, cook butterscotch pieces, at **HIGH** for 2½ to 3 minutes, till melted, stirring once. Blend in milk, peanut butter, vanilla, and salt. Cook, uncovered, at **HIGH** for 1½ to 2 minutes, just till bubbly. Turn into buttered 8×8×2-inch baking dish. Chill till firm. Cut into squares. Keep refrigerated. Makes 2 pounds.

CHICKEN TAMALE PIE

Be sure to unwrap the canned tamales from their corn husk "coats" before arranging atop the casserole—

Total cooking time: 17 minutes

5	12						

- 1 11-ounce can condensed cheddar cheese soup
- 1 8-ounce can tomato sauce
- 2 5-ounce cans boned chicken *or* 1½ cups cubed cooked chicken
- ¾ cup uncooked packaged precooked rice

• • •

- 2 15-ounce cans tamales

In 8×8×2-inch baking dish, combine soup, tomato sauce, chicken, and rice. Heat, covered, at **HIGH** for 5 minutes, stirring once. Drain tamales, reserving liquid. Stir liquid into casserole. Arrange tamales atop; heat, covered, at **HIGH** for 12 minutes more, till tamales are hot and rice is done. Makes 4 to 6 servings.

QUICKIE CHICKIE

Total cooking time: 20 minutes

20							

- 1 package seasoned coating mix for chicken
- 2½ pounds chicken drumsticks (about 10)

Shake and coat drumsticks according to directions on coating mix. Arrange in baking dish. Bake, covered loosely, at **MEDIUM HIGH (7)** for 20 minutes, till tender, giving dish quarter turns every 5 minutes. Makes 4 servings.

PEANUT BUTTER PLUS

Total cooking time: 12 seconds

0:12							

- 1 slice toast
- Peanut butter
- Options: jelly, marshmallow creme, chocolate bar squares, crumbled bacon, banana slices

Place toast on paper napkin, towel, or plate. Spread with peanut butter; top with desired topping. Cook, uncovered, at **HIGH** for 12 to 15 seconds, till peanut butter softens and just begins to melt. Makes 1 serving. *Note:* You can do 4 at once on paper towel, 40 seconds.

LUNCHEON LOAF HAWAIIAN

Total cooking time: 5 minutes

5							

- 1 12-ounce can luncheon meat
- Prepared mustard
- 2 canned pineapple slices, halved
- 2 tablespoons brown sugar

Cut luncheon meat about ⅔ of the way through into 8 sections. Place on serving plate. Spread cut surfaces lightly with mustard. In every other slice, insert a pineapple half-slice. Sprinkle all with brown sugar. Bake, covered, at **HIGH** for 5 minutes. Makes 4 servings.

HOT CIDER AND DOUGHNUTS

Total cooking time: 4 minutes

3	1						

- 1½ cups (12 ounces) cider
- Dash pumpkin pie spice
- 4 doughnuts, glazed or sugared or frosted

Sprinkle cider with a dash pumpkin pie spice; pour into 2 mugs or cups. Heat, uncovered, at **HIGH** for 3 minutes. Place the 4 doughnuts on paper toweling or plates. Place in oven along with cider and heat, covered with waxed paper, at **HIGH** for 1 minute. Makes 2 servings.

JIFFY SPAGHETTI AND MEATBALLS

Total cooking time: 23 minutes

3	20							

- ½ cup chopped onion
- ½ cup chopped green pepper
- 2 tablespoons water
- 2 20-ounce jars Italian cooking sauce
- ⅓ recipe (24) frozen Basic Meatballs (page 161)
- 1 clove garlic, minced
- 1 tablespoon sugar
- ½ teaspoon chili powder
  - Hot cooked spaghetti
  - Grated Parmesan cheese

In 2½- or 3-quart casserole, combine onion, green pepper, and water. Cook, covered, at **HIGH** for 3 to 4 minutes. (Do not drain.) Stir in cooking sauce, frozen meatballs, garlic, sugar, and chili powder. Cook, covered, at **MEDIUM HIGH (7)** for 20 to 25 minutes, till sauce is hot and meatballs are heated through. Serve over hot spaghetti. Pass Parmesan cheese. Makes 6 to 8 servings.

CORNY BEEF DINNER FIX-UP

Total cooking time: 18 minutes

15	3							

- 1 pound ground beef
- 1 8-ounce package cheese-burger-hamburger dinner mix
- 1 12-ounce can whole kernel corn, drained
- ½ cup dairy sour cream
- 2 tablespoons snipped parsley

Crumble beef into 2-quart casserole. Add the dinner mix ingredients; mix well. Add ⅓ cup *less* liquid than called for on package. Cook, covered, at **MEDIUM (5)** for 15 to 20 minutes or till meat is cooked. Stir in corn. Cook, covered, at **HIGH** for 3 minutes or till macaroni is tender. Stir in sour cream. Top with parsley. Makes 4 to 6 servings.

PARTY MINI REUBENS

Total cooking time: 1 minute 15 seconds

1:15								

- 36 slices rye melba toast
  - Thousand Island dressing
- 4 ounces thinly sliced cooked corned beef
- 1 8-ounce can sauerkraut, drained and snipped
- 6 slices (6 ounces) process Swiss cheese

Spread each slice rye with salad dressing. Set aside. Cut slices of corned beef in half. Place slices of corned beef on plates. Cover each with a teaspoon sauerkraut. Cut each slice of cheese into 6 pieces; put one piece atop each. Heat 12 at a time, uncovered, at **HIGH** for 1¼ to 1½ minutes till cheese melts. Serve on melba toast. Makes 36.

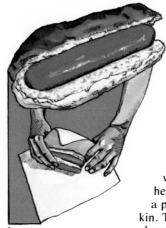

Hot dogs are a good get-started recipe to acquaint young cooks with the microwave oven. Each frank is heated in a bun wrapped in a paper towel or paper napkin. The paper absorbs steam, keeps the sandwich together, and makes serving simple. Tell younger children to unwrap the bundles with care because of the hot steam.

Butter split buns; add a frankfurter and wrap each loosely in a separate paper towel or paper napkin. Arrange in oven. Heat at **HIGH** till meat is warmed according to the chart.

Number	Time
1	30 seconds
2	50 seconds
3	1 minute 20 seconds
4	1 minute 30 seconds
5	1 minute 50 seconds
6	2 minutes

PEANUT CRISP BARS

Total cooking time: 4 minutes 30 seconds

3	1:30							

- ½ cup granulated sugar
- ½ cup light corn syrup
- 1 cup peanut butter
- 2 cups crisp rice cereal
- 4 tablespoons butter or margarine
- ¼ cup packed brown sugar
- 1 tablespoon milk
- ½ teaspoon vanilla
- 1¼ cups sifted powdered sugar

In 2-quart casserole or baking dish, combine granulated sugar, corn syrup, and dash salt. Heat, uncovered, at **HIGH** for 3 minutes, till sugar dissolves, stirring twice. Blend in peanut butter; then add rice cereal. Pat into foil-lined 8×8×2-inch baking dish.

In small mixing bowl, combine butter and brown sugar. Heat, uncovered, at **HIGH** for 1½ minutes, till melted and sugar dissolves, stirring once. Stir in milk and vanilla; add powdered sugar and stir till smooth. Remove cereal mixture from dish; peel off foil. Immediately spread top with frosting. Cut in bars. Makes 48.

Easy Opera Fudge, Snowballs, Pheeney's Chocolate Fudge, Caramel Snappers, Rocky Road, Mint Wafers (recipe page 90)

TIMETABLE

1. Chill punch.
2. Make Easy Opera Fudge; refrigerate.
3. Make Pheeney's Chocolate Fudge; refrigerate.
4. Make Rocky Road; refrigerate.
5. Make Snowballs, Mint Wafers, and Caramel Snappers.
6. Make Wholesome Cereal Snack.
7. Arrange candies on serving tray.

MENU

Wholesome Cereal Snack
Easy Opera Fudge
Caramel Snappers   Mint Wafers
Pheeney's Chocolate Fudge
Rocky Road   Snowballs
Fruit Punch

CANDIES AND SNACKS

PHEENEY'S CHOCOLATE FUDGE

Total cooking time: 2 minutes

2							

- ½ cup butter or margarine
- ⅓ cup water

• • •

- 4½ cups sifted powdered sugar
- ½ cup nonfat dry milk powder
- ½ cup unsweetened cocoa powder
- Dash salt

In 2-quart bowl, combine butter and water. Cook at **HIGH** for 2 minutes or till boiling. Stir together sugar, milk powder, cocoa powder, and salt. Beat into butter mixture. Pour into buttered 8×8×2-inch baking dish. Cool; score with knife. Garnish with walnut halves, if desired. Refrigerate several hours. Cut into squares. Makes 3 dozen 1-inch pieces.

WHOLESOME CEREAL SNACK

Total cooking time: 11 minutes

1	10						

- ½ cup honey
- ¼ cup packed brown sugar
- 4 tablespoons butter or margarine

• • •

- 5 cups puffed wheat cereal
- 1 cup pretzel sticks
- 1 cup salted peanuts
- ⅓ cup toasted sunflower seeds
- ¼ cup wheat germ

In 3-quart bowl, combine honey, brown sugar, and butter. Cook at **HIGH** for 1 minute. Stir until smooth. Add remaining ingredients, tossing to coat evenly. Heat, uncovered, at **MEDIUM LOW (3)** for 10 minutes or till warmed, stirring occasionally. Cool, stirring occasionally. Break up to separate. Makes 10 cups.

SNOWBALLS

Total cooking time: 2 minutes

2							

- 1 6-ounce package (1 cup) semisweet chocolate pieces
- ⅓ cup evaporated milk
- 1¼ cups sifted powdered sugar
- ½ cup chopped walnuts
- 1 3½-ounce can (1⅓ cups) flaked coconut

In 2-quart bowl, combine semisweet chocolate pieces and milk. Cook, uncovered, at **HIGH** for 2 minutes or till melted, stirring twice to blend. Stir in powdered sugar and nuts. Chill 30 minutes. Form into 1-inch balls using 1 rounded teaspoon of mixture for each; roll in coconut. Makes about 30.

ROCKY ROAD CANDY

Total cooking time: 4 minutes

4							

- 2 8-ounce bars milk chocolate, broken up
- 3 cups tiny marshmallows
- ¾ cup coarsely broken walnuts

Place chocolate in 2-quart bowl. Heat, uncovered, at **HIGH** for 4 minutes or till melted, stirring once. Beat till smooth. Stir in marshmallows and nuts. Spread in buttered 8×8×2-inch baking dish. Chill to firm chocolate 30 minutes. Cut in squares. Store in refrigerator. Makes 1½ pounds.

EASY OPERA FUDGE

For chocolate fudge, use one package each chocolate and vanilla pudding mixes in place of coconut pudding—

Total cooking time: 4 minutes 30 seconds

1:30	3						

- ⅓ cup maraschino cherries, chopped
- ½ cup butter or margarine
- 2 3⅛- or 3⅝-ounce packages *regular* coconut cream pudding mix
- ½ cup milk
- ½ teaspoon vanilla
- 1 pound sifted powdered sugar (4½ cups)
- ½ cup chopped walnuts

Drain cherries on paper toweling. In 2-quart bowl, cook butter at **HIGH** for 1½ minutes, or till melted and bubbly. Stir in dry pudding mixes and milk. Cook at **HIGH** for 3 minutes or till mixture comes to a full boil, stirring once each minute. Stir in vanilla. Gradually beat in powdered sugar till smooth. Stir in walnuts and cherries. Spread evenly in buttered 10×6×1½-inch baking dish. Garnish with cherry halves, if desired. Chill before cutting. Store in refrigerator. Makes 32 pieces.

CARAMEL SNAPPERS

Total cooking time: 2 minutes 40 seconds

0:50	0:50	1					

- 144 small pecan halves (about 1¼ cups)
- 36 light caramels
- ½ cup semisweet chocolate pieces

Butter a glass pizza plate or large chop plate. On it arrange *half* the pecans, flat side down, in groups of 4. Place 1 caramel on each cluster of pecans. Heat at **HIGH** for 50 to 60 seconds, till caramels soften. Give plate half turn after 30 seconds. Flatten caramels over pecans, using a buttered spatula. Cool slightly; remove to waxed paper. Repeat with remaining pecans and caramels. Place chocolate pieces in small bowl. Cook at **HIGH** for 1 minute or till melted; stir. Swirl melted chocolate atop caramel. Makes 36.

MINT WAFERS

Try coffee liqueur or creme de cacao, too—

Total cooking time: 3 minutes

1	2						

- **4 tablespoons butter or margarine**
- **⅓ cup green creme de menthe**
- **1 15.4-ounce package white creamy-type frosting mix**

In 2-quart bowl, combine butter and creme de menthe. Cook at **HIGH** for 1 to 1½ minutes or till butter melts. Stir in frosting mix till smooth. Cook at **HIGH** for 2 minutes, stirring twice. Drop from teaspoon onto waxed paper, swirling tops of candies with teaspoon. If mixture thickens, add a few drops hot water and cook at **HIGH** for 30 seconds. Cool till firm. Makes about 5 dozen.

CURRIED CORN-NUT SNACK

Total cooking time: 11 minutes

1	10						

- **4 tablespoons butter or margarine**
- **2 teaspoons curry powder**
- **1 teaspoon onion salt**
- **½ teaspoon ground ginger**
- **6 cups bite-sized shredded corn squares**
- **1 12-ounce can (2 cups) mixed nuts**
- **1 3-ounce can chow mein noodles**
- **1 cup raisins**

In 3-quart bowl, combine butter, curry, onion salt, and ginger. Heat at **HIGH** for 1 minute; mix well. Stir in cereal, nuts, and noodles till coated. Cook, uncovered, at **MEDIUM LOW (3)** for 10 minutes or till warm, stirring occasionally. Add raisins. Cool. Makes 11½ cups.

BUTTER PECAN ROLL

Total cooking time: 2 minutes

2							

- **1 6-ounce package (1 cup) butterscotch pieces**
- **2 tablespoons butter or margarine**
- **1 slightly beaten egg**
- **1½ cups sifted powdered sugar**
- **½ teaspoon vanilla**
- **½ cup flaked coconut**
- **½ cup chopped pecans**

In 2-quart bowl, combine butterscotch pieces and butter. Cook, uncovered, at **HIGH** for 2 minutes or till melted, stirring twice to blend. Cool to lukewarm. Beat in egg till smooth and glossy. Add powdered sugar, vanilla, and dash salt; mix well. Stir in coconut and pecans. Chill 30 minutes. Form into a 10-inch-long roll. Wrap and chill till firm, several hours or overnight. To serve, slice chilled roll ¼ inch thick with thin bladed sharp knife. Makes 40 slices.

PEANUT CLUSTERS

Total cooking time: 9 minutes

3	6						

- **1 3⅝-ounce package *regular* chocolate pudding mix**
- **1 cup sugar**
- **½ cup evaporated milk**
- **1 tablespoon butter or margarine**
- **1 cup dry roasted salted peanuts**
- **1 teaspoon vanilla**

In 2-quart bowl, combine dry pudding mix, sugar, milk, and butter. Cook at **HIGH** for 3 minutes or till mixture comes to a full rolling boil. Mix well and cook at **MEDIUM (5)** for 6 minutes. Stir in nuts and vanilla. Beat till candy thickens and begins to lose its gloss (5 to 8 minutes). Quickly drop from teaspoons into clusters on waxed paper. Makes 2 dozen.

QUICK PENUCHE

Total cooking time: 9 minutes

6	3						

- **1 7-ounce jar marshmallow creme**
- **1 5⅓-ounce can evaporated milk**
- **6 tablespoons butter or margarine**
- **1¾ cups sugar**
- **¼ teaspoon salt**

• • •

- **1 6-ounce package (1 cup) butterscotch pieces**
- **1 cup coarsely chopped walnuts**

In 2-quart bowl, combine marshmallow creme, milk, butter, sugar, and salt. Cook at **HIGH** for 6 to 7 minutes or till mixture comes to a full boil, stirring twice. Mix well. Cook at **MEDIUM (5)** for 3 minutes, stirring once. Add butterscotch pieces and stir till smooth. Stir in nuts.

Pour into 8×8×2-inch pan that has been lined with foil and buttered. Cool, then chill till firm. Lift foil from pan and remove foil. Cut in squares. Store in refrigerator. Makes 5 dozen.

CARAMEL CRISPIES

Total cooking time: 4 minutes

4							

- **1 14-ounce package caramels**
- **4 tablespoons butter or margarine**
- **2 tablespoons water**
- **3 cups crisp rice cereal**
- **1 cup dry roasted peanuts**

Unwrap caramels and place in 2-quart bowl. Add the butter and water. Cook, uncovered, at **HIGH** for 4 minutes. Stir well after each minute. Stir in cereal and peanuts. Press evenly into buttered 8×8×2-inch baking dish. Cool and cut in squares. Makes 36.

CARAMEL CREAM CHEESE FROSTING

Total cooking time: 3 minutes

1	2							

- 7 vanilla caramels (2 ounces)
- 1 tablespoon hot water
- 1 3-ounce package cream cheese
- 2½ cups sifted powdered sugar
  Dash salt

In 2-cup glass measure, combine caramels and 1 tablespoon hot water. Heat, uncovered, at **HIGH** for 1 to 2 minutes, till melted. Cool. In small mixer bowl, place cream cheese; cook at **LOW (1)** for 2 minutes or till softened. Beat in powdered sugar. Stir in caramels and salt; mix well. Makes about 1 cup frosting or enough for a 1-layer cake or 18 cupcakes.

SHORTCUT CREME BRULEE

Total cooking time: 5 minutes

2	3							

- 1 3- or 3¼-ounce package *regular* vanilla pudding mix
- 1¾ cups milk
- ½ cup frozen whipped dessert topping, thawed
  • • •
- 3 tablespoons brown sugar

In 4-cup glass measure, combine pudding mix and milk. Heat, uncovered, at **HIGH** for 2 minutes; stir. Cook at **HIGH** 3 to 4 minutes longer, stirring once each minute, till mixture thickens and bubbles. Cover surface with waxed paper; cool 10 to 15 minutes. Fold in topping. Spoon into 4 individual bakers or custard cups; chill.

Sprinkle about 2 teaspoons brown sugar atop each dessert. Place in shallow pan and surround with ice cubes and a little cold water. Broil conventionally for 2 minutes, till a bubbly brown crust forms on each. Serve immediately. Makes 4 servings.

CHOCOLATE CHOW MEIN CLUSTERS

Total cooking time: 2 minutes

2								

- 14 vanilla caramels (4 ounces)
- ¼ cup semisweet chocolate pieces
- 2 tablespoons chunky peanut butter
- 2 tablespoons water
  • • •
- 1 3-ounce can (2 cups) chow mein noodles

In 4-cup glass measure or bowl, combine caramels, chocolate pieces, peanut butter, and water. Heat, uncovered, at **HIGH** for 2 minutes, till all is melted, stirring once to blend. Add noodles; stir gently till evenly coated. Drop from teaspoon onto waxed paper. Let stand till firm. Makes 2½ dozen.

TUTTI-FRUTTI CAKE TOPPER

Especially good on orange or lemon cake mix—

Total cooking time: 2 minutes

2								

- 1 package 2-layer-size cake mix (no pudding in the mix)
- 1 12-ounce jar (1 cup) apricot preserves
- 1 tablespoon lemon juice
- 1 3½-ounce can (1⅓ cups) flaked coconut
- 1½ cups miniature marshmallows

Prepare your favorite cake. Bake in two 8-inch round cake dishes as directed on page 175. Combine preserves, ¼ cup water, lemon juice, coconut, and marshmallows; spread atop hot cakes. Heat, one at a time, at **HIGH,** uncovered, for 2 to 4 minutes, till marshmallows are about melted. Cool before serving.

HOT FRUIT COMPOTE

Total cooking time: 4 minutes

2	2							

- 1 16-ounce can peach slices, drained
- 1 8¼-ounce can pineapple tidbits (undrained)
- ¼ teaspoon ground cinnamon
  Dash salt
- ⅓ cup port wine
  • • •
- 1 banana, sliced

In a 1½-quart casserole, combine all ingredients except the banana. Cook, covered, at **HIGH** for 2 minutes, stirring once. Add banana slices; cook, covered, at **HIGH** for 2 more minutes. Makes 4 servings.

QUICK PEACH CRUMBLE

Total cooking time: 18 minutes 15 seconds

1:15	5	12						

- ½ cup butter or margarine
- 1 package 2-layer-size butter brickle cake mix
- 1 3½-ounce can (1⅓ cups) flaked coconut
- 1 teaspoon ground cinnamon
- 1 29-ounce can sliced peaches, drained
  Vanilla ice cream

In 12×7½×2-inch baking dish, melt butter at **HIGH** for about 1 minute 15 seconds. Stir in dry cake mix, coconut, and cinnamon; mix well. Remove 1⅓ cups of the mixture; press remaining into dish. Cook, uncovered, at **HIGH** for 5 minutes, giving dish half turn once.

Top with peach slices. Crumble remaining coconut mixture over top. Cook, uncovered, at **HIGH** for 12 minutes, giving dish half turn once. Serve warm or cool topped with ice cream. Makes 10 to 12 servings.

ENTERTAINING WITH EASE

Special occasions are the perfect time to show off your new micro-mastery to admiring guests. And we have party ideas galore for you—from hot beverages and appetizers to elegant main dishes and spectacular desserts. The next time company's coming, why not serve them Pompano en Papillote and Strawberry Cheesecake Pie (recipes next page) to tantalize their palates?

MICRO MENU PLANNER

TIMETABLE

1. Early in the day, bake the Crescent Rolls and make Strawberry Cheesecake Pie.
2. Chill the wine; set the table.
3. Get salad ingredients ready to toss at the table.
4. Prepare the Pompano en Papillote.
5. Meanwhile, cook asparagus on *conventional* range.
6. Warm Crescent Rolls according to chart on page 36.

POMPANO EN PAPILLOTE

Total cooking time: 17 minutes

5	2	10					

    1 pound fresh or frozen pompano or snapper
    1 10-ounce package frozen Welsh rarebit
    2 tablespoons all-purpose flour
    ¼ cup dry white wine
            • • •
    1 cup (4 ounces) medium-sized cooked or canned
        shrimp (18 to 20 shrimp)
    1 3-ounce can sliced mushrooms, drained
    Dash garlic powder

Thaw frozen fish according to directions on page 186. Divide into 4 portions. Cut 4 pieces baking parchment into 10-inch squares. Place one portion fish on half of each piece parchment; set aside.

Remove rarebit from foil container; place in 1-quart bowl. Cook, covered, at **HIGH** for 5 minutes, stirring once, till thawed. Blend flour and wine; stir into rarebit. Cook, uncovered, at **HIGH** for 2 to 3 minutes, till thickened and bubbly, stirring once. Stir in shrimp, mushrooms, and garlic powder. Spoon over fish. Fold half of parchment over fillets to form four individual cases; fold edges to seal. Place in 13×9×2-inch baking dish.

Cook at **MEDIUM HIGH (7)** for 10 to 11 minutes, rearranging cases once. Transfer to dinner plates; cut each open to serve. Makes 4 servings.

STRAWBERRY CHEESECAKE PIE

Total cooking time: 2 minutes 30 seconds

0:30	2						

    1 10¾- or 11-ounce package cheesecake mix
    ⅓ cup chopped toasted almonds
            • • •
    1 quart strawberries
    ⅓ cup sugar
    2 teaspoons cornstarch
    2 tablespoons strawberry-flavored gelatin
    2 teaspoons lemon juice

Prepare crust according to package directions, melting the butter called for in 9-inch pie plate at **HIGH** for 30 to 45 seconds. Press crust into pie plate. Prepare cheesecake filling according to package directions; stir in almonds. Spread in crust; chill 1 hour.

Mash 1 cup strawberries; add water to mashed mixture to make ⅔ cup. In 2-cup glass measure, combine sugar and cornstarch. Stir in strawberry mixture. Cook, uncovered, at **HIGH** for 2 to 3 minutes, till thickened, stirring every 30 seconds. Add dry gelatin; stir till dissolved. Stir in lemon juice. Strain. Chill strawberry mixture till partially set.

Spread *half* the gelatin glaze over pie filling. Dip remaining berries in remaining glaze then arrange, point up, around edge of pie. Carefully spoon remaining glaze over berries. Chill till set.

Stuffed Mushrooms Italiano, Beer Cheese Fondue, Artichoke Appetizer

TIMETABLE

1. Prepare Hot Spiced Wine Punch.
2. Prepare mushroom filling; spoon into mushrooms.
3. Set the cocktail table; light the candles.
4. Cook the two artichokes; keep warm.
5. Cook Beer Cheese Fondue; cover or use fondue burner.
6. Cook the stuffed Mushrooms Italiano.
7. Heat butter dip and serve with Artichoke Appetizer.
8. Reheat wine punch by the cup as needed.

MENU

Mushrooms Italiano

Beer Cheese Fondue

Artichoke Appetizer

Hot Spiced Wine Punch (page 99)

APPEALING APPETIZERS

STUFFED MUSHROOMS ITALIANO

Total cooking time: 6 minutes

2	4						

12 **large fresh mushrooms (5 ounces)**
1 **tablespoon butter or margarine**
¼ **cup finely chopped onion**
¼ **cup diced pepperoni (1 ounce)**
2 **tablespoons finely chopped green pepper**
½ **small clove garlic, minced**

• • •

¼ **cup finely crushed rich round crackers (6 crackers)**
1½ **tablespoons grated Parmesan cheese**
2 **teaspoons snipped parsley**
¼ **teaspoon seasoned salt**
⅛ **teaspoon dried oregano, crushed**
Dash pepper

Wash mushrooms; remove and finely chop the stems. Drain caps on paper toweling. In 1-quart bowl, combine butter, chopped stems, onion, pepperoni, green pepper, and garlic. Cook, covered, at **HIGH** for 2 to 3 minutes, till tender. Stir in crumbs, cheese, parsley, salt, oregano, and pepper; mix well. Mound mixture in the mushroom caps. Place caps in 10×6×1½-inch baking dish. Cook, covered, at **MEDIUM (5)** for 4 minutes, till mushrooms are hot. Makes 12 appetizers.

BEER CHEESE FONDUE

Since cheese can toughen quickly when overcooked, the medium setting is used for gentle melting. Crusty French bread also makes a good fondue dipper—

Total cooking time: 7 minutes

2	5						

2 **cups (8 ounces) shredded process Swiss cheese**
1 **cup (4 ounces) shredded sharp natural cheddar cheese**
1 **tablespoon all-purpose flour**
¾ **cup beer**
Dash bottled hot pepper sauce

• • •

Cubed bagels
Warmed beer

Stir together Swiss cheese, cheddar cheese, and the flour. In 1½-quart glass or ceramic serving bowl, heat the ¾ cup beer, uncovered, at **HIGH** for 2 minutes, till it bubbles. Add pepper sauce. Stir in cheese mixture. Cook, uncovered, at **MEDIUM (5)** for 5 minutes, till cheese is melted and mixture is blended, stirring twice. Serve immediately as is or turn into fondue pot and place heated mixture over fondue burner. Serve with cubed bagels as dippers.

To eat, spear bagel chunk with fondue fork; dip in the hot fondue mixture, swirling to coat. If cheese mixture becomes too thick upon standing, stir in a little additional warmed beer. Makes 2 cups fondue.

ARTICHOKE APPETIZER

Total cooking time: 8 minutes

6	0:30	1:30					

2 **medium artichokes**
3 **tablespoons lemon juice**
4 **tablespoons butter or margarine**
¼ **cup beer**
½ **teaspoon dried dillweed or 2 teaspoons fresh dill**

Cut 1 inch off artichoke tops; remove the stems and snip tips off the artichoke leaves. Brush cut edges and tops with lemon juice. Wrap artichokes in waxed paper turning ends under. Cook at **HIGH** for 6 to 7 minutes, till leaf pulls out easily. Drain; serve hot with Dill-butter dip.

Dill-butter Dip: In small bowl, melt butter at **HIGH** for 30 seconds. Stir in beer and dill; heat again at **HIGH** 1½ to 2 minutes or till hot. Makes ½ cup.

Note: For 1 artichoke cook at **HIGH** 4 to 5 minutes; for 4 artichokes cook at **HIGH** 9 to 10 minutes.

OYSTERS LAFITTE

Total cooking time: 10 minutes 20 seconds

2:30	4	1	2:30	0:20			

2 **tablespoons butter or margarine**
1 **cup chopped fresh mushrooms (3 ounces)**
2 **tablespoons chopped green onion**
2 **tablespoons snipped parsley**
1 **clove garlic, minced**
3 **tablespoons all-purpose flour**
12 **fresh oysters, shucked or 1 8-ounce can oysters, drained**
¼ **cup light cream**
½ **teaspoon salt**
Dash cayenne pepper
2 **tablespoons dry white wine**
½ **cup chopped cooked shrimp**

• • •

2 **tablespoons butter or margarine**
⅓ **cup fine dry bread crumbs**
⅛ **teaspoon paprika**

In 1-quart casserole, combine the first 2 tablespoons butter, mushrooms, onion, parsley, and garlic. Cook, covered, at **HIGH** for 2½ minutes. Stir in flour. Drain oysters, reserving ⅓ cup liquid. Add oyster liquid, cream, salt, and cayenne pepper to vegetables. Cook, uncovered, at **HIGH** for 4 to 4½ minutes, till thickened and bubbly, stirring after each minute. Stir in wine and oysters; cook at **HIGH** 1 minute more. Add shrimp.

Spoon into four 4-ounce baking shells. Place shells in 12×7½×2-inch baking dish. Cook, uncovered, at **HIGH** for 2½ minutes, till heated through, giving dish a half turn once.

In small bowl or 1-cup glass measure, melt 2 tablespoons butter at **HIGH** for 20 seconds; stir in bread crumbs and paprika. Sprinkle over oysters. Makes 4 servings.

RIBAKI

Total cooking time: 25 minutes

15	10						

    2 **pounds pork spareribs, cut in half crosswise**

       •   •   •

 ¼ **cup soy sauce**
    2 **tablespoons cooking oil**
    2 **tablespoons molasses**
    2 **teaspoons ground ginger**
    1 **teaspoon dry mustard**
    1 **clove garlic, minced**

Cut ribs into 1-rib pieces. Place in 12×7½×2-inch baking dish. Cook, covered, at **MEDIUM HIGH (7)** for 15 minutes. Drain; turn and rearrange ribs. Combine remaining ingredients; pour over ribs. Cook, covered, at **MEDIUM HIGH (7)** for 10 minutes. Serve hot. Makes about 36 pieces.

COCKTAIL NUTS PEPITA

Total cooking time: 7 minutes 30 seconds

0:30	7						

In 10×6×1½-inch baking dish, combine 1 tablespoon butter or margarine, 1½ teaspoons Worcestershire sauce, 1 teaspoon salad seasoning, ½ teaspoon garlic salt, ¼ teaspoon bottled hot pepper sauce, and several dashes pepper. Cook, uncovered, at **HIGH** for 30 to 45 seconds, till melted. Add 8 ounces shelled walnut halves, almonds, or filberts, stirring to coat. Heat, uncovered, at **HIGH** for 7 minutes, stirring 3 times. Cool on paper toweling. Store nuts in tightly covered container. Makes 2 cups.

SHRIMP-PINEAPPLE NIBBLES

Total cooking time: 9 minutes

6	3						

 12 **ounces shelled and deveined fresh or frozen shrimp**
  1 **13¼-ounce can pineapple chunks**
  1 **cup canned marinara sauce**
  2 **tablespoons brown sugar**
  2 **teaspoons prepared mustard**
  1 **medium green pepper, cubed**

       •   •   •

  1 **tablespoon cornstarch**
  1 **tablespoon cold water**

Thaw shrimp if frozen (see page 186). Drain pineapple, reserving ¼ cup syrup. In 1½ quart casserole, combine marinara sauce, reserved syrup, brown sugar, and mustard. Add shrimp, pineapple, and green pepper. Cook, covered, at **HIGH** for 6 minutes, stirring every 2 minutes.

    Combine cornstarch and water; stir into mixture. Cook, uncovered, at **HIGH** for 3 to 4 minutes, till thickened, stirring after each minute. Serve hot with wooden picks. Makes 8 to 10 servings.

CHICKEN LIVERS LUCIFER

Total cooking time: 7 minutes

0:30	6	0:30					

  8 **ounces (about 10) chicken livers**
  2 **tablespoons butter or margarine**
 ½ **cup fine dry bread crumbs**

       •   •   •

  2 **tablespoons Dijon-style mustard**
  1 **tablespoon catsup**
  1 **tablespoon water**
  1 **tablespoon butter or margarine**
  2 **teaspoons Worcestershire sauce**
 ½ **teaspoon onion powder**
    Few drops bottled hot pepper sauce

Cut livers in half; cut any large pieces in half again. In a small bowl, melt the 2 tablespoons butter at **HIGH** for 30 seconds. Dip livers in the butter, then in the crumbs to coat. Place in 10×6×1½-inch baking dish. Heat, uncovered, at **MEDIUM (5)** for 6 minutes, turning and rearranging once, till livers are done. (Cut into livers to check doneness. They may appear slightly pink on outside but may be done inside.)

    In small glass bowl, combine remaining ingredients. Cook, uncovered, at **HIGH** for 30 to 45 seconds, till hot; stir to blend in butter. Spear livers with wooden picks; dip in hot sauce. Makes 20 appetizers.

ESCARGOT BOURGUIGNONNE

Total cooking time: 7 minutes 10 seconds

0:10	7						

 ½ **cup butter or margarine**
  1 **tablespoon thinly sliced green onion**
  1 **tablespoon snipped parsley**
  1 **small clove garlic, minced**
 ⅛ **teaspoon salt**
    Dash pepper

       •   •   •

  1 **3-ounce can snails, drained (12 snails)**
  1 **tablespoon fine dry bread crumbs**
 ¼ **cup dry white wine**
    French bread

In small bowl, combine butter, onion, parsley, garlic, salt, and pepper. Cook, uncovered, at **HIGH** 10 seconds to soften butter; mix well. Thoroughly drain and rinse snails and 12 snail shells. Place some butter mixture in bottom of each shell. Add a snail and more butter mixture. Sprinkle opening of each shell lightly with crumbs. Place 6 filled shells in each of 2 snail dishes or small plates; pour 2 tablespoons wine into each dish.

    Cook, uncovered, at **MEDIUM LOW (3)** for 7 minutes, till butter bubbles and snails are heated through, giving dishes a half turn once. Makes 2 servings.

    To eat: Remove snail from shell, pouring liquid into snail plate. Eat snail; dip French bread in wine mixture.

HOT BEVERAGES

HOT COFFEE EGGNOG

Total cooking time: 7 minutes

7								

In 4-cup glass measure, beat 2 eggs slightly. Add 1 cup *each* milk and light cream, ¼ cup coffee liqueur, 2 tablespoons whiskey, 2 teaspoons sugar, and 1 teaspoon instant coffee powder. Heat, uncovered, at **MEDIUM (5)** for 7 to 8 minutes, till mixture thickens, stirring after 3 minutes, then after each minute.

Pour into heat-proof mugs; sprinkle each serving with ground coriander. Makes 5 servings.

TEST KITCHEN TIPS

Exotic international coffees make marvelous substitutes for dessert. And they're so simple for a busy host or hostess to prepare.

Brew hot strong coffee as usual, ahead of time if you wish. For each serving, pour either hot or room temperature coffee into coffee cups or heat-proof mugs, about ½ cup each. Then stir in the flavorings, and heat at **HIGH** according to the chart. Top with a fluff of whipped cream and the garnish as directed.

Cafe Colombian: Add 2 tablespoons coffee liqueur and 2 tablespoons chocolate syrup. Heat and garnish with whipped cream and ground cinnamon.

Cafe Israel: Add 1 tablespoon orange-chocolate liqueur and 2 tablespoons chocolate syrup. Heat; garnish with whipped cream and orange peel twist.

Cafe Hollander: Add 1 tablespoon chocolate mint liqueur and 1 teaspoon creme de cacao. Heat and garnish with whipped cream and a chocolate curl.

Cafe Irish: Add 2 tablespoons Irish whiskey and a dash sugar. Heat and garnish with whipped cream.

Cafe Brandy Royale: Add 2 tablespoons brandy and a dash ground cinnamon. Heat and garnish with whipped cream and grated orange peel.

Number of coffee cups	Time using hot coffee	Time using room temperature coffee
1	30 seconds	1 minute
2	1 minute	2 minutes
3	1 minute 45 sec.	3 minutes
4	2 minutes 15 sec.	4 minutes

CREOLE CHOCOLATE

Total cooking time: 17 minutes

6	11							

  3 1-ounce squares unsweetened chocolate, cut up
½ cup sugar
1 teaspoon ground cinnamon
¼ teaspoon ground nutmeg
4 cups milk
    Frozen whipped dessert topping, thawed

In 2-quart casserole or bowl, combine chocolate, sugar, spices, ¼ teaspoon salt, and 1½ cups water. Heat, uncovered, at **HIGH** for 6 minutes, or till chocolate melts, stirring twice. Stir in milk; heat, uncovered, at **HIGH** for 11 to 12 minutes, till heated through. Beat mixture with rotary beater till foamy. Ladle into mugs; top with whipped topping. Makes 6 servings.

HOT SPICED WINE PUNCH

Total cooking time: 15 minutes

10	5							

In 2-quart pitcher or bowl, combine 3 cups apple cider or juice, ⅓ cup sugar, 9 inches stick cinnamon, and 1 teaspoon whole cloves. Remove peel from ¼ lemon; cut in strips and add to mixture. Cook, uncovered, at **HIGH** for 10 minutes, till sugar is dissolved and mixture heated through, stirring once.

Add 1 fifth dry white wine and 2 tablespoons lemon juice; heat again, uncovered, at **HIGH** for 5 minutes. Strain out spices. Makes 6½ cups.

Or, make ahead and reheat punch in 1-cup portions. Heat each cup, uncovered, 1½ to 2 minutes at **HIGH.**

WASSAIL WITH APPLE FLOATERS

Total cooking time: 22 minutes

10	12							

  1 cup packed brown sugar
1 cup brandy
12 inches stick cinnamon, broken
1 teaspoon *each* whole cloves and whole allspice
6 small apples
2 fifths dry red wine (6½ cups)
1 fifth dry sherry (3¼ cups)

In a 3-quart bowl or casserole, stir together brown sugar, brandy, and 1 cup water. Tie spices in cheesecloth bag. Add spices and apples to brandy syrup. Cook, covered loosely with waxed paper, at **HIGH** for 10 minutes or till apples are just tender. Remove apples, reserving syrup. Add wines to syrup. Cook, uncovered, at **HIGH** for 12 minutes, or till heated through. Remove spice bag. Pour into punch bowl; add cooked apples to float in bowl. Makes 12 cups (or 16 six-ounce servings).

Wallbanger Wassail, Mocha Toddies, Cranberry Wine Cup, Hot Pineapple Punch, Spicy Apple Grog

TIMETABLE

1. Make Mocha Toddies mix; chill.
2. Make Cider Citrus Punch.
3. Make Curried Corn-nut Snack.
4. Make caramel fondue.
5. Make appetizers; chill.
6. Reheat appetizers as needed.
7. Reheat drinks in mugs as needed.

MENU

Ribaki (recipe on page 98)
Shrimp-pineapple Nibbles (recipe on page 98)
4-way Rumaki (recipe on page 142)
Curried Corn-nut Snack (recipe on page 90)
Caramel Apple Fondue (recipe on page 153)
Mocha Toddies   Cider Citrus Punch

HOT BEVERAGES *(continued)*

WALLBANGER WASSAIL

Total cooking time: 21 minutes

10	7	4						

- **1 12-ounce can frozen orange juice concentrate**
- **1 6-ounce can frozen lemonade concentrate**
- **6 cups water**
- **¼ to ⅓ cup sugar**
- **6 inches stick cinnamon**
- **1 teaspoon whole cardamom seeds**
- **1 cup vodka**
- **½ cup Galliano liqueur**

In 3-quart bowl, combine undiluted juice concentrates, water, and sugar. Cook at **HIGH** for 10 minutes or till mixture almost boils and sugar is dissolved. Tie cinnamon sticks and cardamom seeds in cheesecloth bag; add to bowl. Cook at **HIGH** for 7 to 8 minutes or till heated through. Discard spice bag. Stir in vodka and Galliano. Cook at **HIGH** for 4 to 5 minutes or till hot. Garnish with orange slices. Makes 9 cups.

SPICY APPLE GROG

Total cooking time: 15 minutes

10	5							

- **3 cups apple cider**
- **2 cups white grape juice**
- **1 16-ounce jar spiced crab apples**
- **1 fifth (3¼ cups) pop apple wine**
- **1 cup brandy**

In 4-quart bowl, combine cider, grape juice, and crab apples with syrup. Cook at **HIGH** for 10 minutes. Stir in wine and brandy. Cook at **HIGH** for 5 minutes or till hot. Serve in mugs with crab apples. Makes 10 cups.

HOT CRANBERRY WINE CUP

Total cooking time: 15 minutes

10	5							

- **2 cups cranberry juice cocktail**
- **1 cup water**
- **½ cup sugar**
- **Peel of ¼ lemon, cut in strips**
- **2 inches stick cinnamon**
- **6 whole cloves**
- **1 fifth (3¼ cups) dry red wine**
- **2 tablespoons lemon juice**

In 3-quart bowl, combine cranberry juice, water, sugar, and lemon peel. Tie cinnamon sticks and cloves in cheesecloth bag; add to bowl. Cook at **HIGH** for 10 minutes or till mixture almost boils and sugar dissolves. Discard spice bag and lemon peel. Add wine and lemon juice. Cook at **HIGH** for 5 minutes or till hot. Garnish with skewered cranberries and lemon peel. Makes 6 cups.

MOCHA TODDIES

Total cooking time: 3 minutes

1	2							

- **¼ cup water**
- **1 2-ounce jar (¾ cup) instant coffee crystals**
- **1 16-ounce can (1½ cups) chocolate syrup**
- **1 cup rum**
- **1 tablespoon vanilla**

• • •

Milk
Vanilla ice cream

In 1-quart glass measure, heat water at **HIGH** for 1 minute. Add coffee crystals; stir till dissolved. Stir in syrup, rum, and vanilla. Store, covered, in refrigerator.

To serve, place 2 tablespoons mocha base in each heat-proof mug. Add ¾ cup milk to each mug. Stir to combine. Heat at **HIGH**: 1 mug = 2 minutes, 2 mugs = 3 minutes, 3 mugs = 4 minutes, 4 mugs = 5 minutes. Top with a scoop of vanilla ice cream. Makes 3 cups mocha base, enough for 24 servings.

HOT PINEAPPLE PUNCH

Total cooking time: 15 minutes

10	5							

- **1 46-ounce can unsweetened pineapple juice**
- **½ cup sugar**
- **¼ cup lime juice**
- **¼ teaspoon ground nutmeg**
- **1 fifth (3¼ cups) dry white wine**

In 3-quart bowl, combine pineapple juice, sugar, lime juice, and nutmeg. Cook, uncovered, at **HIGH** for 10 minutes or till mixture almost boils. Stir to dissolve sugar. Stir in wine. Cook at **HIGH** for 5 minutes or till hot. Garnish with pineapple spears. Makes 9 cups.

CIDER CITRUS PUNCH

Total cooking time: 20 minutes

10	10							

- **2 quarts apple cider or apple juice (8 cups)**
- **½ of 6-ounce can (⅓ cup) frozen lemonade concentrate**
- **½ of 6-ounce can (⅓ cup) frozen orange juice concentrate**
- **¼ cup packed brown sugar**
- **1½ teaspoons whole cloves**
- **1½ teaspoons whole allspice**

In 3-quart bowl, combine cider, undiluted juice concentrates, and the brown sugar. Cook at **HIGH** for 10 minutes or till mixture almost boils and sugar is dissolved; stir. Tie cloves and allspice in cheesecloth bag; add to cider mixture. Cook at **HIGH** for 10 minutes or till hot. Remove spice bag and discard. Makes 8¼ cups.

Ham Steak with Burgundy Sauce

TIMETABLE

1. Early in the day, prepare the Butter Brickle Chocolate Dessert; freeze. Heat Tomato Broth Appetizer; chill.
2. Set the table; open the wine.
3. Cook Herb-buttered New Potatoes; cover and keep warm.
4. Drain canned peaches; arrange on lettuce.
5. Bake biscuits in a conventional oven.
6. Prepare Ham Steak and Burgundy Sauce.
7. Reheat Tomato Broth Appetizer in serving bowls.

MENU

Tomato Broth Appetizer
Ham Steak with Burgundy Sauce
Herb-buttered New Potatoes
Cling Peach Halves

Buttermilk Biscuits   Honey
Burgundy
Butter Brickle Chocolate Dessert
Coffee

ELEGANT MEAT ENTREES

TOMATO BROTH APPETIZER

If you wish, prepare broth mixture ahead; cover and chill. To serve, pour into 6 serving bowls. Cook 3 bowls at a time, uncovered, at HIGH for 5 to 6 minutes—

Total cooking time: 21 minutes

5	10	6					

3 cups tomato juice
½ cup sliced celery
2 thin slices onion
1 bay leaf
4 whole cloves
2 dashes bottled hot pepper sauce

• • •

1 10½-ounce can condensed beef broth
⅓ cup dry white wine
4 thin slices lemon, halved
Crackers

In 2-quart casserole or heat-proof pitcher, combine tomato juice, celery, onion, bay leaf, cloves, and hot pepper sauce. Heat at **HIGH,** uncovered, for 5 to 6 minutes, till mixture boils. Reduce setting to **MEDIUM (5);** cook, uncovered, for 10 minutes.

Strain juice, discarding seasonings. Return to casserole; add beef broth and wine. Heat, uncovered, at **HIGH** 6 to 8 minutes more, till mixture boils again. To serve, spoon into bowls; float a lemon slice on each. Serve with crackers. Makes 6 to 8 servings.

HAM STEAK WITH BURGUNDY SAUCE

Total cooking time: 18 minutes

1:30	2:30	7	7				

2 tablespoons butter or margarine
1 tablespoon sliced green onion
2 tablespoons sugar
1 tablespoon cornstarch
¾ cup burgundy or dry red wine

• • •

1 cup (6 ounces) seedless green grapes, halved
Dash ground ginger
Fully cooked ham slice, 1 inch thick (2 pounds)

In 4-cup glass measure, combine butter and the sliced green onion. Cook, uncovered, at **HIGH** for 1½ minutes, till tender. Stir in sugar and cornstarch. Blend in wine. Cook, uncovered, at **HIGH** 2½ to 3 minutes, till mixture is thickened and bubbly, stirring 3 or 4 times. Stir in grapes and ginger; set aside.

Place ham in 12×7½×2-inch baking dish. Cook, covered with waxed paper, at **MEDIUM HIGH (7)** for 7 minutes; turn ham slice over. Pour on grape sauce. Cook, covered with waxed paper, at **MEDIUM HIGH (7)** for 7 minutes, till ham slice is heated through.

To serve, place ham on platter; spoon some sauce over; pass remaining. Garnish platter with pineapple and grapes, if desired. Makes 6 servings.

HERB-BUTTERED NEW POTATOES

Total cooking time: 18 minutes 30 seconds

18	0:30						

1½ pounds new potatoes
2 tablespoons butter or margarine
2 teaspoons lemon juice
1 tablespoon snipped parsley
1 tablespoon chopped chives
½ teaspoon dried dillweed
Dash *each* salt and pepper

Pare a strip around center of each potato if desired. Place in a 2-quart casserole or bowl with 2 cups water and ½ teaspoon salt. Cook, covered, at **HIGH** for 18 minutes, till potatoes are tender, stirring once or twice. Drain and set aside.

In same casserole, combine butter and remaining ingredients; heat, uncovered, at **HIGH** for 30 to 45 seconds, till melted. Add potatoes; toss. Makes 6 servings.

SPINACH ORIENTAL

Total cooking time: 3 minutes

1	2						

Wash 16 ounces (12 cups) fresh spinach; pat dry. Remove and cut stems into 1-inch pieces. Tear leaves into bite-size pieces. In 3-quart casserole, combine ¼ cup cooking oil, 3 tablespoons soy sauce, and 1 tablespoon lime juice. Heat, uncovered, at **HIGH** for 1 minute.

Stir in 2 cups diagonally sliced zucchini and ½ cup sliced water chestnuts. Add spinach leaves and stems. Heat, uncovered, at **HIGH** for 2 minutes, tossing after every 30 seconds. Serve at once. Makes 4 to 6 servings.

BUTTER BRICKLE CHOCOLATE DESSERT

Total cooking time: 1 minute

0:30	0:30						

4 tablespoons butter or margarine
¼ cup packed brown sugar
1½ cups wheat germ
⅓ cup chopped walnuts

• • •

1 quart butter brickle ice cream, softened
1 pint chocolate ice cream, softened

In 8×8×2-inch baking dish, melt butter at **HIGH** for 30 to 45 seconds. Stir in brown sugar. Heat, uncovered, at **HIGH** till bubbly, 30 to 45 seconds. Stir in wheat germ and nuts; mix well. Set aside 1 cup wheat germ mixture. Press remaining into dish to form crust. Chill.

Spoon softened butter brickle and chocolate ice creams alternately over crust. Sprinkle with reserved wheat germ mixture. Cover with plastic wrap or foil and freeze. Cut into squares. Makes 12 servings.

ELEGANT MEAT ENTREES *(continued)*

LEMON PEPPER STEAK STRIPS

Total cooking time: 5 minutes 30 seconds

0:30	3	2					

- 1 pound boneless beef sirloin steak, 1 inch thick
- 2 tablespoons Lemon Pepper Butter (see Tips right)
- 1 3-ounce can sliced mushrooms, drained
- 3 tablespoons dry white wine
- 1 teaspoon Worcestershire sauce

Cut the steak into strips ¼ inch wide and 2 inches long (partially frozen meat is easier to cut). Allow meat to thaw completely. Sprinkle with a little salt. In 8×8×2-inch baking dish, melt the Lemon Pepper Butter at **HIGH** for 30 to 45 seconds. Add the meat; cook, uncovered, at **HIGH** for 3 minutes, stirring after 1½ minutes. Add mushrooms, wine, and Worcestershire. Cook, loosely covered, at **HIGH** for 2 to 3 minutes, till hot. Makes 2 to 3 servings.

SAUSAGE-STUFFED PORK ROAST

Total cooking time: 59 minutes

5	10	35	3	6			

- 4- pound pork loin rib roast (at least 6 ribs)
- 1 pound bulk pork sausage
- ½ cup chopped onion
- 1 clove garlic, minced
- 1¾ cups herb-seasoned stuffing mix
- ¼ cup grated Parmesan cheese
- 1 7½-ounce can spinach, drained and chopped
- 2 slightly beaten eggs
- 2 to 4 tablespoons chicken broth
  Herb Gravy (optional)

Have meatman loosen backbone on rib roast. Cut 6 pockets in roast corresponding to the 6 ribs. In 2-quart casserole, crumble sausage; add onion and garlic. Cook, covered, at **HIGH** for 5 minutes, stirring 3 times; drain. Add stuffing mix, Parmesan, spinach, and eggs. Add 2 to 4 tablespoons broth as needed to make mixture hold together. Stuff about ¼ cup inside each pocket of the roast. Place remaining stuffing in small casserole.

Place roast, fat side down, on microwave roasting rack or inverted saucers in 13×9×2-inch baking dish. Cook, uncovered, at **HIGH** for 10 minutes. Turn meat fat side up. Reduce setting to **MEDIUM HIGH (7)** and cook, uncovered, for 35 minutes more (till meat thermometer* registers 165°). Cover; let stand. Heat remaining stuffing, covered, at **HIGH** for 3 to 4 minutes. Makes 6 servings.

Herb Gravy: Pour meat juices from roasting dish into 4-cup glass measure. Skim off fat. Add enough chicken broth (about 1½ cups) to equal 2 cups liquid. Combine ⅓ cup all-purpose flour and ½ cup cold water; stir into juice mixture with ½ teaspoon dried crushed basil and ½ teaspoon kitchen bouquet. Heat, uncovered, at **HIGH** for 6 to 8 minutes, till mixture thickens and bubbles, stirring after 2 minutes, then after each minute. Add salt and pepper to taste. Makes 2½ cups.

TEST KITCHEN TIPS

Lemon Pepper Butter—whip this up, stash in the refrigerator, and use it to jazz up plain fare at a moment's notice. Brush this sensational butter on fish or steaks; stir it into tender hot vegetables. Try it on English muffins to start a hot sandwich or melt it and use as a dip for shellfish and artichokes.

In a small mixer bowl, place 1 pound (2 cups) butter or margarine. Cook at **LOW (1)** for 3 to 4 minutes, till slightly softened. With electric mixer, beat till butter is light and fluffy. Add ¼ cup snipped fresh or freeze-dried chives, 1½ teaspoons grated lemon peel, 2 tablespoons lemon juice, and ½ teaspoon fresh ground black pepper. Mix thoroughly.

Store in refrigerator in a tightly covered container. Makes 2 cups butter.

PORK ROAST WITH CHERRY GLAZE

Total cooking time: 47 minutes

10	35	2					

- 4- pound boneless pork loin roast, rolled and tied
- 1 12-ounce jar (1 cup) cherry preserves
- 2 tablespoons light corn syrup
- 1 tablespoon red wine vinegar
- ¼ teaspoon *each* salt, ground cinnamon, ground nutmeg, and ground cloves
- ¼ cup slivered toasted almonds

Season roast with salt and pepper. Place roast, fat side down, on microwave roasting rack or inverted saucers in 12×7½×2-inch baking dish. Cook, uncovered, at **HIGH** for 10 minutes. Turn fat side up. Reduce setting to **MEDIUM HIGH (7)**; cook, uncovered, 35 minutes more (till meat thermometer* registers 165°), brushing with some of the *Cherry Glaze* during the last 5 minutes of cooking. Remove from oven; cover and let stand 15 minutes.

Meanwhile, heat remaining glaze, uncovered, at **HIGH** for 2 to 3 minutes or till boiling. Add almonds. Serve with roast. Makes 8 servings.

Cherry Glaze: In small bowl, combine preserves, corn syrup, vinegar, salt, and spices.

*DO NOT USE A CONVENTIONAL THERMOMETER INSIDE THE MICROWAVE OVEN. SPECIAL MICROWAVE THERMOMETERS ARE AVAILABLE.

BEEF STROGANOFF

Total cooking time: 15 minutes

3	8	4					

- 1 pound boneless beef sirloin steak
- ½ cup chopped onion
- 1 clove garlic, minced
- 4 tablespoons butter or margarine
- 1 tablespoon tomato paste
- 1 10½-ounce can condensed beef broth
- ½ teaspoon salt
- 5 ounces (2 cups) fresh mushrooms, sliced

• • •

- ½ cup dairy sour cream
- ⅓ cup all-purpose flour
- 2 tablespoons dry white or red wine
- 4 servings hot cooked noodles

Cut the steak into strips ¼ inch wide and 2 inches long (partially frozen meat is easier to cut). Allow meat to thaw completely. In 3-quart casserole, cook onion and garlic in butter, uncovered, at **HIGH** about 3 minutes, till tender. Stir in tomato paste, beef broth, and salt. Add beef and mushrooms. Cook, covered, at **HIGH** for 8 minutes, or till meat is nearly done, stirring twice.

Combine sour cream and flour; blend in wine and about ½ cup of the hot liquid from beef mixture; add to beef mixture. Cook, uncovered, at **HIGH** for 4 minutes, till thickened and bubbly, stirring after each minute. Serve over noodles. Makes 4 servings.

LEMON-HERBED LAMB CHOPS

Total cooking time: 18 minutes

12	6						

- 4 shoulder lamb chops, cut ½ inch thick
- 2 tablespoons lemon juice
- 1 teaspoon Worcestershire sauce
- ¼ teaspoon dried oregano, crushed
- ¼ teaspoon dried rosemary, crushed
- 1 tablespoon cornstarch
- ¼ teaspoon grated lemon peel

Slash fat edge of chops at 1-inch intervals. (If desired, brown chops in skillet in 2 tablespoons hot oil on conventional range or use browning skillet in microwave oven omitting oil.) Place chops in 12×7½×2-inch baking dish; combine ⅓ cup water, the lemon juice, Worcestershire sauce, ½ teaspoon salt, dash pepper, and herbs; pour over chops. Cook, covered, at **MEDIUM (5)** for 12 minutes, till tender, rearranging once. Remove chops to platter; cover and keep warm.

Pour cooking juices into 2-cup glass measure; skim off fat. Add water if needed to make ¾ cup liquid. Combine cornstarch and 2 tablespoons cold water; add to juices, along with lemon peel. Heat, uncovered, at **HIGH** for 6 minutes, till thickened and bubbly, stirring after each minute. Pass with meat. Makes 4 servings.

BEEF BURGUNDY

Total cooking time: 18 minutes

4	12	2					

- 1 pound boneless beef sirloin steak
- 5 ounces (2 cups) fresh mushrooms, sliced
- ½ cup chopped onion
- 1 clove garlic, crushed
- 4 tablespoons butter or margarine
- 1 tablespoon snipped parsley
- 1 bay leaf
- ¾ teaspoon salt
  Dash freshly ground pepper
- 1 cup burgundy
- ¼ cup all-purpose flour
  Hot cooked rice

Cut the steak into strips ¼ inch wide and 2 inches long (partially frozen meat is easier to cut). Thaw meat completely. In 3-quart casserole, cook mushrooms, onion, and garlic in butter, covered, at **HIGH** for 4 minutes, stirring once. Add steak, parsley, bay leaf, salt, and pepper. Stir in wine. Cook, covered, at **HIGH** for 12 minutes.

Combine flour and ¾ cup cold water; stir into mixture. Cook, uncovered, at **HIGH** for 2 minutes, stirring once. Serve over hot rice. Makes 3 to 4 servings.

HUNGARIAN GOULASH ZOLTAN

Total cooking time: 47 minutes

7	35	5					

- ⅓ cup all-purpose flour
- 1 teaspoon salt
- 1 pound boneless veal, cut in ½-inch cubes
- 1 pound boneless pork, cut in ½-inch cubes
- 1½ cups water
- ¼ cup chopped onion
- 2 tablespoons catsup
- 2 chicken bouillon cubes
- 1 teaspoon paprika
- 2 bay leaves
- ½ cup dairy sour cream
- 1 teaspoon caraway seed
- 1 27-ounce can sauerkraut, drained
- 6 hot boiled potatoes

In paper or plastic bag, combine flour, salt, and dash pepper. Add meat cubes, a few at a time, and shake to coat. Transfer meat to 2-quart casserole. Add water, onion, catsup, bouillon cubes, paprika, and bay leaves. Cook, covered, at **HIGH** for 7 to 8 minutes, till mixture bubbles. Reduce setting to **MEDIUM (5)** and cook 35 to 45 minutes, till meat is tender, stirring twice. Remove bay leaves.

Blend a small amount (⅓ cup) hot mixture into sour cream; return to hot mixture. Combine caraway and sauerkraut in a 12×7½×2-inch baking dish. Heat, uncovered, at **HIGH** for 5 to 6 minutes. Serve meat mixture over sauerkraut; pass hot potatoes. Makes 6 servings.

Chicken Saltimbocca

TIMETABLE

1. Early in the day, scoop ice cream for dessert; prepare the cranberry salad; freeze.
2. Prepare Chicken Saltimbocca; cover and keep warm.
3. Meanwhile, cook rice on top of conventional range.
4. Cook Spinach Stuffed Tomatoes; cut salad to serve.
5. Warm 6 bakery croissants on paper toweling or in a serving basket with a napkin for 40 seconds at **HIGH.**
6. At dessert time, make sauce for Bananas Foster.

MENU

Chicken Saltimbocca
Herbed White and Wild Rice
Spinach-stuffed Tomatoes
Frozen Cranberry Salad
Croissants   Butter
Bananas Foster or Fresh Pears
Coffee

106

COMPANY-PLEASING POULTRY AND SEAFOOD

CHICKEN SALTIMBOCCA

Check the chicken after 10 minutes and rearrange, moving less cooked rolls to the outside of the dish—

Total cooking time: 20 minutes 30 seconds

0:30	20							

  3 large chicken breasts, skinned, boned, and halved lengthwise (1½ pounds)
  6 thin slices boiled ham
  3 slices process Swiss cheese, halved
  1 medium tomato, seeded and chopped
  ½ teaspoon dried sage, crushed
  ⅓ cup fine dry bread crumbs
  2 tablespoons grated Parmesan cheese
  2 tablespoons snipped parsley
  4 tablespoons butter or margarine

Place chicken, boned side up, on cutting board. Cover with plastic wrap. Working from the center out, pound lightly with meat mallet to about 6×5 inches. Remove wrap. Place a ham slice and half slice of cheese on each cutlet, trimming to fit. Top with some tomato and a dash of sage. Tuck in sides; roll up like a jelly roll, pressing to seal well.

Combine crumbs, Parmesan, and parsley. In 12×7½×2-inch baking dish, melt butter at **HIGH** for 30 to 45 seconds. Dip chicken in butter, then roll in crumb mixture. Arrange chicken rolls, seam side down, in the baking dish so rolls do not touch. Cook, covered, at **MEDIUM HIGH (7)** for 20 minutes or till done, rearranging rolls and giving dish a half turn once. Place rolls on serving platter. Stir to blend mixture remaining in baking dish; spoon over chicken rolls. Makes 6 servings.

SPINACH-STUFFED TOMATOES

Total cooking time: 9 minutes 30 seconds

6	1:30	2						

  6 medium (1½ pounds) tomatoes
  1 tablespoon all-purpose flour
  ½ teaspoon salt
  ½ cup milk
  1 slightly beaten egg yolk
  1 10-ounce package frozen chopped spinach
  1 tablespoon butter or margarine

Cut a slice ¼ inch thick off top of each tomato. Scoop out insides of each tomato, leaving a shell ¼ inch thick. Sprinkle with salt. Place on serving plate.

In small bowl, combine flour and salt; blend in milk. Stir in egg yolk. In 1-quart casserole, cook spinach according to directions on page 183 at **HIGH** for 6 to 8 minutes. Drain well. In same casserole, stir butter into spinach till melted; add milk mixture. Heat, uncovered, at **HIGH** till mixture simmers, about 1½ minutes.

Fill tomatoes with hot creamed mixture. Cook, uncovered, at **HIGH** for 2 minutes or till tomatoes and the spinach filling are hot. Makes 6 servings.

BANANAS FOSTER

Total cooking time: 3 minutes 50 seconds

1:30	2	0:20					

  1 quart vanilla ice cream
  4 tablespoons butter or margarine
  ⅔ cup packed brown sugar
  2 tablespoons milk
  ¼ teaspoon ground cinnamon
  3 cups (4 medium) bananas, sliced
  ¼ cup light rum

Scoop ice cream into 6 balls; freeze. In 1½-quart casserole or serving dish, combine butter, brown sugar, milk, and cinnamon. Heat, uncovered, at **HIGH** for 1½ minutes, till melted and bubbly, stirring once. Add banana slices; heat, uncovered, at **HIGH** for 2 minutes, till fruit is warmed, stirring mixture once.

In 1-cup glass measure, heat rum at **HIGH** for 20 seconds; pour over bananas and flame at once. In sherbet dishes or bowls, spoon sauce over ice cream balls and serve immediately. Makes 6 to 8 servings.

CRAB-STUFFED CHICKEN BREASTS

Total cooking time: 25 minutes

2	20	3					

  6 chicken breasts, skinned and boned (2 pounds)
  3 tablespoons butter or margarine
  ½ cup chopped onion
  ½ cup chopped celery
  3 tablespoons dry white wine
  1 7½-ounce can crab meat, drained, flaked, and carti-lage removed
  ½ cup herb-seasoned stuffing mix
    Paprika
  1 envelope (1⅛ ounces) hollandaise sauce mix
  ⅔ cup milk
  ½ cup (2 ounces) shredded process Swiss cheese
  2 tablespoons dry white wine

Place chicken, boned side up, on cutting board; cover with plastic wrap. Pound lightly to flatten each to about 8×6 inches. Remove wrap. Sprinkle with a little salt and pepper. Set aside. In mixing bowl, combine butter, onion, and celery. Cook, covered, at **HIGH** 2 minutes, stirring once. Stir in the 3 tablespoons wine, crab, and stuffing mix. Divide stuffing among chicken breasts. Roll up like a jelly roll, pressing to seal well. Place seam side down in 12×7½×2-inch baking dish so rolls do not touch. Sprinkle with paprika. Cook, covered, at **MEDIUM HIGH (7)** for 20 minutes or till done, giving dish half turn once. Cover to keep warm.

In 2-cup glass measure, blend sauce mix and milk. Add cheese. Cook, uncovered, at **HIGH** 3 minutes, till mixture boils, stirring after 1 minute, then every 30 seconds. Stir in remaining 2 tablespoons wine. Serve sauce over chicken. Makes 6 servings.

CHICKEN AND ARTICHOKE ELEGANTE

Total cooking time: 37 minutes

3	4	25	5				

2 small carrots, cut in julienne strips (¾ cup)
1 cup fresh mushrooms, sliced
½ cup sliced green onions
4 tablespoons butter or margarine
½ cup water chestnuts, drained and sliced
⅛ teaspoon dried thyme, crushed
¾ cup chicken broth
⅓ cup dry white wine
4 large chicken breasts, split and skinned
1 9-ounce package frozen artichoke hearts
2 tablespoons cornstarch

In small bowl, cook carrots in ¼ cup water, covered, at **HIGH** for 3 minutes; drain. In 12×7½×2-inch baking dish, cook mushrooms, onions, and butter, covered, at **HIGH** for 4 minutes. Stir in carrots, water chestnuts, thyme, ½ teaspoon salt, and ⅛ teaspoon pepper. Add broth and wine. Add chicken and artichokes to casserole; sprinkle lightly with additional salt. Cook, covered, at **MEDIUM HIGH (7)** for 25 minutes, till chicken is done, giving dish a half turn once. Remove chicken breasts; cover.

Combine cornstarch and 2 tablespoons cold water; add to broth and vegetables in baking dish. Cook, uncovered, at **HIGH** for 5 minutes, till thickened, stirring after each minute. Makes 8 servings.

BURGUNDY-BASTED DUCKLING

Total cooking time: 32 minutes

16	16						

1 4- to 5-pound duckling
¼ cup burgundy
¼ cup lemon juice
1 tablespoon Worcestershire sauce
¼ teaspoon bottled hot pepper sauce
1 clove garlic, minced
1 teaspoon dried marjoram, crushed
1 small onion, sliced and separated into rings

Prick duck skin all over. Combine burgundy, lemon juice, Worcestershire, pepper sauce, garlic, marjoram, 1 teaspoon salt, and ¼ teaspoon pepper. Brush inside of duckling with wine mixture; fill with onion rings. Tie legs together and wings close to body. Place duckling, breast side down, on microwave roasting rack or inverted saucers in 12×7½×2-inch baking dish.

Cook, uncovered, at **HIGH** for 16 minutes, brushing with sauce and draining off fat. Turn breast up; cook, uncovered, at **MEDIUM HIGH (7)** for 16 to 20 minutes, brushing with sauce and draining fat (till meat thermometer* registers 175°). Cover; let stand 10 to 15 minutes (till thermometer* registers 185°). Makes 2 to 3 servings.
*DO NOT USE A CONVENTIONAL THERMOMETER INSIDE THE MICROWAVE OVEN. SPECIAL MICROWAVE THERMOMETERS ARE AVAILABLE.

VELVET-SAUCED SOLE

Total cooking time: 11 minutes 35 seconds

4	0:35	5	1	1			

1 pound fresh or frozen sole fillets
2 tablespoons butter or margarine
2 tablespoons all-purpose flour
½ teaspoon salt
1 cup milk
¼ cup dry white wine
1 slightly beaten egg yolk
¼ cup grated Parmesan cheese

Thaw frozen fish according to directions on page 186. Separate sole into 4 pieces and arrange in 12×7½×2-inch baking dish. Cook, covered, at **MEDIUM HIGH (7)** for 4 minutes or till fish flakes easily. Drain. Cover; let stand.

In 2-cup glass measure, melt butter at **HIGH** for 35 seconds. Blend in flour, salt, and dash pepper. Stir in milk and wine. Cook, uncovered, at **MEDIUM (5)** for 5 to 5½ minutes, stirring every 30 seconds, till mixture thickens and bubbles. Stir about ½ cup hot mixture into egg yolk; return mixture to glass measure. Cook, uncovered, at **HIGH** for 1 minute, stirring once. Heat fish, covered, at **HIGH** for 1 minute. Pour sauce over fish. Sprinkle with Parmesan cheese. Makes 4 servings.

HADDOCK ROLLUPS PROVENCALE

Total cooking time: 14 minutes

2	5	4	3				

1½ to 2 pounds fresh or frozen haddock fillets (6)
¼ cup chopped onion
1 clove garlic, minced
1 tablespoon butter or margarine
½ cup dry white wine
2 small tomatoes, peeled, seeded, and chopped
1 3-ounce can chopped mushrooms, drained
2 tablespoons snipped parsley
1 vegetable bouillon cube
1 teaspoon sugar
2 teaspoons cornstarch

Thaw frozen fish according to directions on page 186. Separate into fillets (6). Sprinkle boned side of each fillet with a little salt and paprika. Roll up fillets, boned side out; secure with wooden picks. In small bowl, combine onion, garlic, and butter. Cook, uncovered, at **HIGH** for 2 minutes, till tender. In 10×6×1½-inch baking dish, combine onion mixture, wine, tomatoes, mushrooms, parsley, bouillon cube, and sugar. Heat, uncovered, at **HIGH** for 5 minutes, till boiling; stir to dissolve bouillon. Add fish rollups. Cook, covered, at **MEDIUM HIGH (7)** for 4 minutes, till fish flakes. Remove to platter; cover.

Combine cornstarch and 2 tablespoons cold water; add to tomato mixture. Heat, uncovered, at **HIGH** for 3 minutes, till mixture is thickened and bubbly. Spoon sauce over fish rolls. Makes 6 servings.

HADDOCK FLORENTINE

Total cooking time: 17 minutes

3	10	4					

    2 pounds fresh or frozen haddock fillets
    1 medium onion, sliced
    4 tablespoons butter or margarine
    ¼ teaspoon dried thyme, crushed
      Dash lemon pepper marinade
    4 cups fresh spinach (6 ounces)
    3 cups sliced fresh mushrooms
    ½ cup dry white wine
    2 tablespoons cornstarch

Thaw frozen fish according to directions on page 186. Cut into 6 rectangular portions. In 13×9×2-inch baking dish, combine onion and *half* the butter; cook, uncovered, at **HIGH** for 3 to 4 minutes, till tender. Add fish portions; sprinkle with 1 teaspoon salt, the thyme, and lemon pepper. Add spinach, mushrooms, and wine. Dot with remaining butter. Cook, covered, at **MEDIUM HIGH (7)** for 10 minutes, till fish flakes easily when tested with a fork. Remove fish to platter; keep warm.

Combine cornstarch, ½ teaspoon salt, and ¼ cup cold water. Stir into .spinach mixture. Cook, uncovered, at **HIGH** for 4 to 5 minutes, till mixture thickens and bubbles. Spoon over fish. Makes 6 servings.

COQUILLES ST. JACQUES

Total cooking time: 9 minutes 30 seconds

1:30	4	3	1				

    1 pound fresh or frozen unbreaded scallops
    ⅓ cup sliced fresh mushrooms
    1 tablespoon butter or margarine
    2 tablespoons *each* snipped chives and parsley
    ¼ cup dry white wine
    1 tablespoon lemon juice
          •   •   •
    2 teaspoons cornstarch
    2 tablespoons milk
    4 teaspoons fine dry bread crumbs

Thaw frozen scallops in 2-quart casserole according to directions on page 186. Rinse scallops; cut up large pieces. In same casserole, combine mushrooms and butter. Heat, uncovered, at **HIGH** for 1½ to 2 minutes, till tender. Add scallops, chives, parsley, wine, and lemon juice. Cook, covered, at **HIGH** for 4 minutes, or till scallops are tender. Lift scallops and mushrooms from liquid with slotted spoon; divide among 4 coquilles shells.

Stir together cornstarch and milk; add to liquid in casserole. Cook, uncovered, at **HIGH** for 3 to 4 minutes, till mixture thickens and bubbles, stirring after each minute. Sprinkle with a little salt and pepper.

Spoon over scallops in coquilles shells. Combine crumbs and a little paprika; sprinkle atop. Cook, uncovered, at **HIGH** 1 to 2 minutes, till hot. Makes 4 servings.

SEAFOOD ASPARAGUS DIVAN

Total cooking time: 24 minutes

13	7	4					

    2 8-ounce packages frozen cut asparagus
    1 7½-ounce can crab meat, drained, flaked and carti-
      lage removed
    1 cup shelled cooked shrimp *or* 1 4½-ounce can medi-
      um shrimp, drained
    3 hard-cooked eggs, sliced
    2 packages (1⅛ ounces each) hollandaise sauce mix
  1½ cups milk
    ½ cup dairy sour cream
    1 tablespoon grated Parmesan cheese

Place cartons of frozen asparagus side by side in 10×6-×1½-inch baking dish. Make small slit through top of each carton. Cook at **HIGH** for 13 minutes; drain well. Layer asparagus, crab meat, and shrimp in the 10×6×1½-inch dish. Top with egg slices. Cook, covered, at **HIGH** for 7 minutes, till heated through. Cover and keep warm.

In 4-cup glass measure, combine the hollandaise sauce mix and milk. Cook, uncovered, at **HIGH** 4 minutes, or till mixture boils, stirring after each minute. Stir in sour cream; spoon over casserole. Top with cheese. Serve immediately. Makes 6 servings.

BOUILLABAISSE

Total cooking time: 25 minutes

5	5	3	12				

    8 ounces frozen lobster tail
   10 ounces fresh or frozen snapper or sole fillets
    1 pound fresh or frozen cod or haddock fillets
   12 ounces fresh or frozen scallops
    1 pound clams in shells
  1½ cups chopped onion
    1 clove garlic, minced
    2 tablespoons olive oil or cooking oil
    1 16-ounce can tomatoes, cut up
    ¼ cup snipped parsley
    1 bay leaf
    1 teaspoon dried thyme, crushed
    ¼ teaspoon saffron, crushed

Thaw frozen shellfish and fish according to directions on page 186. Split lobster in half lengthwise; cut crosswise to make 6 to 8 pieces. Cut blocks of fish fillets into 1-inch pieces. Cut large scallops in half. Wash clams well. Set all aside.

In 3-quart casserole, combine onion, garlic, and oil; cook, covered, at **HIGH** for 5 minutes, stirring once. Add 1½ cups water, tomatoes, parsley, bay leaf, thyme, saffron, 2 teaspoons salt, and dash pepper. Cook, uncovered, at **HIGH** 5 to 6 minutes. Add lobster; cook, uncovered, at **HIGH** for 3 minutes. Add fish, scallops, and clams; cook, uncovered, at **HIGH** for 12 minutes, stirring every 3 minutes. Makes 6 to 8 servings.

Corn-stuffed Onions

TIMETABLE

1. Early in the day, prepare Herb Loaves; proof in the microwave oven. Bake in a conventional oven.
2. Prepare Butterscotch Cheesecake; chill.
3. Drain canned pineapple slices for salad; arrange on lettuce with fresh mint leaves. Set the table.
4. Prepare Corn-stuffed Onions.
5. While onions cook, broil lamb chops conventionally.
6. Warm Herb Loaf according to directions on page 36.

MENU

Broiled Lamb Chops

Corn-stuffed Onions

Pineapple Mint Salad

Herb Loaf (page 75)   Butter

Butterscotch Cheesecake (page 115)

Coffee

VEGETABLE SPECIALS

CORN-STUFFED ONIONS

Total cooking time: 26 minutes

16	3	1	6					

6 medium onions (1½ pounds)
1 12-ounce can corn with green pepper and pimiento
2 tablespoons butter or margarine
1 10¾-ounce can condensed cream of celery soup
1 cup (4 ounces) shredded process American cheese

Hollow out onions; chop centers to make 1 cup. Fill onions with corn; place in 8×8×2-inch baking dish. Cook, covered, at **HIGH** 16 minutes, turning dish once. In 4-cup glass measure, combine butter and chopped onion; cook, uncovered, at **HIGH** for 3 to 4 minutes, stirring once. Stir in soup, any remaining corn, and cheese. Cook at **HIGH** 1 minute, stirring once. Spoon sauce over onions; cook, uncovered, at **HIGH** 6 minutes. Makes 6 servings.

PEA PODS AND ALMONDS

Total cooking time: 6 minutes 30 seconds

2:30	2:30	1:30						

1 cup fresh mushrooms, sliced
¼ cup sliced green onions with tops
2 tablespoons butter or margarine
1 teaspoon cornstarch
1 teaspoon instant chicken bouillon granules
2 teaspoons soy sauce
1 6-ounce package frozen pea pods, thawed
2 tablespoons toasted slivered almonds

In 1-quart casserole, cook mushrooms, onion, and butter, covered, at **HIGH** for 2½ minutes. Combine cornstarch, ⅓ cup cold water, bouillon granules, and soy; add to mixture. Cook, uncovered, at **HIGH** for 2½ to 3 minutes, till thickened, stirring twice. Stir in pea pods. Cook at **HIGH** for 1½ minutes. Toss with almonds. Serves 3 or 4.

BRUSSELS SPROUTS EGG BAKE

Total cooking time: 10 minutes

10								

3 hard-cooked eggs, sliced
2 10-ounce packages frozen Brussels sprouts, cooked
1 cup (4 ounces) shredded process American cheese
⅓ cup milk
1 10¾-ounce can condensed cream of mushroom soup
½ cup cornflake crumbs
2 tablespoons butter or margarine, melted

Arrange egg slices atop sprouts in 10×6×1½-inch baking dish; sprinkle with cheese. Blend milk and soup; pour over all. Cook, covered, at **MEDIUM HIGH (7)** for 10 minutes, till hot, turning dish once. Combine crumbs and butter; sprinkle atop. Makes 6 to 8 servings.

QUICK SPINACH RAREBIT

Total cooking time: 13 minutes 30 seconds

8	5	0:30						

2 10-ounce packages frozen chopped spinach
½ of 8-ounce can water chestnuts, drained and sliced
1 10-ounce package frozen Welsh rarebit, thawed
8 slices bacon, crisp-cooked and crumbled
½ of 3-ounce can French fried onions

Place spinach in 10×6×1½-inch baking dish. Cook, covered with waxed paper, at **HIGH** 8 minutes, stirring once; drain well. Stir in water chestnuts, ⅓ of the rarebit, and a little salt. Sprinkle with bacon. Spread remaining rarebit atop. Cook, uncovered, at **HIGH** for 5 minutes, giving dish half turn once. Top with onion rings; cook at **HIGH** 30 seconds. Makes 6 servings.

CREAMED ONIONS

Total cooking time: 17 minutes 30 seconds

12	0:30	3	2					

Peel 1½ pounds small whole onions; place in 2-quart casserole with 2 tablespoons water. Cook, covered, at **HIGH** for 12 to 15 minutes; drain and set aside. In same casserole, melt 2 tablespoons butter at **HIGH** for 30 to 45 seconds. Stir in 3 tablespoons all-purpose flour, ½ teaspoon salt, and dash white pepper. Add 1 cup light cream. Cook, uncovered, at **HIGH** for 3 to 4 minutes, stirring after each minute, till thickened and bubbly.

Add ⅓ cup dry white wine and the onions. Heat, uncovered, at **HIGH** for 2 minutes. Sprinkle with grated Parmesan cheese before serving. Makes 6 to 8 servings.

BUFFET VEGETABLE BAKE

Total cooking time: 24 minutes

15	9							

2 10-ounce packages frozen peas and carrots
1 9-ounce package frozen cut green beans
2 cups (8 ounces) shredded process American cheese
1 10¾-ounce can condensed cream of mushroom soup
1 8-ounce can water chestnuts, drained and sliced
1 3-ounce can sliced mushrooms, drained
⅓ cup dry white wine
1 teaspoon Worcestershire sauce
  Dash bottled hot pepper sauce
½ cup rich round cracker crumbs (12 crackers)

Place peas, carrots, and beans in 12×7½×2-inch baking dish; add ¼ cup water. Cook, covered, at **HIGH** 15 to 18 minutes, stirring twice. Drain; return to dish. Combine cheese, soup, water chestnuts, mushrooms, wine, Worcestershire, and pepper sauce; stir into vegetables. Cook, uncovered, at **HIGH** 9 minutes, giving dish a half turn once. Top with crumbs. Makes 12 servings.

111

EASY-MIXED VEGETABLE CASSEROLE

Tightly fitting covers are important when cooking vegetables. To avoid steam burns, use hot pads and lift the lid towards the wall instead of towards you. Piercing plastic wrap with a fork before removing it allows hot steam to escape, too—

Total cooking time: 20 minutes

3	15	2					

   1 envelope (1¼ ounces) sour cream sauce mix
   1 10-ounce package Parisian-style vegetables with sauce cubes
   1 envelope (1¼ ounces) cheese sauce mix
   ¼ teaspoon salt
   ¾ cup milk
   1 10-ounce package frozen peas and onions
   1 10-ounce package frozen cauliflower
   ½ of 3-ounce can (1 cup) French fried onions

In small bowl, prepare sour cream sauce mix according to package directions. Set aside.

In 2-quart casserole or serving dish, place Parisian-style vegetables with sauce cubes. Add liquid as directed on package; cook, covered, at **HIGH** for 3 minutes stirring once to blend sauce. Stir in the dry cheese sauce mix and the salt; gradually stir in the milk. Stir in frozen peas and onions. Cut up large pieces of cauliflower; add to mixture. Cook, covered, at **HIGH** for 15 minutes, till vegetables are tender, stirring twice.

Stir in the prepared sour cream sauce. Sprinkle top of casserole with French fried onions. Heat, uncovered, at **HIGH** 2 minutes. Makes 8 to 10 servings.

MUSHROOM CASSEROLE

Total cooking time: 8 minutes

3	5						

   ½ cup chopped onion
   2 tablespoons butter or margarine
   1 cup beef broth
   3 tablespoons dry white wine
   2 tablespoons cornstarch
   ¼ teaspoon dried marjoram, crushed
   2 6-ounce cans (2 cups) sliced mushrooms, drained
   2 tablespoons snipped parsley
                  • • •
   ¼ cup coarsely crumbled saltines (4 crackers)
   1 tablespoon grated Parmesan cheese
   1 tablespoon butter or margarine, melted

In 1-quart casserole, combine onion and the 2 tablespoons butter. Cook, uncovered, at **HIGH** for 3 minutes, till tender. Combine beef broth, wine, cornstarch, and marjoram; add to mixture in casserole. Add mushrooms and parsley; cook, uncovered, at **HIGH** for 5 minutes, till thickened and bubbly, stirring 3 times.

Combine saltine crumbs, Parmesan, and remaining butter; sprinkle atop to serve. Makes 4 to 6 servings.

SWEET POTATOES TROPICALE

Total cooking time: 12 minutes

1	10	1					

   4 tablespoons butter or margarine
   2 18-ounce cans vacuum-packed sweet potatoes
   3 eggs
   ½ cup sugar
   ½ cup chopped pecans
   ½ cup flaked coconut
   ½ cup orange juice
   ½ teaspoon vanilla
   1 cup miniature marshmallows

In mixer bowl, melt butter, uncovered, at **HIGH** for 1 minute. Add potatoes; mash. Beat in eggs, sugar, pecans, coconut, orange juice, vanilla, and ½ teaspoon salt. Turn into 2-quart casserole. Cook, covered, at **HIGH** for 10 minutes. Top with marshmallows. Cook, uncovered, at **HIGH** for 1 to 1½ minutes. Serves 8 to 10.

ASPARAGUS GOLDENROD

Total cooking time: 6 minutes

2	4						

In 10×6×1½-inch baking dish, arrange two 10-ounce packages frozen asparagus spears, cooked.

In 2-cup glass measure, combine 1 package (1⅛ ounces) hollandaise sauce mix and water called for on package. Cook, uncovered, at **HIGH** for 2 minutes, till thickened and bubbly, stirring every 30 seconds.

Stir in ¼ cup frozen whipped dessert topping, thawed, ½ teaspoon grated lemon peel, and 1 teaspoon lemon juice. Spoon over asparagus. Sprinkle with 2 chopped hard-cooked eggs. Cook, uncovered, at **HIGH** for 4 to 5 minutes, giving dish half turn once. Makes 6 servings.

ZUCCHINI ITALIANO

Total cooking time: 19 minutes

12	6	1					

   2½ pounds zucchini, cut in ⅜-inch slices (8 cups)
   ½ cup chopped onion
   ½ cup chopped green pepper
   1 3-ounce can sliced mushrooms, drained
   1 package (1½ ounces) spaghetti sauce mix
   1 8-ounce can tomato sauce
   ½ cup (2 ounces) shredded mozzarella cheese

In 2-quart casserole, combine zucchini, onion, pepper, and ½ cup water. Cook, covered, at **HIGH** for 12 to 15 minutes, till tender-crisp, stirring every 4 minutes; drain. Stir in mushrooms, dry sauce mix, tomato sauce, and 1 cup water; mix well. Cook, covered, at **HIGH** for 6 to 7 minutes, till mixture is hot. Sprinkle with cheese; cook at **HIGH** 1 minute more. Makes 8 servings.

GREEN BEANS ELEGANTE

Total cooking time: 19 minutes

10	2:30	4:30	2				

    1 pound (3 cups) fresh green beans, cut in
        1-inch pieces
    1 cup fresh mushrooms, sliced
    1 tablespoon chopped onion
    2 tablespoons butter or margarine
    3 tablespoons all-purpose flour
    ½ teaspoon salt
    ¼ teaspoon dried thyme, crushed
    2 cups milk
    4 slices bacon, crisp-cooked, drained, and crumbled
    6 patty shells (baked in a conventional oven)

Place green beans in 1-quart casserole; add ⅓ cup water. Cook, covered, at **HIGH** for 10 to 15 minutes, till tender; drain and set aside.

In same casserole, combine mushrooms, onion, and butter. Cook, covered, at **HIGH** for 2½ minutes, till tender. Stir in flour, salt, thyme, and dash pepper; add milk all at once. Cook, uncovered, at **HIGH** for 4½ to 5 minutes, stirring after 3 minutes, and then after each minute, till mixture thickens and bubbles.

Add beans; heat again at **HIGH**, uncovered, for 2 minutes, till all is heated through. Stir in bacon; spoon into hot patty shells to serve. Makes 6 servings.

FRESH MUSHROOM SALAD

Total cooking time: 3 minutes

1	2						

    2 cups water
      Few drops lemon juice
    1 medium onion, halved and sliced
    4 cups (10 ounces) fresh mushrooms, sliced
    ¼ cup cooking oil
    2 teaspoons prepared mustard
    ¼ cup white wine vinegar
    ¼ teaspoon salt
    ¼ teaspoon dried marjoram, crushed
    ¼ teaspoon dried chervil, crushed
    ⅛ teaspoon freshly ground pepper
      Bibb lettuce leaves
      Snipped parsley

In 2-quart casserole, combine water, lemon juice, onions, and dash salt. Cook, uncovered, at **HIGH** for 1 minute. Add mushrooms; cook, uncovered, at **HIGH** for 2 to 3 minutes or till vegetables are barely tender, stirring after each minute. Drain. Place vegetables on paper toweling.

In screw-top jar, combine oil, mustard, vinegar, and seasonings. Cover; shake well to mix. Return onions and mushrooms to casserole. Pour vinegar mixture over vegetables. Cover; chill 1½ to 2 hours.

To serve, drain vegetables; arrange on lettuce leaves; top with parsley. Makes 6 to 8 servings.

ONION-STUFFED ACORN SQUASH

Total cooking time: 17 minutes 30 seconds

8	2:30	3:30	3	0:30			

    2 medium acorn squash
    1 9-ounce package frozen tiny onions with
        cream sauce cubes
    ½ cup (2 ounces) shredded process American cheese

Pierce squash with meat fork. Place the two whole squash in 12×7½×2-inch baking dish. Cook at **HIGH** 8 minutes. Let stand 5 to 8 minutes while preparing onions.

In 1-quart bowl or casserole, heat the ⅔ cup water and 1 tablespoon butter called for on the onion package at **HIGH** for 2½ minutes. Add onions and sauce cubes. Cook, covered, at **HIGH** for 3½ minutes, stirring once.

Cut squash in half and remove seeds. Place cut side up in a 12×7½×2-inch baking dish. Sprinkle with a little salt and spoon in the onion mixture. Cook, covered, at **HIGH** for 3 minutes. Top with cheese. Cook, uncovered, at **HIGH** for 30 seconds. Makes 4 servings.

TEST KITCHEN TIPS

Crown a baked potato with *Regal Cheese Sauce* and it's ready for royalty. This fluffy sauce combines sour cream, butter, sharp cheese, and green onions—each a great potato topper in its own right and even better when served together.

Regal Cheese Sauce: In a small glass mixer bowl, combine ½ cup dairy sour cream and 4 tablespoons butter or margarine. Cook, uncovered, at **MEDIUM (5)** for 1 minute. Add 1 cup (4 ounces) shredded sharp process American cheese and 2 tablespoons sliced green onion. Cook, uncovered, at **MEDIUM (5)** for 30 to 45 seconds, till cheese is warm but not melting. Beat with electric mixer at high speed till fluffy, 3 to 5 minutes. Makes 1¼ cups sauce.

If you're caught short without these potato topping ingredients, however, set out an array of sprinkles and spoon-ons for guests to choose from: crisp crumbled bacon, blue cheese, green pepper, snipped fresh herbs (chives, parsley, dill, basil), caviar, anchovies, finely chopped ham, horseradish, Parmesan cheese, plain yogurt, potato chip dip, toasted almonds, whipped cream cheese, mustard, or salad dressing: Thousand Island, creamy garlic, green goddess, or creamy onion.

Four Fruit Pizza

TIMETABLE

1. Early in the day, make Whole Wheat Bread; proof in the microwave oven. Bake in conventional oven.
2. Prepare Four Fruit Pizza; chill at least 2 hours.
3. Prepare Sausage-stuffed Pork Roast; cook.
4. Cook potatoes on conventional range; mash and cover.
5. Set the table; make salad and dressing.
6. While pork roast stands, prepare Herb Gravy.
7. Warm bread according to chart on page 36.

MENU

Sausage-stuffed Pork Roast and Herb Gravy (page 104)

Mashed Potatoes

Honey Whole Wheat Bread (page 75)   Butter

Bibb Lettuce Salad

Four Fruit Pizza

Coffee

DESSERT SPECTACULARS

FOUR FRUIT PIZZA

Total cooking time: 10 minutes

5	2	3					

- 1 roll refrigerated sugar cookie dough
- 1 8-ounce package cream cheese
- 6 tablespoons sugar
- 1 16-ounce can apricot halves
- 2 tablespoons cornstarch
- ¼ teaspoon pumpkin pie spice
- ½ cup red currant jelly
- 1 pint fresh strawberries, halved
- ½ cup fresh raspberries or blueberries
- 1 canned pineapple slice

Heat unwrapped roll cookie dough at **LOW (1)** for 5 minutes, turning over once. Unwrap and pat in 12-inch pizza pan. Bake in *conventional* 375° oven 15 to 16 minutes. Cool.

Remove cream cheese from wrapper. In small bowl, heat cream cheese, uncovered, at **LOW (1)** for 2 minutes; stir in *4 tablespoons* of the sugar. Spread on crust. Drain apricots, reserving ⅔ cup syrup. In 4-cup glass measure, combine cornstarch, remaining sugar, and spice. Stir in reserved syrup; add jelly. Cook, uncovered, at **HIGH** for 3 to 4 minutes, till boiling. Arrange fruits atop cheese. Spoon on syrup; chill. Cut in wedges. Makes 10 servings.

BRANDIED PUMPKIN PIE

Total cooking time: 1 hour 3 minutes

45	3	15					

- 1 9-inch pastry shell
- 1 16-ounce can pumpkin
- 1 13-ounce can evaporated milk
- ⅔ cup packed brown sugar
- 2 slightly beaten eggs
- ¼ cup brandy
- ½ teaspoon salt
- 1 teaspoon ground cinnamon
- ½ teaspoon ground ginger
- ¼ teaspoon *each* ground nutmeg and cloves
- 1 2-ounce envelope dessert topping mix
- 2 tablespoons chilled brandy

Bake the pastry shell conventionally; cool. Combine remaining ingredients except topping mix and the chilled brandy. Pour *3½ cups* into pastry shell. Cook, uncovered, at **MEDIUM LOW (3)** for 45 minutes, giving dish half turn once, till knife inserted near center comes out clean. Cool.

Before serving, prepare topping mix according to package directions, substituting the chilled brandy for 2 tablespoons of the liquid called for. Spoon atop pie.

Pour remaining pumpkin mixture into two 6-ounce custard cups. In 8×8×2-inch baking dish, heat 2 cups water at **HIGH** for 3 minutes. Place custard cups in hot water. Cook, uncovered, at **MEDIUM LOW (3)** for 15 to 19 minutes; turning each cup once. (Mixture will barely be set in centers.) Cool. Makes 1 pie and 2 individual servings.

PRALINE SUNDAE SAUCE

Total cooking time: 2 minutes 30 seconds

2:30							

- 1½ cups packed brown sugar
- 1 6-ounce can (⅔ cup) evaporated milk
- 1 tablespoon butter or margarine
- ½ teaspoon *each* rum flavoring and vanilla
- ⅓ cup chopped pecans

In 4-cup glass measure, combine brown sugar, evaporated milk, and butter. Heat, uncovered, at **HIGH** for 2½ to 3 minutes, till smooth and syrupy, stirring after each minute. Stir in flavorings and nuts. Serve over ice cream. Makes about 1¾ cups sauce.

BUTTERSCOTCH CHEESECAKE

Try chocolate pudding in place of butterscotch—

Total cooking time: 35 minutes

1	2	2	5	21	4		

- 10 tablespoons butter or margarine
- 2½ cups graham cracker crumbs
- ½ cup granulated sugar
- 1 3¾- or 4-ounce package *regular* butterscotch pudding mix
- ½ cup granulated sugar
- 1½ cups milk
- 3 8-ounce packages cream cheese, softened
- 3 eggs
- 1 teaspoon vanilla
- 2 cups dairy sour cream
- ½ cup sifted powdered sugar

In bowl, melt butter at **HIGH** for 1 to 1½ minutes. Add crumbs and the ½ cup granulated sugar; mix well. Press half the mixture in a 9-inch pie plate; press remaining into 6 custard cups. Bake pie shell, uncovered, at **MEDIUM HIGH (7)** for 2 minutes; press out bubbles. Bake the 6 custard cups at **MEDIUM HIGH (7)** for 1 to 2 minutes. Cool.

In 4-cup glass measure, combine pudding mix, remaining ½ cup granulated sugar, and the milk. Cook, uncovered, at **HIGH** for 5 to 6 minutes, till thickened and bubbly, stirring after 3 minutes, then after each minute. Cover surface with plastic wrap. Set aside to cool.

In large mixer bowl, beat cream cheese till fluffy; add eggs and beat to blend well. Add vanilla and cooled pudding; blend well. Pour 4 cups mixture into pie shell. Bake, uncovered, at **MEDIUM (5)** for 21 to 23 minutes, till center seems firm when shaken, turning dish three times. Pour remaining filling into 6 custard cups; bake, uncovered, at **MEDIUM (5)** for 4 to 4½ minutes.

Stir together sour cream and powdered sugar; spread half on the pie, remaining on individuals. Garnish with banana slices and chocolate curls, if desired. Makes one pie (10 servings) and 6 individual servings.

115

STRAWBERRY PARTY CAKE

Keep this attractive cake in mind for your next bridal shower or anniversary party—

Total cooking time: 14 minutes

9	5						

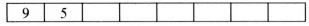

- 1 package 2-layer-size white cake mix (no pudding in the mix)
- 1 16-ounce package frozen strawberry halves, thawed
- 1 3-ounce package strawberry-flavored gelatin
- 1 cup boiling water
- 2 2-ounce packages dessert topping mix

Prepare cake mix according to package directions. Turn into ungreased 13×9×2-inch baking dish. Spread batter in dish. Cook, uncovered, at **MEDIUM (5)** for 9 minutes, giving dish half turn once. Cook at **HIGH** for 5 to 6 minutes longer, till cake tests done, giving dish half turn once. (Top will be moist in places.) Cool 10 minutes.

Meanwhile, drain berries, reserving ½ cup syrup. Dissolve gelatin in boiling water; stir in reserved syrup. Set aside at room temperature.

Using a long-tined fork, punch deep holes in cake, making even rows across surface (be sure to include corners). Slowly spoon gelatin over top of cake. Chill.

Prepare topping; fold in berries. Spread over cake. Chill. (Refrigerate leftover cake.) Makes 16 servings.

CHOCO-CHERRY CAKE

Total cooking time: 17 minutes

5	2	10					

- 1 16-ounce can pitted dark sweet cherries
- 1 tablespoon cornstarch
- 2 tablespoons sugar
- 2 tablespoons dry red wine
- 1 8-ounce package cream cheese
- ¼ cup sugar
- 2 tablespoons milk
- ½ of 2-layer-size package chocolate cake mix (no pudding in the mix)

Drain cherries, reserving syrup. In 4-cup glass measure, combine cornstarch and the 2 tablespoons sugar. Blend in reserved cherry syrup. Cook, uncovered, at **HIGH** for 5 minutes, till thickened and bubbly, stirring after each minute. Stir in wine and cherries; chill.

In bowl, warm cream cheese, uncovered, at **LOW (1)** for 2 minutes. Stir in ¼ cup sugar; blend in milk. Set aside.

Prepare cake batter according to package directions. Pour *2 cups* batter into a greased and waxed paper-lined 8×1½-inch round baking dish. Cook, uncovered, at **MEDIUM (5)** for 10 minutes, or till cake tests done, giving dish a half turn after 5 minutes. Cool 5 to 10 minutes; invert and remove from dish. Cool cake completely. Cut in wedges and serve with a dollop of cream cheese mixture; spoon cherry sauce atop. (Use remaining cake batter for cupcakes—page 175.) Makes 6 servings.

TEST KITCHEN TIPS

Flaming Dessert Sundaes—here's a trio of showy desserts to dazzle your dinner guests. You'll look like a master chef, yet all it takes is a little planning. Ahead of time, scoop ice cream into serving dishes and keep them in the freezer. Measure the sauce ingredients and have ready. At dessert time, carry ice cream, a serving ladle, and some long-handled matches to the table. Prepare fruit sauce and liqueur in the microwave. Dim the lights at the table. Pour the hot liqueur over the warm fruit; quickly light a match and touch it to the surface of the sauce. Voila! (Let the flames burn out completely before serving.)

Pineapple Jubilee: In 1-quart casserole or serving dish, combine ½ cup orange marmalade, 2 tablespoons brown sugar, and 2 cups chopped fresh pineapple. Blend together 1 tablespoon cornstarch and 1 tablespoon water; stir into mixture. Heat, uncovered, at **HIGH** for 4 minutes, stirring after each minute, till thick and bubbly. In 1-cup glass measure, heat ¼ cup orange liqueur at **HIGH** for 20 seconds; pour over fruit and flame at once. Serve over ice cream. Makes 2 cups.

Strawberries and Nectarines Flambe: Mash 1 cup fresh strawberries. Cut another 1 cup berries in halves. In 1-quart casserole, combine ¼ cup sugar and 1 tablespoon cornstarch. Gradually stir in pureed berries. Heat, uncovered, at **HIGH** for 2 to 3 minutes, stirring after each minute, till thick and bubbly. Add 1 cup sliced peeled nectarines. Heat, covered, at **HIGH** for 1 minute. Add halved berries and heat at **HIGH** 1 minute more. In 1-cup glass measure, heat ¼ cup rum at **HIGH** for 20 seconds; pour over fruit and flame at once. Serve over ice cream. Makes 2 cups.

Flaming Bananas and Raspberries: Thaw one 10-ounce package frozen raspberries (see page 82); sieve. In 1½-quart casserole or serving dish, melt 2 tablespoons butter or margarine at **HIGH** for 30 to 45 seconds. Add raspberry puree, 2 tablespoons sugar, and 2 tablespoons orange liqueur. Heat, covered, at **HIGH** for 2 minutes, stirring once. Add 4 cups banana slices; cook, covered, at **HIGH** for 1 minute. In 1-cup glass measure, heat 4 tablespoons orange liqueur at **HIGH** for 20 seconds. Pour over fruit and flame at once. Serve over ice cream. Makes 4 cups.

CHOCOLATE FONDUE

Total cooking time: 4 minutes 30 seconds

2:30	2							

- 8 ounces semisweet chocolate (8 squares)
- 1 15-ounce can *sweetened condensed* milk (1⅓ cups)
- ⅓ to ½ cup milk
- 2 tablespoons instant coffee powder *or* 4 ounces cream-filled mint patties, broken up *or* ⅓ cup orange liqueur *or* ¼ cup brandy
  Angel cake or pound cake cubes
  Banana chunks, pineapple chunks, and strawberries

In 1-quart casserole or non-metal fondue pot, cook chocolate, uncovered, at **HIGH** for 2½ to 3½ minutes, till melted, stirring after 2 minutes. Stir in *condensed* milk and the ⅓ cup milk till blended. Heat, uncovered, at **HIGH** for 2 minutes more, till heated through. Stir in coffee powder, mint patties, orange liqueur, or brandy as desired. Transfer to fondue burner.

Thin with a little more milk if necessary. Use remaining ingredients as dippers. Makes 2½ cups sauce.

PASTRY SHELL

Total cooking time: 6 minutes

6							

Mix one pie crust stick or a recipe for a single crust pastry shell. Roll out to ⅛-inch thickness. Fit into 9-inch pie plate. Prick well with a fork. Cook, uncovered, at **MEDIUM HIGH (7)** for 6 to 8 minutes, removing just when brown spots begin to appear. Cool before filling.

Tart Shells: Mix and roll as above. Cut in four 5-inch rounds. Fit over inverted custard cups, pinching pleats in 5 or 6 places. Prick well with fork. Cook, uncovered, at **MEDIUM HIGH (7)** for 4½ minutes, removing just when brown spots appear. Cool a few minutes; remove from cups. Makes 4.

PEAR-BERRY COMPOTE

Total cooking time: 10 minutes

3	7						

- 1 16-ounce can whole cranberry sauce
- 2 tablespoons sugar
- 1 tablespoon lemon juice
- ¼ teaspoon ground cinnamon
- ¼ teaspoon ground ginger
- 6 fresh pears, pared, cored, and quartered
- 2 medium oranges, peeled, sliced, and quartered

In 2-quart casserole, combine cranberry sauce, sugar, lemon juice, cinnamon, and ginger; cook, covered, at **HIGH** 3 to 4 minutes till mixture boils, stirring once.

Add pears and oranges; cook, covered, at **HIGH** for 7 minutes more, till pears are tender, stirring after 3 minutes. Serve warm. Makes 6 servings.

PINEAPPLE SOUR CREAM PIE

Total cooking time: 7 minutes

5	2							

- ¾ cup sugar
- ¼ cup all-purpose flour
- ½ teaspoon salt
- 1 20-ounce can crushed pineapple
- 1 cup dairy sour cream
- 1 tablespoon lemon juice
- 3 slightly beaten egg yolks
- 1 baked 9-inch pie shell
- 3 egg whites
- ½ teaspoon vanilla
- ¼ teaspoon cream of tartar
- 6 tablespoons sugar

In 2-quart casserole, combine the ¾ cup sugar, flour, and salt. Stir in *undrained* pineapple and the sour cream, mixing well. Heat, uncovered, at **HIGH** for 5 to 6 minutes, till mixture is thickened and bubbly, stirring after 2 minutes, then after each minute. Add lemon juice. Stir ⅓ of the hot mixture into egg yolks; return all to hot mixture. Cook, uncovered, at **HIGH** for 2 minutes, till thickened. Spoon into pie shell.

In mixer bowl, beat egg whites, vanilla, and cream of tartar till soft peaks form. Gradually add the remaining 6 tablespoons sugar, beating to stiff peaks. Spread meringue atop filling, sealing to edges of pastry. Bake *conventionally* in 350° oven for 12 to 15 minutes.

SNAPPY CARAMEL DESSERT

Total cooking time: 6 minutes

6								

- 8 ounces vanilla caramels (about 28)
- 1½ cups milk
- 1 envelope unflavored gelatin
- ¼ cup cold water
- 1 teaspoon vanilla
- 1 cup whipping cream
- ⅓ cup coarse vanilla wafer crumbs (7 wafers)
- ¼ cup chopped pecans
- 1 tablespoon butter or margarine, melted

In 2-quart casserole or mixing bowl, combine caramels and milk. Heat, uncovered, at **HIGH** for 6 to 7 minutes, stirring occasionally till all are melted and blended. Meanwhile, soften gelatin in cold water; add to caramel mixture, stirring till gelatin is dissolved. Stir in vanilla. Chill till mixture mounds slightly when spooned.

Beat with rotary or electric beater till smooth. Whip cream; fold into caramel mixture. Spoon about ¼ cup mixture into 6 sherbet glasses. Combine crumbs, pecans, and the melted butter; sprinkle about 1 tablespoon mixture atop pudding in each glass. Spoon on the remaining caramel pudding; top each with remaining crumb mixture. Chill. Makes 6 servings.

117

WHEN 1 OR 2 IS A CROWD

When you think in terms of small servings, think microwave! This is where your new kitchen helper can really shine. Whether it's heating a plateful of food for late-comers, cooking just one bowl of soup, or fixing dinner for two every night, micro-cooking can make it all a breeze. As a matter of fact, our Cornish Hens with Granola Rice Stuffing and Harvest Salad Molds (recipes next page) are so easy and fast to cook why not light some candles and serve them tonight?

MICRO MENU PLANNER

MAIN DISHES

HEARTY SOUPS, SALADS & SANDWICHES

DESSERTS

Cooking for one or two needn't be a bore—all it takes is a little creativity. Take a plain everyday egg. Now add a pinch of imagination. You'll enjoy serving our *Mexican-style Eggs* (recipe on page 128) for a casual brunch. Or, how about *Puffy Mushroom Omelet* (recipe on page 132) for brunch on the fancy side. And for a late night supper, you just can't beat *Scrambled Supper* (recipe on page 134). Then to challenge your cooking skills even more, take a look at our *Exotic Eggs* concoctions in the test kitchen tip box on page 124.

For a dinner with lots of planned-over possibilities, cook up a storm with *Roast Turkey Breast* (recipe on page 129). Remove the leftover meat from the bones. Freeze in one or two serving size packages. You then have a world of delicious dishes right at your fingertips. For example, substitute turkey for the chicken in *Chicken Cheese Strata* (recipe on page 123) or *Chicken Enchiladas* (recipe on page 128). There's always hot turkey sandwiches—warm up turkey slices in canned or leftover gravy, then serve over your favorite bread. Another time, make a basic white sauce (recipe on page 37) substituting chicken broth for part of the milk. Stir in turkey, mushrooms, and pimiento for a fast turkey a la king to spoon over rice, noodles, mashed potatoes, or patty shells.

Curried Fruit Ham Ring (recipe on page 127) and *Stroganoff Meat Ring* (recipe on page 127) both can make tasty encores. Cut in chunks and heat with macaroni and cheese. Serve thin slices of meat loaf as the "bread" and creamy potato or rice salad as the "filling" for a fun new sandwich. Or slice some French bread diagonally and sandwich a slice of meat loaf in each cut. Drizzle with garlic butter; top with cheese, and heat a minute or two in the microwave oven.

The Micro Menu Planner above can help you create more menus for one or two with a flair.

MENU

Puffy Mushroom Omelet (page 132)
Broiled Tomatoes
English Muffins   Jams
Fresh Fruit Basket
Coffee

MENU

Roast Turkey Breast (page 129)
Mashed Potatoes
Buttered Peas and Onions
Cranberry Sauce (page 73)
Hot Rolls   Butter
Brandied Pumpkin Pie (page 115)

MENU

Barbecued Ham (page 123)
Macaroni Salad
Italian Green Beans
Spiced Peaches
Chocolate Cupcakes (page 133)
Coffee

MENU

Cheesy Halibut (page 124)
Buttered Broccoli Spears
Fresh Orange Salad   Celery Seed Dressing
Crescent Rolls   Butter
Five Layer Bars (page 133)
Coffee

MENU

Saucy Pork Tenderloin (page 129)
Fluffy Hot Cooked Rice
Buttered Asparagus
Cinnamon Applesauce
S'mores (page 85)

MENU

Cornish Hens with Granola Rice Stuffing (right)
Buttered Carrots
Harvest Fruit Molds (right)
Mini Bread Loaf   Butter
Chablis
Creme de Menthe Parfaits
Coffee

TIMETABLE

1. Prepare Harvest Fruit Molds early in the day.
2. Make Creme de Menthe Parfaits; freeze.
3. Chill wine and set the table.
4. Stuff and cook Cornish hens.
5. Cook carrots conventionally while hens cook.
6. Unmold salads and heat bread loaf.

CORNISH HENS WITH GRANOLA RICE STUFFING

Total cooking time: 26 minutes 30 seconds

2	0:30	12	12				

2 1¼-pound Cornish hens, thawed
2 tablespoons butter or margarine
¼ teaspoon paprika
1 medium orange
¾ cup cooked rice
½ cup granola
⅓ cup chopped pared apple
¼ teaspoon salt
⅛ teaspoon ground cinnamon
3 tablespoons chopped celery
2 tablespoons chopped onion
1 tablespoon butter or margarine

Save giblets for another use or discard. Wash hens; pat dry. Sprinkle cavities with salt. Stuff with *Granola Rice Stuffing*, below. Tie legs together and wings to body with string. Place on microwave roasting rack, breast side down, in 12×7½×2-inch baking dish.

In custard cup, melt the 2 tablespoons butter at **HIGH** for 30 seconds; add paprika. Brush some on hens. Cook, covered, at **MEDIUM HIGH (7)** for 12 minutes. Turn breast up, reversing outside edges to inside. Brush with remaining butter mixture. Cook, covered, at **MEDIUM HIGH (7)** for 12 minutes more or till 185°.* Cover with foil and let stand 10 minutes. Makes 2 servings.

Granola Rice Stuffing: Peel and section orange over bowl to catch juices. Set juice aside. Chop orange sections; measure ⅓ cup. In bowl, combine rice, granola, apple, chopped orange, salt, and cinnamon. In small bowl, cook celery, onion, and 1 tablespoon butter, uncovered, at **HIGH** for 2 to 3 minutes, till tender. Add to rice mixture; toss to mix. Add reserved orange juice, if desired, to moisten.
*DO NOT USE A CONVENTIONAL THERMOMETER INSIDE THE MICROWAVE OVEN. SPECIAL MICROWAVE THERMOMETERS ARE AVAILABLE.

HARVEST SALAD MOLDS

Total cooking time: 10 minutes

10							

6 ounces mixed dried fruits
1½ cups water
3 tablespoons sugar
1 3-ounce package lemon-flavored gelatin
¾ cup water
¼ cup dry sherry

Pit prunes; cut up all fruit. In 1½-quart casserole, combine the dried fruits and 1½ cups water. Cook, covered, at **MEDIUM (5)** for 10 minutes, till tender. Stir in sugar and gelatin to dissolve. Stir in remaining ¾ cup water and the sherry. Chill till partially set. Pour into four 1-cup individual ring molds. Chill till firm. Makes 4 servings.

121

Wiener Schnitzel California-style

TIMETABLE

1. Set the table.
2. Cut up vegetable relishes; cover with ice water.
3. Begin cooking noodles on conventional range.
4. Cook Wiener Schnitzel California-style.
5. Drain noodles thoroughly; arrange with veal on a serving platter. Place bread sticks in a basket.
6. At dessert time, prepare Baked Apples in Wine.

MENU

Wiener Schnitzel California-style
Green Noodles
Iced Garden Relishes
Bread Sticks   Butter
Baked Apples in Wine
Coffee

HURRY-UP SUPPERS

WIENER SCHNITZEL CALIFORNIA-STYLE

The timing for preheating and cooking with a browning dish may vary from one type to another. Be sure to follow the directions for the one you have—

Total cooking time: 15 minutes

4	5	1:30	1:30	1	2		

   8 to 10 ounces veal sirloin steak, cut in 2 pieces
   1 beaten egg
  ⅓ cup fine dry bread crumbs

     • • •

   1 package (1¾ ounces) stroganoff sauce mix (with real sour cream, already in the mix)
1⅓ cups milk
   1 tablespoon cooking oil
   1 small avocado, cut in 4 wedges
   1 small tomato, cut in wedges
  ¼ cup (1 ounce) shredded Monterey Jack cheese
    Hot cooked green noodles

With meat mallet, pound each piece of veal till very thin—about 6×5 inches. Sprinkle with a little salt and pepper. Dip in beaten egg, then in crumbs; set aside.

In 2-cup glass measure, combine dry sauce mix and milk. Cook, uncovered, at **HIGH** for 4 minutes, till sauce is thickened and bubbly, stirring after each minute. Cover and set sauce aside.

Preheat browning dish according to directions for meat, at **HIGH** about 5 minutes. Measure oil into browning dish. Swirl veal in dish to coat with oil. Cook at **HIGH** about 1½ minutes or till browned. Turn meat over. Cook at **HIGH** 1½ minutes more.

Spoon some sauce over meat. Place the 2-cup measure with remaining sauce in the microwave along with the veal in the browning dish. Cook, uncovered, at **HIGH** for 1 minute. Place avocado and tomato wedges atop meat; cook at **HIGH** 2 minutes more till hot. Sprinkle with cheese. Serve meat on platter with noodles. Pour sauce into serving bowl and pass with meat. Makes 2 servings.

BAKED APPLES IN WINE

Total cooking time: 3 minutes 30 seconds

3:30							

   2 large baking apples
   2 tablespoons brown sugar
  ⅛ teaspoon ground nutmeg
   2 teaspoons butter or margarine
  ¼ cup rose wine

Core apples; pare strip from top of each. Place in 1-quart casserole. Stir together brown sugar and nutmeg; spoon into apple centers. Top each with 1 teaspoon butter; pour wine into casserole. Bake, uncovered, at **HIGH** for 3½ to 4 minutes, rearranging and spooning sauce over once. Makes 2 servings.

If desired, double recipe to make 4 servings; cook, uncovered, at **HIGH** for 5 to 5½ minutes.

BARBECUED HAM

Total cooking time: 7 minutes

2	3	2					

   1 8¾-ounce can pineapple tidbits
   2 tablespoons bottled barbecue sauce
  ½ medium green pepper, cut in strips
   1 tablespoon cornstarch
   1 cup (4 ounces) cubed cooked ham
    Hot cooked rice

Drain pineapple, reserving syrup. In 1-quart bowl, combine reserved syrup and barbecue sauce. Add green pepper; cook, uncovered, at **HIGH** for 2 minutes. Blend cornstarch and ½ cup cold water; stir into pepper mixture. Cook, uncovered, at **HIGH** for 3 to 4 minutes, till thickened. Stir in pineapple and ham. Cook, uncovered, at **HIGH** 2 minutes more. Serve over hot rice. Makes 2 servings.

SPEEDY SHRIMP STROGANOFF

Total cooking time: 6 minutes

2	3	1					

   1 10¾-ounce can condensed cream of shrimp soup
  ¼ cup milk
   1 teaspoon snipped parsley or dried parsley flakes
   1 teaspoon instant minced onion
   1 4½-ounce can shrimp, drained
  ¼ cup dairy sour cream
    Hot cooked rice

In 1-quart casserole, combine soup, milk, parsley, and onion. Heat, uncovered, at **HIGH** 2 to 3 minutes, or till mixture boils, stirring once. Add shrimp; heat, uncovered, at **HIGH** 3 to 5 minutes. Stir some hot mixture into sour cream; return to casserole. Cook at **HIGH** 1 minute. Serve over rice. Pass condiments such as raisins, peanuts, chopped tomato, and shredded coconut, if desired. Makes 2 servings.

CHICKEN CHEESE STRATA

Total cooking time: 6 minutes

5	1						

   2 slices firm textured bread
   1 10¾-ounce can condensed chicken noodle soup
   2 beaten eggs
  ¼ cup (1 ounce) shredded process American cheese

Cut bread into bite-size cubes. Place in bottom of two 5×5×1½-inch ceramic baking dishes. Cut up soup noodles; combine soup with noodles and eggs. Pour over bread.

Cook, uncovered, at **MEDIUM HIGH (7)** for 5 minutes. Top with cheese and cook, covered, at **MEDIUM HIGH (7)** 1 minute more (mixture will be almost set). Let stand 5 minutes to finish cooking. Makes 2 servings.

HOT SAUSAGE POTATO SALAD

Total cooking time: 17 minutes

8	1:30	1:30	2	4			

  2 **cups peeled and cubed potatoes (2 potatoes)**

• • •

  2 **slices bacon, chopped**
 ¼ **cup chopped onion**
  1 **tablespoon all-purpose flour**
  2 **tablespoons sugar**
 ¾ **teaspoon salt**
 ¼ **teaspoon celery seed**
   Dash pepper
 ¼ **cup water**
  3 **tablespoons vinegar**

• • •

  2 **Polish sausages, halved crosswise**
  2 **tablespoons snipped parsley**

Combine cubed potatoes and ½ cup water in 1-quart casserole. Cook at **HIGH** for 8 to 10 minutes, stirring once. Drain in colander and set aside.

In same casserole, place bacon; cover with paper toweling. Cook at **HIGH** for 1½ to 2 minutes. Remove toweling and bacon and set aside. Reserve bacon drippings in casserole. Add onion to casserole; cook, uncovered, at **HIGH** for 1½ minutes. Stir in flour, sugar, salt, celery seed, and pepper. Add water and vinegar; cook, uncovered, at **HIGH** for 2 minutes, till mixture thickens and bubbles. Add potatoes. Arrange sausages on top. Sprinkle with parsley. Heat, covered, at **HIGH** for 4 to 6 minutes, till hot, turning dish once. Makes 2 servings.

PORK SWEET-SOUR

Total cooking time: 9 minutes

3	3	3					

 ½ **pound boneless pork, cut in strips**
  1 **tablespoon cooking oil**
  1 **cup zucchini slices cut in half**
 ½ **cup sliced unpared apple**
  4 **teaspoons cornstarch**
  2 **tablespoons brown sugar**
 ⅔ **cup pineapple juice**
  2 **tablespoons vinegar**
  1 **tablespoon soy sauce**
   Chinese noodles or hot cooked rice

In 1-quart casserole, combine pork and oil. Heat, uncovered, at **HIGH** for 3 minutes, stirring after 2 minutes. Remove meat and set aside. Add zucchini and apple to dish; cook, covered, at **HIGH** for 3 minutes, till tender, stirring once. Return meat to mixture.

Combine cornstarch and brown sugar; blend in pineapple juice, vinegar, and soy sauce. Add to meat mixture; cook, uncovered, at **HIGH** for 3 minutes, till thickened and bubbly, stirring once or twice. Serve over Chinese noodles or cooked rice with soy sauce. Makes 2 servings.

TEST KITCHEN TIPS

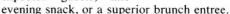

Exotic Eggs. Turn your place into a restaurant and whip up some fancy omelets in a flash. They're great for a quick supper for one or two, dinner for unexpected guests, late-evening snack, or a superior brunch entree.

Simply begin with the *Fluffy Scrambled Eggs* recipe on page 48. Then add a filling, topping, and a garnish as suggested below. Improvise with your combinations—you may be delightfully surprised.

For each person, a two-egg scramble is ideal. Use a small dish for cooking. Add about ¼ cup of the filling you desire, and cook, covered, at **MEDIUM HIGH (7)** for 2 to 2½ minutes, stirring often. Turn onto a plate and spoon on topping and garnish.

Fillings: Shrimp, chicken livers, ham, crumbled pork sausage, artichoke hearts, cottage cheese, cubed cooked potatoes, sauteed zucchini, green peppers, pineapple chunks, bananas.

Toppings: Warmed tomato sauce, hollandaise sauce, seafood cocktail sauce, shredded cheese, chutney, apple slices, sour cream, orange marmalade, strawberry halves, blueberries, whipped cream cheese, maple-flavored syrup, honey.

Garnishes: Snipped fresh chives, parsley, crisp-cooked crumbled bacon, caviar, brown sugar, shaved chocolate, toasted almonds.

CHEESY HALIBUT

Total cooking time: 5 minutes

4	1						

  2 **frozen halibut steaks, thawed**
   Dash salt
   Dash pepper
  2 **tablespoons bottled tartar sauce**
 ¼ **cup (1 ounce) shredded process American cheese**

Place fish steaks in 10×6×1½-inch baking dish. Sprinkle with salt and pepper. Bake fish, uncovered, at **HIGH** for 4 minutes, giving dish half turn after 2 minutes, till fish is nearly done. Spread steaks with tartar sauce; sprinkle with cheese. Cook, uncovered, at **HIGH** 1 minute more, till fish flakes easily. Makes 2 servings.

SALMON TETRAZZINI

Total cooking time: 8 minutes 30 seconds

0:30	3	5					

- ⅓ cup uncooked spaghetti, broken up
- 1 cup milk
- 1 teaspoon instant minced onion
- 1 7¾-ounce can salmon
- 1 tablespoon butter or margarine
- 1 tablespoon all-purpose flour
- ⅛ teaspoon salt
  Dash pepper
- 2 tablespoons grated Parmesan cheese
- 2 tablespoons dry white wine
- 1 3-ounce can sliced mushrooms, drained
  • • •
- 1 teaspoon butter or margarine, melted
- 2 tablespoons dry bread crumbs

Cook spaghetti on top of range; drain well. Combine milk and onion; let stand 5 minutes. Drain salmon; break into pieces, remove skin and bones.

In 3-cup casserole or medium mixing bowl, melt the 1 tablespoon butter, uncovered, at **HIGH** for 30 to 45 seconds. Blend in flour, salt, and pepper. Add milk-onion mixture. Cook, uncovered, at **HIGH** for 3 to 4 minutes, till mixture thickens and bubbles. Add Parmesan and wine. Stir in spaghetti, mushrooms, and salmon.

Combine the 1 teaspoon butter and the crumbs; sprinkle on top. Cook, uncovered, at **HIGH** for 5 to 6 minutes, till heated through. Makes 2 servings.

For 2 individual casseroles, divide the mixture between 2 casseroles. Top each with crumbs. Cook, uncovered, at **HIGH** for 7 to 8 minutes, till hot.

TUNA FISHYSSOISE

Total cooking time: 7 minutes 30 seconds

2	4	1:30					

- 2 tablespoons chopped onion
- 1 tablespoon butter or margarine
- 1 10¾-ounce can condensed cream of potato soup
- ¾ cup milk
- 2 tablespoons dry white wine
- ¼ teaspoon Worcestershire sauce
- 1 7-ounce can tuna, drained and broken in chunks
- 2 slices French bread, toasted
- 2 slices (2 ounces) process American cheese

In 1-quart casserole or mixing bowl, combine onion and butter. Cook, uncovered, at **HIGH** for 2 to 3 minutes, till tender. Add soup; gradually stir in milk, wine, and Worcestershire sauce. Add tuna; heat, uncovered, at **HIGH** for 4 minutes, till boiling.

Pour into two 2-cup or 20-ounce casseroles; top with toast and cheese, trimming if necessary. Place immediately in microwave; heat, uncovered, at **HIGH** for 1½ to 2 minutes. Makes 2 servings.

CHILI BEEF BAKE

Total cooking time: 17 minutes 30 seconds

2	15	0:30					

- 4 ounces lean ground beef
- ¼ cup finely chopped onion
- 1 tablespoon chopped green pepper
- 1 8-ounce can (1 cup) tomatoes, cut up
- 1 8-ounce can red kidney beans, undrained
- ¼ cup uncooked packaged precooked rice
- ¼ teaspoon chili powder
- ¼ teaspoon salt
- ⅛ teaspoon garlic powder
- ¼ cup (1 ounce) shredded process American cheese

In 1-quart casserole, crumble beef; add onion and green pepper. Cook, uncovered, at **HIGH** for 2 minutes, stirring once. Drain. Stir in remaining ingredients except cheese. Cover; cook at **MEDIUM HIGH (7)** for 15 minutes, stirring once, till rice is tender. Top with cheese; heat, uncovered, at **MEDIUM HIGH (7)** for 30 seconds more. Serves 2.

WINE SAUCED BURGER STEAK

Total cooking time: 5 minutes 30 seconds

4:30	1						

Combine 12 ounces lean ground beef, ½ teaspoon salt, and dash pepper; mix well. Shape in 2 patties ½-inch thick. Place in 8×8×2-inch baking dish. Cook, covered loosely, at **HIGH** for 4½ minutes, turning patties after 3½ minutes.

Remove patties to plates; drain fat from dish. Add 2 tablespoons dry red wine, 1 teaspoon lemon juice, ¼ teaspoon Worcestershire sauce, 2 teaspoons dried parsley flakes, and ½ teaspoon instant minced onion to baking dish. Heat sauce, uncovered, at **HIGH** for 1 minute, till boiling. Pour over burger steaks. Makes 2 servings.

REUBEN'S CASSEROLE

Total cooking time: 5 minutes

2:30	2:30						

- 1 8-ounce can sauerkraut, drained
- 1 small tomato, sliced
- 2 tablespoons Thousand Island dressing
- 1 3-ounce package sliced corned beef, cut up
- ⅛ teaspoon caraway seed
- ½ cup soft rye bread crumbs (1 slice bread)
- 1 tablespoon butter or margarine, melted
- ½ cup (2 ounces) shredded process Swiss cheese

Spread sauerkraut in 3-cup baking dish. Top with tomato slices, dressing, corned beef, then caraway. Cook, uncovered, at **HIGH** for 2½ minutes; give dish a half turn once. Toss crumbs with butter. Sprinkle cheese on casserole; top with crumbs. Cook, uncovered, at **HIGH** for 2½ minutes more. Makes 2 servings.

Curried Fruit Ham Ring

TIMETABLE

1. Prepare Marinated Vegetable Salad; chill.
2. Mix and shape Curried Fruit Ham Ring; cook 7 minutes.
3. Meanwhile, set the table. Cover meat and let stand.
4. Cook 2 sweet potatoes about 7 minutes (see page 183).
5. Add glaze to ham ring; cook. Add fruit; cook again.
6. Warm bakery rolls according to directions on page 36.
7. At dessert time, prepare Hot Fudge Rum Turtle Sundaes. Or, make sauce ahead and reheat it at serving time.

MENU

Curried Fruit Ham Ring

Baked Sweet Potatoes

Marinated Vegetable Salad

Sesame Seed Rolls   Butter

Hot Fudge Rum Turtle Sundaes

Coffee

WEEKDAY DINNERS

CURRIED FRUIT HAM RING

Total cooking time: 13 minutes

7	3	3						

    1 egg
    ¾ cup soft bread crumbs (1 slice bread)
    ¼ cup finely chopped onion
    ¼ cup milk
    ¾ pound ground cooked ham
    ½ pound ground fresh pork
        • • •
    1 tablespoon butter or margarine, softened
    2 tablespoons brown sugar
    ½ to 1 teaspoon curry powder
    1 17-ounce can fruits for salads, drained

Combine egg, crumbs, onion, and milk. Add meats and mix well. In 8×8×2-inch baking dish, shape meat mixture into a 6-inch ring. (If desired, place a 6-ounce custard cup, right side up, in center of dish and mold mixture around the cup.) Cook, covered with waxed paper, at **HIGH** for 7 minutes. (Remove cup.) Drain off meat juices.

Combine butter, brown sugar, and curry; spread over ham loaf. Give dish a half turn; cook, covered, at **HIGH** 3 minutes. Spoon fruit over and around loaf. Cook, covered, at **HIGH** 3 minutes. Transfer meat ring to serving plate; spoon on juices and fruits. Serve with cashews, coconut, and chutney, if desired. Makes 4 servings.

STROGANOFF MEAT RING

Total cooking time: 12 minutes

10	2							

    ½ of 10¾-ounce can (⅔ cup) condensed golden mush-
        room soup
    ⅓ cup dairy sour cream
    1 beaten egg
    1½ cups soft bread crumbs (2 slices bread)
    ¼ cup wheat germ
        Dash garlic salt
    ¼ teaspoon dried basil, crushed
        Dash ground pepper
    1 pound lean ground beef
        • • •
    1 tablespoon dry white wine

Combine ¼ *cup* of the soup, ¼ *cup* of the sour cream, the egg, crumbs, wheat germ, and seasonings. Let stand 5 minutes. Add beef, mix well. In a 9-inch glass pie plate, shape meat mixture into a ring. (If desired, place a 6-ounce custard cup, right side up, in center of plate and mold mixture around cup.) Cook, covered with waxed paper, at **HIGH** for 10 minutes, giving plate half turn twice. Let stand 5 minutes. (Remove cup.) Drain off meat juices.

In 2-cup glass measure or serving bowl, stir together *remaining* soup, *remaining* sour cream, and the wine. Cook, uncovered, at **HIGH** for 2 to 3 minutes, till hot. Spoon some over meat loaf; pass remaining. Makes 4 servings.

MARINATED VEGETABLE SALAD

Total cooking time: 3 minutes

3								

    2 cups thinly sliced zucchini
    ¼ cup cream-style cottage cheese with chives
    2 tablespoons dairy sour cream
    1½ teaspoons lemon juice
    ⅛ teaspoon garlic salt
    2 tablespoons chopped green pepper
    2 medium tomatoes, sliced
        Curly endive

Place zucchini in 1-quart casserole; add 2 tablespoons water. Cook, covered, at **HIGH** for 3 to 4 minutes, till tender-crisp; drain well. Combine cottage cheese, sour cream, lemon juice, and garlic salt. Add zucchini and green pepper; toss to coat. Chill. Stir before serving on tomato slices; garnish with endive. Makes 2 servings.

HOT FUDGE RUM TURTLE SUNDAES

Total cooking time: 1 minute

1								

    ½ cup semisweet chocolate pieces
    ½ cup tiny marshmallows
    2 tablespoons milk
    2 tablespoons light rum
        Vanilla ice cream
        Pecan halves, toasted

In 2-cup glass measure, combine chocolate pieces, marsh-mallows, and milk. Cook, uncovered, at **HIGH** for 1 to 1½ minutes, stirring once, till melted together. Stir in rum. Scoop 2 servings ice cream into serving dishes; top with hot sauce and nuts. Makes 2 servings.

PEACH-A-BERRY TARTS

Total cooking time: 1 minute

1								

    2 tart shells (recipe on page 117)
    2 canned peach halves with syrup
    2 tablespoons brandy
    ½ teaspoon unflavored gelatin
    ¼ cup peach preserves
    ½ cup fresh blueberries

Drain peach halves, reserving 2 tablespoons syrup. In 2-cup glass measure, combine syrup and brandy. Stir in gelatin; let stand to soften. Add preserves. Heat, uncover-ed, at **HIGH** for 1 minute. Stir; cool to thicken slightly.

Spread a little glaze in tart shells over bottom and sides. For each tart: place 2 tablespoons blueberries in shell, then peach half, cut side up. Add 2 tablespoons more berries; spoon on glaze. Chill. Makes 2 tarts.

CHICKEN ENCHILADAS

Total cooking time: 6 minutes 30 seconds

0:30	2	3	1				

   6 corn tortillas, thawed
  ¼ cup cooking oil
  2 tablespoons butter or margarine
  2 tablespoons all-purpose flour
    Dash *each* paprika, ground nutmeg, salt, and pepper
  ½ cup chicken broth
  ¾ cup shredded Monterey Jack or sharp cheddar
    cheese
  2 teaspoons lemon juice
  1 tablespoon snipped parsley
  ½ teaspoon grated onion
  1 cup finely diced cooked chicken
    Avocado Sauce and Jalapeño Relish

Dip tortillas in oil in skillet on top of range for 10 seconds on each side, just till limp. Set aside on paper towel.

In 4-cup glass measure, melt butter, uncovered, at **HIGH** for 30 seconds. Blend in flour and seasonings. Add chicken broth; heat, uncovered, at **HIGH** for 2 minutes, till thickened and bubbly, stirring every 30 seconds. Add *¼ cup* of the cheese, lemon juice, parsley, and onion; stir in chicken.

Divide mixture among tortillas; roll each up and place in 12×7½×2-inch baking dish. Cook, covered, at **MEDIUM HIGH (7)** for 3 minutes. Sprinkle with remaining cheese; cook, uncovered, at **MEDIUM HIGH (7)** for 1 minute. Pass *Sauce* and *Jalapeño Relish*. Serves 2 or 3.

Avocado Sauce: Seed and peel 1 avocado. In bowl, mash avocado. Stir in ¼ cup dairy sour cream, ½ teaspoon lemon juice, ⅛ teaspoon salt, dash onion powder, and 5 drops bottled hot pepper sauce.

Jalapeño Relish: Combine 1 finely chopped small tomato, 2 tablespoons finely chopped onion, 1 finely chopped jalapeño pepper or regular chili pepper (seeded if desired) and ¼ teaspoon salt. Chill.

CONTINENTAL BEEF BAKE

Total cooking time: 56 minutes

5	45	6					

  8 ounces boneless beef, cut in ½-inch cubes
  ¼ cup chopped onion
  1 8-ounce can (1 cup) tomatoes, cut up
    Dash garlic salt
  1 teaspoon dried parsley flakes
  ⅛ teaspoon dried thyme, crushed
  ¼ cup dry white wine
  ¼ cup uncooked packaged precooked rice

In 1½-quart casserole, combine ⅔ cup water, the beef, onion, tomatoes, ¼ teaspoon salt, garlic salt, parsley, and thyme. Heat, covered, at **HIGH** for 5 minutes, till boiling. Cook, covered, at **MEDIUM (5)** for 45 minutes, stirring twice. Add wine and rice; cook, covered, at **MEDIUM (5)** for 6 minutes, stirring once. Makes 2 servings.

MEXICAN-STYLE EGGS

Total cooking time: 10 minutes

2	5	3					

  4 corn tortillas, thawed
  ¼ cup chopped onion
  1 tablespoon cooking oil
  1 16-ounce can tomatoes, cut up
  2 green chilies, drained, rinsed, seeded, and chopped (3
    tablespoons)
  ¼ teaspoon salt
  ¼ teaspoon chili powder
  ¼ teaspoon garlic powder
       • • •
  4 eggs
  ¼ cup shredded Monterey Jack or American cheese

Dip tortillas in oil as in *Chicken Enchilada* recipe. In 4-cup measure, combine onion and oil. Cook, uncovered, at **HIGH** for 2 minutes. Add tomatoes, chilies, salt, chili powder, and garlic powder. Pour into 9-inch pie plate or divide mixture among 4 individual casseroles.

Cook, uncovered, at **HIGH** for 5 to 7 minutes, till boiling. Break all 4 eggs into pie plate or break 1 egg into each casserole. Cook, covered with waxed paper, at **HIGH** for 3 to 5 minutes, till eggs are almost done. Let stand 2 to 4 minutes, till done. Serve on tortillas; sprinkle with cheese. Makes 2 to 4 servings.

BEER BEEF POT ROAST

Total cooking time: 1 hour 23 minutes

15	15	50	3				

  2-pound beef pot roast
  1 tablespoon all-purpose flour
  2 tablespoons cooking oil
  1 bay leaf
  1 12-ounce can beer
  2 medium potatoes, pared and halved
  2 small carrots, pared and cut in 1-inch pieces
  2 small onions, quartered
  2 tablespoons all-purpose flour

Coat pot roast with the 1 tablespoon flour. If desired, brown in hot oil in skillet on top of range. Place in 12×7½×2-inch baking dish. Add 1 teaspoon salt, dash pepper, bay leaf, and *½ cup* beer. Cover; cook at **MEDIUM (5)** for 15 minutes.

Add remaining beer; arrange vegetables around meat. Cook, covered, at **MEDIUM (5)** for 15 minutes. Turn meat over; rearrange vegetables. Cook, covered, at **MEDIUM (5)** for 50 minutes, turning meat over again after 30 minutes.

Remove meat and vegetables to platter; cover. Pour juices into 4-cup glass measure; skim off fat. Blend together remaining flour and ¼ cup cold water. Stir into juices. Cook, uncovered, at **HIGH** for 3 to 5 minutes, till thickened and bubbly. Season with salt and pepper. Makes 2 large servings plus leftovers.

LAMB CHOPS OLÉ

Total cooking time: 22 minutes

2	20						

½ medium onion, sliced
¼ cup chopped green pepper
¼ cup sliced celery
1 8-ounce can tomato sauce
½ small clove garlic, minced
½ teaspoon chili powder
Dash bottled hot pepper sauce
2 shoulder lamb chops
Hot cooked noodles

In a 10×6×1½-inch baking dish, combine onion, green pepper, and celery. Add 2 tablespoons water. Heat, uncovered, at **HIGH** for 2 minutes. Add tomato sauce, garlic, chili powder, and pepper sauce. Dip chops in mixture to coat; place atop mixture. Cook, covered, at **MEDIUM (5)** for 20 to 22 minutes, turning chops over after 10 minutes. Serve sauce over noodles. Makes 2 servings.

ROAST TURKEY BREAST

Total cooking time: 1 hour

30	30						

Thaw a 4-pound frozen turkey breast according to chart on page 186. Place, breast down, in 8×8×2-inch baking dish. Cook, uncovered, at **HIGH** for 30 minutes, turning dish twice. Turn breast up; cook at **MEDIUM (5)** for 30 to 35 minutes or till done.

VEAL HUNGARIAN

Total cooking time: 14 minutes

12	2						

8 ounces boneless veal, cut in ½-inch cubes
1 8-ounce can (1 cup) tomatoes, cut up
½ cup water
½ cup chopped onion
2 tablespoons chopped green pepper
¼ cup elbow macaroni
1 teaspoon paprika
½ teaspoon salt
⅛ teaspoon dried marjoram, crushed
1 tablespoon all-purpose flour
¼ cup dairy sour cream

In 1½-quart casserole, combine all ingredients except flour and sour cream. Cook, covered, at **MEDIUM HIGH (7)** for 12 to 14 minutes, till macaroni is tender and meat is done, stirring after 6 minutes. Combine flour and 2 tablespoons water; stir into meat mixture. Cook at **MEDIUM HIGH (7)** for 2 to 3 minutes, till thickened, stirring twice. Stir about ¼ cup hot mixture into sour cream; return to meat mixture. Serve at once. Makes 2 servings.

TEST KITCHEN
TIPS

Spontaneous soups. If you have a piece of celery, an onion, some parsley, and perhaps a carrot or two, you have the makings for soup. A dab of leftover meat or pasta can add even more flavor.

Save the neck and giblets next time you buy a whole chicken; add them to a cup or two of water in a bowl and simmer some stock. Use the **MEDIUM (5)** setting, and season the brew with herbs. Discard bones and giblets, freeze broth till needed, then reheat with some cooked chicken, yesterday's rice, and that bit of broccoli.

No time to make stock? Start with a canned cream or clear soup, or a mix. Additions like fresh mushrooms, green onions, slivers of ham, a little dry wine, and Parmesan cheese make it a hearty supper with some warm crusty bread.

Try starting a soup "pot" in your freezer. Whenever you have some extra broth, vegetable cooking liquid or the like, add a layer to the pot. Make more layers daily with dabs of leftover vegetables, meat, or noodles. After a quart or so has accumulated (or three weeks have passed) warm the frozen wonder in your microwave. Season according to your tastes.

Make smaller quantities of soup in the microwave oven; large amounts cook faster on the range top.

SAUCY PORK TENDERLOIN

Total cooking time: 27 minutes 30 seconds

0:30	2	25					

4 pieces pork tenderloin (1 pound)
1 tablespoon butter or margarine
¼ cup chopped onion
½ of 10¾-ounce can condensed cream of mushroom soup
2 tablespoons milk
1 3-ounce can sliced mushrooms, drained
¼ teaspoon curry powder

Pound meat to flatten. In 8×8×2-inch baking dish, melt butter at **HIGH** for 30 seconds. Cook onion in butter at **HIGH** for 2 minutes. Top with meat. Combine soup, milk, mushrooms, curry, and dash pepper; pour over meat. Cook, covered, at **MEDIUM (5)** for 25 to 28 minutes. Serve with rice, if desired. Makes 2 servings.

Clambake for Two

TIMETABLE

1. Early in the day, make Fruit Glazed Cheese Pie; chill.
2. Chill beer; put two beer mugs in the freezer to frost.
3. Soak the clams; prepare salad ingredients and chill.
4. Set the table or a picnic table outside.
5. Precook lobster on top of range; arrange all the Clambake ingredients in the oven bag and cook.
6. Meanwhile, bake the rolls in a *conventional* oven.
7. Toss the salad with your favorite dressing.

MENU

Clambake for Two

Boston Lettuce with Tomato Wedges

Brown and Serve Rolls   Butter

Beer

Fruit Glazed Cheese Pie or Watermelon

Coffee

130

FRANKLY FANCY DINNERS

CLAMBAKE FOR TWO

Total cooking time: 15 minutes

8	7							

- 12 hard-shelled clams
- 1 live lobster (1½ pounds)

• • •

- 2 chicken quarters
- 2 ears corn in husks (silks removed)
- ½ cup butter or margarine, melted

Rinse clams; cover with salt water and let stand 15 minutes; drain. Repeat twice. Boil a large kettle of water on top of range. Plunge the live lobster head first into the boiling water. Cook 2 minutes; drain.

Flour a large oven roasting bag according to package directions. Place bag in 12×7½×2-inch baking dish. Arrange clams, cooked lobster, chicken quarters, and corn in the bag. Tie bag closed with string (do not use a paper- or foil-covered wire). Cook at **HIGH** for 8 minutes. Open bag. Turn corn over; retie and continue cooking at **HIGH** for 7 to 8 minutes more.

Remove lobster. Split tail of lobster and if still translucent in center, cook alone at **HIGH**, 45 seconds to 1 minute more. Sprinkle chicken with paprika. Serve with melted butter. Makes 2 servings.

PAELLA

Remove the shrimp or lobster shells before cooking, if you want. Shellfish cook in the same amount of time with or without the shell—

Total cooking time: 22 minutes

3	15	4						

- 4 to 6 ounces fresh or frozen shrimp *or* 4- to 6-ounce lobster tail *or* 4 small clams in shells

• • •

- 1 small chicken breast, boned and cut up
- 4 ounces chorizo or Italian sausage, casings removed
- 2 tablespoons chopped onion

• • •

- ¾ cup chicken broth
- ⅓ cup uncooked long-grain rice
- 1 tomato, peeled and chopped (½ cup)
- 1 small clove garlic, minced
- ⅛ teaspoon saffron, crushed
- ⅛ teaspoon dried oregano, crushed

Thaw shrimp and lobster, if frozen, as directed on page 186. In 1-quart casserole, combine chicken, sausage, and onion. Heat, uncovered, at **HIGH** for 3 minutes, till chicken is tender. Spoon off fat.

Add chicken broth, rice, tomato, garlic, saffron, and oregano. Cook, covered, at **MEDIUM (5)** for 15 minutes, till rice is done, stirring every 5 minutes.

Top with seafood; cook, covered, at **MEDIUM (5)** for 4 to 5 minutes, till seafood is done. Makes 2 servings.

LEMON BUTTERED LOBSTER TAILS

Total cooking time: 11 minutes 30 seconds

0:30	11							

- 2 8-ounce fresh or frozen lobster tails
- 4 tablespoons butter or margarine
- 1 tablespoon snipped parsley
- 1 to 2 tablespoons lemon juice

Thaw frozen lobster tails as directed on page 186. In 1-cup glass measure or small bowl, combine butter, parsley, and lemon juice. Heat, uncovered, at **HIGH** for 30 seconds, till melted. Split each lobster tail through the top shell, cutting to but not through the softer undershell. Spread tails open so meat is on top.

Place in 10×6×1½-inch baking dish. Heat, covered, at **MEDIUM HIGH (7)** for 11 minutes, giving dish a quarter turn every 3 minutes and brushing with butter sauce. Pass remaining butter sauce for dipping. Makes 2 servings.

FRUIT GLAZED CHEESE PIE

Total cooking time: 12 minutes

2	10							

- 1 9-inch graham cracker pie shell
- 1 8-ounce package cream cheese
- 1 cup dairy sour cream
- ½ cup sugar
- ½ teaspoon vanilla

• • •

- 1 17-ounce can fruits for salad, chilled
- ⅓ cup orange marmalade

Prepare pie shell according to directions on page 81. Place cream cheese in small mixer bowl. Heat, uncovered, at **LOW (1)** for 2 minutes. Add sour cream, sugar, and vanilla; beat till smooth. Pour into pie shell.

Bake, uncovered, at **MEDIUM (5)** for 10 to 11 minutes or till set, giving dish 3 quarter turns. Cool, then chill. Drain fruits thoroughly. Arrange in circle atop pie. Stir marmalade; spoon over fruits on pie to glaze.

CAFE MOCHA

If you use hot instead of room temperature coffee, see chart on page 99 for warming this delectable brew—

Total cooking time: 1 minute

1								

- ½ jigger brandy (1½ tablespoons)
- ½ jigger dark creme de cacao (1½ tablespoons)
- ½ jigger coffee-flavored liqueur (1½ tablespoons)
- ¾ cup room temperature strong coffee

In coffee cup, combine brandy, creme de cacao, and coffee liqueur. Add coffee to fill cup. Heat, uncovered, at **HIGH** for 1 minute. Makes 1 serving.

VEAL STEAK FLORENTINE

Total cooking time: 11 minutes

6	0:30	4	0:30				

- 2 **veal steaks (about 10 ounces)**
- 2 **tablespoons fine dry bread crumbs**
- ⅛ **teaspoon mixed Italian herbs**
- 1 **slightly beaten egg**
- 2 **tablespoons grated Parmesan cheese**
- 1 **10-ounce package frozen spinach**
- 3 **tablespoons butter or margarine**
- 2 **tablespoons shredded process Swiss cheese**

Pound veal to 6×5-inch pieces. Combine crumbs and herbs. Dip meat in egg, then Parmesan, then crumbs.

Cook spinach, covered, in 8×8×2-inch baking dish at **HIGH** for 6 minutes. Drain well in colander. Stir *1 tablespoon* of the butter into *half* the spinach. (Refrigerate remaining spinach for use another time.)

In same 8×8×2-inch dish, melt remaining 2 tablespoons butter at **HIGH** for 30 seconds. Add veal; cook, uncovered, at **HIGH** for 4 minutes, turning after 3 minutes. Place veal atop spinach on platter. Sprinkle with Swiss cheese. Cook at **HIGH** 30 seconds, till cheese melts. Makes 2 servings.

PUFFY MUSHROOM OMELET

Total cooking time: 15 minutes 30 seconds

2	2:30	0:30	2:30	8			

- **Mushroom Sauce**
- 2 **tablespoons butter or margarine**
- 2 **tablespoons all-purpose flour**
- ¼ **teaspoon dry mustard**
- ½ **cup milk**
- 1 **cup (4 ounces) shredded cheddar cheese**
- 2 **egg yolks**
- 2 **egg whites**

Mushroom Sauce: In 2-cup glass measure, combine ½ cup sliced fresh mushrooms, 2 tablespoons finely sliced green onion, and 2 tablespoons butter. Cook, uncovered, at **HIGH** for 2 minutes. Stir in 1 tablespoon flour. Add ½ cup milk, 1 tablespoon snipped parsley, ¼ teaspoon salt, and dash pepper. Cook, uncovered, at **HIGH** for 2½ minutes, stirring after 1 minute. Cover; set aside.

Puffy Omelet: In 4-cup glass measure, melt butter at **HIGH** for 30 seconds. Add flour, dry mustard, ¼ teaspoon salt, and dash cayenne pepper. Blend in milk; cook, uncovered, at **HIGH** for 2½ to 3 minutes, stirring after each minute, till thickened. Add cheese, stirring till melted.

In small mixer bowl, beat egg yolks 3 to 4 minutes at high speed of electric mixer. By hand, slowly add cheese mixture to yolks, stirring constantly. Cool slightly. In large mixer bowl, beat egg whites to stiff peaks. Gradually pour yolk mixture over whites; fold together.

Pour into ungreased 3-cup souffle dish. Bake, uncovered, at **MEDIUM (5)** for 8 minutes. (Mixture will puff high then fall.) Serve at once with *Mushroom Sauce*. Serves 2.

DUCKLING A L'ORANGE

Total cooking time: 38 minutes

16	20	2					

- 1 **4½- to 5-pound duckling**
- 1 **orange**
- 2 **teaspoons sugar**
- 2 **teaspoons cornstarch**
- ½ **cup beef broth**
- 1 **tablespoon dry red wine**
- 1 **tablespoon red wine vinegar**
- 1 **teaspoon orange liqueur**
- **Dash bitters**
- **Paprika**

Prepare and cook duckling as directed on page 108, at **HIGH** for 16 minutes, then at **MEDIUM HIGH (7)** for 20 minutes. Let stand 10 minutes.

While duckling stands, cut peel from orange; slice ¼ of the peel into julienne strips, discarding the white membrane and the remaining peel. Set peel aside. Section orange and set aside. In 2-cup glass measure, combine sugar and cornstarch; blend in beef broth and wine. Cook, uncovered, at **HIGH** 2 minutes, till thickened and bubbly, stirring after each minute. Add vinegar, orange liqueur, bitters, and the orange sections.

Spoon some sauce on duckling; sprinkle with peel and paprika. Makes 2 servings.

BEEF BURGUNDY PIE

Total cooking time: 54 minutes

7	10	30	7				

- ¾ **pound beef stew meat, cut in small cubes**
- 1 **beef bouillon cube**
- 2 **tablespoons all-purpose flour**
- ¼ **cup burgundy**
- ½ **cup thinly sliced carrots**
- ¼ **cup chopped onion**
- 1 **clove garlic, minced**
- ½ **teaspoon Worcestershire sauce**
- ¼ **teaspoon salt**
- ¼ **teaspoon mixed salad herbs**
- ¼ **teaspoon kitchen bouquet**
- **Dash pepper**
- ½ **cup packaged biscuit mix**

In 1½-quart casserole, combine beef, 1¾ cups water, and bouillon cube. Cook, covered, at **HIGH** for 7 minutes, till boiling. Stir. Cook, covered, at **MEDIUM (5)** for 10 minutes.

In small bowl, blend flour and wine; stir into mixture. Add carrots, onion, garlic, Worcestershire, salt, salad herbs, kitchen bouquet, and pepper. Cook, covered, at **MEDIUM (5)** for 30 minutes.

Combine biscuit mix and 3 tablespoons water; spoon atop mixture, making 4 dumplings. Cook, covered, at **MEDIUM (5)** for 7 minutes, till dumplings are done. Makes 2 servings.

PETITE DESSERTS

FIVE LAYER BARS

Total cooking time: 8 minutes 45 seconds

0:45	8							

  4 tablespoons butter or margarine
  1 cup graham cracker crumbs

        •   •   •

  1 6-ounce package (1 cup) semisweet chocolate pieces
  1 6-ounce package (1 cup) butterscotch pieces
  1 3½-ounce can (1⅓ cups) flaked coconut
  ½ cup chopped walnuts
  1 15-ounce can (1⅓ cups) *sweetened condensed* milk

In 12×7½×2-inch baking dish melt butter at **HIGH** for 45 to 60 seconds. Lift and tilt dish to spread butter. Place an inverted 2½-inch glass in center of dish. Sprinkle crumbs evenly over butter.

Layer chocolate pieces, butterscotch pieces, coconut, and nuts atop crumbs. Pour *sweetened condensed* milk over all. Bake, uncovered, at **HIGH** for 8 minutes, giving dish half turn after 4 minutes. Cool; cut in bars.

TEST KITCHEN TIPS

Try Cupcake Convenience. For a quick snack or last-minute dessert, how about baking cupcakes in a flash. Store the batter, homemade or from a one- or two-layer-size cake mix, in a covered pitcher in the refrigerator. (It will keep up to a week.)

For each, place a paper bake cup inside a glass custard cup. Add about 2 tablespoons batter, filling the cup only half full. Place one cupcake in center of the oven, or arrange 2 to 6 in the oven with one inch of space between cups. Cook, uncovered, at **HIGH** according to the chart. Cupcakes are done when wooden pick inserted in the center comes out clean. Sprinkle with sifted powdered sugar or frost when cooled with canned frosting, whipped cream, or dessert topping.

Number of cupcakes	Time at **HIGH** setting
1	30 to 35 seconds
2	45 to 50 seconds
4	1¼ to 1½ minutes
6	2¼ to 2½ minutes

For more about cake mixes, see page 175.

RASPBERRY FONDUE

Total cooking time: 5 minutes

3	2							

  1 10-ounce package frozen raspberries, thawed
  1 tablespoon red cinnamon candies
  1 tablespoon cornstarch
    Apple and pear wedges, pineapple and banana chunks

Sieve raspberries into 1-quart casserole or ceramic fondue pot. Stir in cinnamon candies; heat, uncovered, at **HIGH** for 3 to 4 minutes, till candies dissolve. Blend cornstarch and 2 tablespoons cold water; stir into mixture. Cook, uncovered, at **HIGH** for 2 to 3 minutes, till mixture thickens and bubbles, stirring after each minute. Serve with fruit dippers. Makes 2 servings.

STRAWBERRIES PORTOFINO

Total cooking time: 1 minute 30 seconds

1	0:30							

  1 cup fresh strawberries, quartered
  ¾ cup port wine
  ½ of 3-ounce package raspberry-flavored gelatin
  1 cup vanilla ice cream

Soak berries in wine for 1 hour. In 2-cup glass measure, heat ½ cup water at **HIGH** for 1 to 1½ minutes, till boiling. Stir in gelatin till dissolved. Add port and berries. Spoon into 2 dessert glasses; chill till firm. In small bowl, soften ice cream at **LOW (1)** for 30 seconds. Spoon atop desserts to serve. Makes 2 servings.

COCONUT OR CHOCOLATE TARTS

Total cooking time: 2 minutes 30 seconds

2	0:30							

  ¼ cup sugar
  1 tablespoon cornstarch
  ⅔ cup milk
  1 slightly beaten egg yolk
  1 tablespoon butter or margarine
  ¼ teaspoon vanilla
  ¼ cup flaked coconut
  2 baked tart shells (recipe on page 117)

In 2-cup glass measure, combine sugar, cornstarch, and dash salt. Blend in milk. Cook, uncovered, at **HIGH** for 2 minutes, till thickened, stirring after 1½ minutes. Stir a moderate amount of hot mixture into egg yolk; return to hot mixture. Cook, uncovered, at **HIGH** for 30 seconds, till thickened, stirring once. Stir in butter, vanilla, and coconut. Pour into tart shells. Top with whipped cream, if desired. Makes 2 tarts.

Chocolate Tarts: Prepare as above *except* omit coconut; increase sugar to ⅓ cup. Add ¼ cup semisweet chocolate pieces with the milk; stir after cooking till melted.

ALL FOR ONE

SCRAMBLED SUPPER

Total cooking time: 4 minutes

2	2							

- ¼ cup coarsely chopped zucchini
- 1 tablespoon butter or margarine
- 2 eggs
- 2 tablespoons milk
- ⅛ teaspoon salt
  Dash pepper
- ¼ of 3-ounce package cream cheese with chives, cut in small cubes

In 8- or 9-inch pie plate, combine zucchini and butter. Cook, uncovered, at **HIGH** for 2 minutes, stirring once. Beat together eggs, milk, salt, and pepper with a fork. Add to baking dish with cheese. Heat, uncovered, at **MEDIUM HIGH (7)** for 2 minutes, stirring every 30 seconds, till eggs are glossy and moist but set. Makes 1 serving.

GERMAN-STYLE STEW

Total cooking time: 9 minutes

7	2							

- 1 10-ounce package frozen beef stew
- 1 tablespoon raisins
- 2 teaspoons brown sugar
- 2 tablespoons dry red wine
- 2 teaspoons vinegar
- 1 gingersnap cookie, crumbled

Place pouch of frozen stew on plate; slit top once or twice. Cook, uncovered, at **HIGH** for 7 to 8 minutes. Pour into small serving bowl or 3-cup casserole. Add raisins, brown sugar, wine, vinegar, cookie, and 3 tablespoons water; cook, uncovered, at **HIGH** for 2 to 3 minutes, stirring after 1 minute, or till hot. Makes 1 serving.

LEMONY DEVILED LAMB CHOP

Total cooking time: 10 minutes

5	5							

- 1 shoulder lamb chop (4 ounces)
- ⅛ teaspoon dried thyme, crushed
  Dash garlic salt
  Prepared mustard
- 1 thin onion slice
- 1 thin lemon slice
- 1 green pepper ring

Sprinkle chop on both sides with thyme and garlic salt. Place in small baking dish. Cook, covered, at **MEDIUM (5)** for 5 minutes; turn meat over. Spread top of chop with prepared mustard; top with onion, lemon, and green pepper. Cook, covered, at **MEDIUM (5)** for 5 to 6 minutes, till tender. Makes 1 serving.

PLUM-GOOD CORNISH HEN

Total cooking time: 12 minutes

12								

- 1- to 1¼-pound cornish hen, thawed
- 1 tablespoon butter or margarine, melted
- 2 tablespoons plum preserves

Rinse bird; sprinkle inside cavity with salt. Place on inverted saucer in 8×8×2-inch baking dish. Brush with melted butter. Cook, covered, at **MEDIUM HIGH (7)** for 12 minutes, brushing again with butter during cooking. Spread with plum preserves. Cover with foil; let stand 10 minutes. Makes 1 serving.

TEST KITCHEN TIPS

Freezer Dinners. Serve a piping hot roast turkey dinner for one person? You can when you make your own TV dinners with paper plates and leftovers. Time from freezer to table is just 6 minutes.

Start with partitioned plates specifically designed for microwave oven use or sturdy round paper plates that have partitioned sections, or make your own compartments with folded waxed paper dividers. Add single portions of cooked meat, gravy, potatoes, and frozen vegetable from the list below. Wrap singly in freezer paper or a plastic freezer bag. Freeze 3 to 4 weeks.

To heat, leave the plate in the freezer wrap and remove closure from freezer bag. Cook, covered, at **HIGH** for 6 to 7 minutes. Slide the paper plate onto a dinner plate; remove cover to serve. Increase the cooking time if you freeze larger portions.

Portion Guide for Each Plate

Three ounces cooked meat: roast sliced beef, turkey, pork, lamb, ham, meat loaf.

⅓ to ½ cup gravy.

½ cup mashed or twice baked potatoes, cooked rice, stuffing, baked or canned sweet potatoes, or frozen potatoes. Top with a pat of butter if you wish. Or substitute a baked muffin for the potato.

½ cup frozen vegetable with ½ teaspoon pat of butter: green beans, mixed vegetables, peas, asparagus, diced carrots, corn, broccoli.

Add 2 to 3 teaspoons cranberry sauce, 2 teaspoons mint jelly, a spiced crab apple, or chutney.

ORIENTAL STEAK

Total cooking time: 5 minutes

2	1	1	1				

  ¼ of medium green pepper, cut in ½-inch strips
  ¼ cup diagonally sliced celery
  2 teaspoons cooking oil
      • • •
  1 beef minute steak, cut in strips (4 ounces)
  3 tablespoons cold water
  1 teaspoon cornstarch
  2 teaspoons soy sauce
  ¼ teaspoon sugar
  ⅛ teaspoon salt
  1 small tomato, peeled (if desired) and cut in wedges
    Gingered Rice

In 8-inch pie plate, combine green pepper strips, celery, and oil. Cook, uncovered, at **HIGH** for 2 minutes, till tender. Lift vegetables from oil; remove and set aside.

Add meat to dish; cook, uncovered, at **HIGH** for 1 minute. Drain off meat juices. Combine water, cornstarch, soy, sugar, and salt; add to meat in dish. Cook, uncovered, at **HIGH** for 1 minute, till thickened and bubbly stirring once or twice. Stir in tomato and vegetables; cook at **HIGH** 1 minute. Spoon atop rice. Makes 1 serving.

Gingered Rice: Cook ¼ cup packaged precooked rice according to package directions for one serving. Toss with dash ground ginger.

CHINESE CHICKEN SOUP

Total cooking time: 8 minutes

3	3	2					

  ½ chicken breast, boned and cut in strips (6 ounces)
  1 tablespoon cooking oil
  1 10½-ounce can condensed chicken vegetable soup
  1 soup can (1¼ cups) water
  1 to 2 tablespoons vinegar
  1 tablespoon soy sauce
  ⅛ teaspoon ground ginger
  ⅛ teaspoon pepper
  1 teaspoon cornstarch
  2 tablespoons cold water
  1 egg
  1 to 2 tablespoons sliced green onion with tops

In 1-quart casserole, combine chicken and oil. Heat, covered, at **HIGH** for 3 minutes, till chicken is tender, stirring once to separate strips. Drain excess fat.

Stir in soup and soup can of water; add vinegar, soy, ginger, and pepper; heat, uncovered, at **HIGH** for 3 to 5 minutes, till mixture is hot.

Stir cornstarch into the 2 tablespoons water; add to soup. Heat, uncovered, at **HIGH** for 2 to 3 minutes, till soup thickens slightly. Beat the egg with a fork; gradually stir into the soup. Stir once gently; top with green onion to serve. Makes 3½ cups soup.

SUPER SAUSAGE SANDWICH

Total cooking time: 4 minutes

2	2						

  2 tablespoons dry red wine
  ½ teaspoon instant minced onion
  2 smoked sausage links
  1 cup shredded cabbage
  2 tablespoons Italian salad dressing
  ⅛ teaspoon celery seed
  1 Kaiser roll or hard roll, split and buttered

In 1-quart casserole, combine wine and onion; let stand 5 minutes. Add sausage; cook, covered, at **MEDIUM (5)** for 2 minutes. Combine cabbage, salad dressing, and celery seed; add to casserole. Cook, covered, at **MEDIUM (5)** for 2 minutes. Spoon into roll with slotted spoon. Drizzle with some wine mixture. Makes 1 sandwich.

WILTED HAM-SPINACH SALAD

Total cooking time: 4 minutes 30 seconds

1	2	1:30					

  1 slice bacon
  2 ounces sliced cooked ham, cut in strips (⅓ cup)
  1 green onion, sliced
  ¼ teaspoon sugar
    Dash *each* dried tarragon, crushed, and pepper
  1 tablespoon lemon juice
  3 cups (4 ounces) torn spinach or leaf lettuce
    Plain croutons

In 1-quart casserole, cook bacon, covered with paper towel, at **HIGH** for 1 to 1¼ minutes. Crumble bacon and set aside; reserve drippings in casserole. Stir in ham, onion, sugar, tarragon, and pepper. Cook, uncovered, at **MEDIUM (5)** for 2 minutes, stirring once. Stir in lemon juice.

Add greens; toss with hot mixture. Heat, covered, at **MEDIUM (5)** for 1½ to 2 minutes, till greens begin to wilt. Serve with bacon and croutons. Makes 1 serving.

FRUIT STUFFED PORK CHOP

Total cooking time: 8 minutes

8							

  1 pork loin chop, 1¼ to 1½ inches thick
  ¼ cup toasted bread cubes
  1 tablespoon chopped unpared apple
  1 tablespoon shredded sharp natural cheddar cheese
    Dash ground cinnamon

Cut a pocket in chop along the fat side. Salt and pepper the inside of the pocket. In small mixing bowl, combine bread cubes, apple, cheese, and cinnamon; toss to mix well. Stuff into the pocket of the chop. Place chop in shallow baking dish. Cook, covered, at **MEDIUM HIGH (7)** for 8 to 8½ minutes, turning meat over once. Makes 1 serving.

MEALS THAT BEAT THE CLOCK

Whether you're a busy mother, swinging single, or harried husband, think of your microwave oven as a new-found friend. It's always ready to thaw what you forgot, cook a dinner in less time than it should take, and cut down on clean up chores. What more can you ask? Feast your eyes on Smoky Pork and Bean Bake, Green and Gold Parfaits, and Cooked Salad Dressing (recipes next page)—and it's just one of our many fast menu ideas!

MICRO MENU PLANNER

APPETIZERS/SNACKS/SAUCES

SALADS/DRESSINGS/VEGETABLES

MAIN DISHES

SANDWICHES & BREADS

DESSERTS

MENU
Frozen Swiss Steak Strips (page 157)
Instant Mashed Potatoes (page 177)
Buttered Canned Corn
Mandarin-banana Salad
Double Chocolate Squares a la Mode (page 153)
Coffee   Milk

MENU
Broiled Ham Slice
Cheesy Potatoes Deluxe (page 150)
Canned Pineapple Salad
Rye Rolls   Butter
Buttered Rum Sundae (page 153)
Coffee   Milk

MENU
Saucy Chicken Dinner (page 147)
Sauteed Zucchini
Molded Cranberry Salad
Raisin-spice Muffins (page 141)   Butter
Shortcut Creme Brulee (page 91)
Coffee   Milk

COOKED SALAD DRESSING

Total cooking time: 5 minutes 30 seconds

0:30	1	3	1					

- 2 tablespoons butter or margarine
- 3 tablespoons all-purpose flour
- 3 tablespoons sugar
- 1 teaspoon salt
- 1 teaspoon dry mustard
- Dash cayenne pepper
- ¾ cup milk
- 2 beaten egg yolks
- ¼ cup vinegar

In 2-cup glass measure, melt butter, uncovered, at **HIGH** for 30 seconds. Blend in flour, sugar, salt, mustard, and cayenne pepper. Stir in milk. Cook, uncovered, at **MEDIUM (5)** for 1 minute; stir. Cook at **MEDIUM (5)** for 3 minutes, stirring well after each 30 seconds, till thickened and bubbly. Gradually blend hot mixture into egg yolks; return to measuring cup and cook, uncovered, at **MEDIUM (5)** for 1 minute, stirring once. Beat in vinegar with rotary beater. Chill. Use as is for potato salad or the variations below. Makes 1¼ cups.

Thousand Island: To 1¼ cups dressing, add 3 tablespoons chili sauce, 2 tablespoons chopped green pepper, 2 tablespoons chopped celery, 1 teaspoon snipped chives, 2 chopped hard-cooked eggs, 1 teaspoon paprika, and ½ teaspoon salt; mix well.

Blue Cheese: To 1¼ cups dressing, add ½ cup (2 ounces) crumbled blue cheese, 2 tablespoons vinegar, few drops bottled hot pepper sauce, 1 tablespoon sugar, ¼ cup dairy sour cream, and dash garlic powder; mix well.

SMOKY PORK AND BEAN BAKE

Total cooking time: 16 minutes 30 seconds

3:30	3	10						

- 4 slices bacon
- ½ cup chopped onion
- 2 14-ounce cans beans and pork in molasses sauce
- 2 teaspoons Worcestershire sauce
- 3 drops liquid smoke

• • •

- Prepared mustard
- 4 smoked pork chops (1 pound)
- Brown sugar
- Catsup

• • •

- 4 onion slices
- 4 lemon slices

Place bacon in 10×6×1½-inch baking dish. Cook, covered with paper toweling, at **HIGH** for 3½ minutes. Crumble bacon; set aside. Cook chopped onion in the bacon drippings at **HIGH** for 3 minutes, stirring once. Spoon ½ cup liquid from cans of beans; discard. Stir beans with remaining liquid along with Worcestershire, liquid smoke, and bacon into onion.

Spread a little mustard on each chop. Top with a little brown sugar, then spread with catsup. Place atop beans. Top each chop with an onion slice and lemon slice. Cook, covered with waxed paper, at **MEDIUM HIGH (7)** for 10 minutes or till hot. Makes 4 servings.

GREEN AND GOLD PARFAITS

Total cooking time: 4 minutes

2	2							

- ⅓ cup sugar
- 4 teaspoons cornstarch
- 1 cup orange juice
- 1 cup peeled and sliced fresh peaches (1 large)
- ½ cup seedless green grapes, halved
- 1 quart pineapple sherbet

In 1½-quart casserole, combine sugar and cornstarch. Stir in orange juice; add peaches. Cook, uncovered, at **HIGH** for 2 minutes or till hot. Cook at **HIGH** 2 minutes, stirring after each 30 seconds, or till mixture is thickened and bubbly. Chill; add grapes. To serve, layer fruit mixture and sherbet in parfait glasses. Garnish with cookies, if desired. Makes 6 to 8 servings.

MENU
Smoky Pork and Bean Bake (above)
Tossed Mixed Green Salad with Artichokes
Thousand Island Dressing (left)
Corn Muffins   Butter
Green and Gold Parfaits (above)
Coffee   Milk

Raisin-spice Muffins, Corny Bacon Muffins, Refrigerator Bran Muffins

TIMETABLE

1. Cut melon in serving wedges; chill.
2. Soften butter: Place ¼ pound stick butter on plate. Heat at **LOW (1)** for 2 minutes.
3. Spoon jam into serving dish. Set table.
4. Prepare muffin batter.
5. Make Peanutty Breakfast Mugs; cover to keep warm.
6. Cook muffins. (To reheat muffins: Heat 2 to 4 muffins at **MEDIUM HIGH (7)** for 20 to 30 seconds.)

MENU

Cantaloupe Wedges

Assorted Muffins

Butter

Strawberry Jam

Peanutty Breakfast Mugs

Coffee

BUSY-DAY BREAKFASTS

RAISIN-SPICE MUFFINS

Total cooking time: 1 minute 30 seconds

1:30							

- 1½ cups packaged biscuit mix
- 2 tablespoons sugar
- ½ teaspoon ground cinnamon

• • •

- 1 beaten egg
- ⅓ cup milk
- 1 tablespoon cooking oil
- ¼ cup raisins

• • •

- 2 tablespoons butter or margarine, melted
- 2 tablespoons sugar
- ½ teaspoon ground cinnamon

In bowl, combine biscuit mix, the first 2 tablespoons sugar, and ½ teaspoon cinnamon. Make well in center. Combine egg, milk, and oil; pour all at once into well. Stir just till moistened. Fold in raisins. Spoon into paper-lined custard cups. Cook, 4 at a time, at **HIGH** for 1½ minutes. While warm, dip tops in butter, then in mixture of remaining sugar and cinnamon. Makes 8.

CORNY BACON MUFFINS

Total cooking time: 7 minutes

2:30	4:30						

- 4 slices bacon
- 3 tablespoons maple-flavored syrup
- 1 8½-ounce package corn muffin mix

Place bacon between paper toweling on plate. Cook at **HIGH** for 2½ to 3 minutes. Crumble *half* the bacon into bottoms of 4 paper-bake-cup-lined 6-ounce custard cups. Drizzle about *1 teaspoon* of syrup into each. Prepare muffin mix using package directions. Spoon *half* the batter over bacon mixture filling each muffin cup about half full. Cook, 4 at a time, uncovered, at **MEDIUM (5)** for 4½ minutes. Place on rack to cool. Repeat with remaining bacon, syrup, and batter. Makes 8.

INSTANT HOT CEREALS

For 1 or 2 servings, measure amount of water shown in chart and dash salt into each serving bowl. Cook at **HIGH** for time shown in chart. Stir in cereal packets till thickened and well blended. For 4 servings, heat water in 1-quart bowl.

Instant Farina			Instant Oatmeal		
1-ounce packets	water (cups)	minutes at **HIGH**	1⅝-ounce packets	water (cups)	minutes at **HIGH**
1	½	1½	1	⅔	1½
2	1	2½	2	1⅓	2½
4	2	4½	4	2⅔	5½

REFRIGERATOR BRAN MUFFINS

- 3 cups whole bran cereal
- 1 cup boiling water
- ½ cup shortening
- 2 cups buttermilk
- 2 beaten eggs
- 2½ cups all-purpose flour
- 1 cup sugar
- 1½ teaspoons baking powder
- 1½ teaspoons baking soda
- 1 teaspoon salt

In large bowl, combine cereal and boiling water; stir in shortening till melted. Add buttermilk and eggs; mix well. Stir together remaining ingredients. Add all at once to cereal mixture, stirring just till moistened. Store in tightly covered container in refrigerator up to 4 weeks. To bake, spoon 2 tablespoons batter into paper-bake-cup-lined custard cup. Bake at **HIGH** according to time chart. Makes 48.

Number of muffins	Cook at **HIGH**
1	35 seconds
2	50 seconds
4	1½ minutes
6	2½ minutes

PEANUTTY BREAKFAST MUGS

Total cooking time: 4 minutes 30 seconds

4	0:30						

- 2 cups milk
- ¼ cup creamy peanut butter
- 1 tablespoon honey
- 4 marshmallows

In blender container combine milk, peanut butter, and honey. Blend till smooth, about 30 seconds. Pour into 4-cup glass measure. Cook, uncovered, at **HIGH** for 4 to 5 minutes or just till bubbly. Pour into four heat-proof mugs. Top each with a marshmallow; cook, uncovered, at **HIGH** for 30 seconds or till marshmallows puff. Makes 4 servings.

FLASH-IN-THE-PAN PANCAKES

Total cooking time: 55 seconds

0:40	0:15						

Pancake mix
Maple syrup

Prepare and cook pancakes according to package directions. Freezer wrap in serving-size packages (3 pancakes) with waxed paper between pancakes. Seal, label, and freeze. To serve: Separate pancakes and place on serving plate lined with paper toweling. Cook, covered, at **HIGH** for 40 to 45 seconds or till piping hot. Remove metal cap from syrup bottle and heat for 15 seconds or till warm.

141

FAST LUNCHES AND SNACKS

FRIED RICE BUNDLES

Total cooking time: 8 minutes 30 seconds

2	5	1:30						

¼ cup sliced green onion
3 tablespoons cooking oil
3 tablespoons soy sauce
⅛ teaspoon pepper
2 cups cooked rice
1 4½-ounce can tiny shrimp, drained
1 cup diced cooked chicken
1 cup fresh or drained canned bean sprouts
½ cup sliced water chestnuts

• • •

2 slightly beaten eggs
12 lettuce leaves

In large glass bowl, cook onion in *2 tablespoons* of the oil, uncovered, at **HIGH** for 2 to 3 minutes. Add soy, pepper, rice, shrimp, chicken, bean sprouts, and water chestnuts. Cook, uncovered, at **HIGH** for 5 minutes, stirring twice. Cover with foil to keep warm.

Place remaining 1 tablespoon oil in pie plate. Add eggs. Cook, uncovered, at **HIGH** for 1½ to 2 minutes, stirring every 30 seconds. Cut up large pieces of egg. Stir eggs into rice mixture. To serve, spoon portions of hot rice mixture into lettuce leaves; roll up. Serve with canned Chinese plum sauce or hoisin sauce, if desired. Makes 4 servings, 3 rolls each.

4-WAY RUMAKI

Total cooking time: 8 minutes

4	4						

1 8-ounce can minced clams
½ cup herb-seasoned stuffing mix
8 slices bacon, halved crosswise
Water chestnuts
Large olives
Frozen fried potato nuggets

Drain clams, reserving ¼ cup liquid. Combine clams, reserved liquid, and stuffing mix. Let stand a few minutes to soften. Meanwhile, partially cook bacon pieces on microwave roasting rack in 12×7½×2-inch baking dish at **HIGH** for 4 to 4½ minutes, rearranging pieces if necessary for even cooking. Drain bacon; wipe dish.

Form clam mixture into 16 balls, using a generous teaspoon of mixture for each. Wrap a piece of bacon around each; secure with wooden picks. Place on rack in same 12×7½×2-inch dish. Cook at **HIGH** for 4 to 4½ minutes, giving dish half turn after 2 minutes, till bacon is done. Makes 16.

If desired, water chestnuts (halved, if large), olives, and/or frozen fried potato nuggets may be substituted for the clam-stuffing mixture. (Place 16 frozen potato nuggets on paper toweling in pie plate; cook at **HIGH** for 2 minutes before wrapping with bacon.)

HOT FRANK AND EGG SALAD ROLLS

Serve with mugs of chicken noodle soup, crisp red apples, and oatmeal cookies—

Total cooking time: 3 minutes

3								

6 frankfurters
¼ cup mayonnaise or salad dressing
1 teaspoon vinegar
1 teaspoon prepared mustard
½ teaspoon dried dillweed
¼ teaspoon salt

• • •

2 hard-cooked eggs, chopped
2 tablespoons sliced green onion
6 frankfurter buns, split and toasted

Slice franks crosswise in ⅛-inch-thick slices. In medium glass bowl, combine mayonnaise, vinegar, mustard, dillweed, and salt. Fold in franks, eggs, and onion. Cook, uncovered, at **HIGH** for 3 minutes, stirring twice. Serve in buns. Makes 6 sandwiches.

PIZZA BUNWICHES

Total cooking time: 5 minutes

5								

½ pound ground cooked ham
¾ cup (3 ounces) shredded mozzarella cheese
¼ cup chopped dill pickle
¼ cup finely chopped onion
2 tablespoons diced green pepper
½ cup canned pizza sauce
6 hamburger buns, split and toasted

In 1½-quart bowl, crumble ham; stir in cheese, pickle, onion, green pepper, and pizza sauce. Cook, uncovered, at **HIGH** for 5 minutes, stirring twice, till cheese is melted and mixture is hot. Serve in buns. Makes 6.

CORNED BEEF AND CABBAGE BUNS

Total cooking time: 5 minutes

5								

2 cups finely shredded cabbage
1 12-ounce can corned beef, crumbled
½ cup mayonnaise or salad dressing
1 teaspoon instant minced onion
1 teaspoon horseradish mustard
8 hamburger buns, split and toasted
Dill pickle slices

In 1½-quart bowl or casserole, combine cabbage, corned beef, mayonnaise, onion, and horseradish mustard. Cook, covered, at **HIGH** for 5 minutes, stirring once. Serve in buns and top with dill pickle slices. Makes 8.

SPUNKY BEAN DUNK

Also good as a rarebit sauce on sandwiches—

Total cooking time: 8 minutes

5	3							

- 1 6-ounce roll garlic-flavored process cheese spread, chilled
- 1 11½-ounce can condensed bean with bacon soup
- 1 cup dairy sour cream
- 2 tablespoons sliced green onion
  Corn chips

Cut cheese spread into chunks. In 1½-quart bowl, combine cheese and soup. Cook, uncovered, at **MEDIUM (5)** for 5 minutes, stirring twice to blend. Stir in sour cream and onion. Cook, uncovered, at **MEDIUM (5)** for 3 minutes, stirring once, till mixture is heated through. Serve hot with corn chips. Makes 2½ cups dip.

PICKLE-SAUSAGE NIBBLES

Total cooking time: 5 minutes

1	4							

- ¼ cup beer
- 1 teaspoon cornstarch
- ½ cup bottled barbecue sauce
- 2 5-ounce cans Vienna sausage
- 9 medium dill pickles, cut in ½-inch slices

Combine beer and cornstarch in 2-cup glass measure. Stir in barbecue sauce. Cook at **HIGH** for 1 to 2 minutes or till bubbly and thickened, stirring after each 30 seconds. Spear Vienna sausage and dill pickle slices on wooden picks. Dip each into sauce; place in 12×7½×2-inch baking dish. Brush with remaining sauce. Cook, uncovered, at **HIGH** for 4 to 5 minutes or till hot. Makes 28.

SPEEDY SEAFOOD FONDUE

Total cooking time: 5 minutes 30 seconds

2:30	1	2						

- 1 8-ounce package cream cheese
- 1 5-ounce jar sharp process cheese spread
- 3 tablespoons milk
- ½ teaspoon Worcestershire sauce
  • • •
- 1 6½- or 7-ounce can tuna *or* salmon *or* crab meat, drained and flaked
  French bread cubes

In medium glass bowl, heat cream cheese and cheese spread at **MEDIUM (5)** till softened, 2½ to 3 minutes. Blend in milk and Worcestershire. Cook, uncovered, at **HIGH** for 1 minute; stir in tuna, salmon, or crab; cook at **HIGH** 2 minutes more, or till heated through, stirring once. Serve hot with French bread cubes as dunkers. Makes about 2⅓ cups fondue.

TEST KITCHEN TIPS

Bite size nibbles you can arrange in advance, then cook and serve on the same plate are ideal.

Zesty Shrimp: Thaw 18 to 20 large frozen cooked shrimp (4 ounces). Drain one 3-ounce can mushroom crowns. On wooden picks, spear a shrimp and a mushroom. Place on serving plate; brush with bottled seafood cocktail sauce. Cook, uncovered, at **HIGH** for 2½ to 3 minutes, till hot. Pass sauce for dipping. Makes 18.

Smoky Chokes: Drain two 6-ounce jars marinated artichoke hearts, reserving marinade. Halve artichokes. Open one 3-ounce package smoked sliced beef; separate slices and cut in half. Wrap one half slice beef around each artichoke; secure with wooden pick. Place *half* the nibbles on serving plate. Brush with *half* the reserved marinade; cook, uncovered, at **HIGH** for 2 to 2½ minutes. Repeat with remaining nibbles. Makes 30.

Sweet-Sour Bites: Cut one 12-ounce can luncheon meat into ¾-inch cubes to make about 40 pieces. Drain one 13½-ounce can pineapple chunks, reserving juice. On wooden picks, spear 2 luncheon meat cubes and one pineapple chunk. (Save extra pineapple in reserved juice.) Place on serving plate; brush with bottled sweet-sour sauce. Cook, uncovered, at **HIGH** for 3 to 4 minutes, rearranging after 2 minutes. Makes 20.

Irish Kabobs: Cut a slit in one 8-ounce package frozen Brussels sprouts; place in 12×7½×2-inch baking dish. Cook at **HIGH** for 6 minutes; drain. Cut small sprouts in half, larger ones in quarters. Cut one chilled 12-ounce can corned beef in ½-inch cubes. On wooden picks, spear a corned beef cube and a sprout; arrange 12 spears in 12×7½×2-inch baking dish and brush with bottled sandwich and salad spread. Cook at **HIGH** for 1½ minutes. Repeat with remaining nibbles. Makes 48.

Cocktail Franks: In 2-quart casserole or serving dish, combine ½ cup chili sauce, ½ cup currant jelly, 1½ tablespoons lemon juice, and 1½ teaspoons prepared mustard. Blend 2 teaspoons cornstarch and 2 teaspoons cold water; stir into chili mixture. Add three 5½-ounce packages (48) cocktail franks and one drained 13¼-ounce can pineapple chunks. Cook, uncovered, at **HIGH** for 8 minutes, stirring 3 times. Makes 48.

Tijuana Chef's Bowl

TIMETABLE

1. Prepare fruit cup and salad except dressing; chill.
2. Prepare rolled and buttered tortillas: Arrange one 12-ounce package frozen tortillas on plate. Cook, uncovered, at **MEDIUM LOW (3)** for 4½ to 5 minutes, separating and placing center tortillas to outside after 4 minutes. Butter and roll up. Keep warm.
3. Prepare cheese dressing; serve at once over salad.
4. Prepare Hot Banana Splits.

144

MENU

Fresh Fruit Cup

Tijuana Chef's Bowl

Rolled and Buttered Tortillas

Hot Banana Splits

Coffee   Milk

QUICK AND EASY DINNERS

TIJUANA CHEF'S BOWL

Total cooking time: 3 minutes

3								

  6 cups torn lettuce
  1 cup shredded carrot (2 carrots)
  1 cup diced celery (2 stalks)
  1 cup cooked ham cut in julienne strips
  1 cup cooked chicken cut in julienne strips
  2 medium tomatoes, diced
  ¼ cup sliced pitted ripe olives
  3 tablespoons sliced green onion with tops
        • • •
  2 cups (8 ounces) shredded sharp process American
     cheese
  ½ cup milk
  ¼ cup chopped seeded canned green chilies
  2 cups corn chips

In large salad bowl, combine lettuce, carrot, and celery. Arrange ham, chicken, tomatoes, olives, and green onion atop. In 4-cup glass measure, combine cheese and milk. Cook, uncovered, at **MEDIUM (5)** for 3 to 4 minutes, stirring twice. Stir till smooth. Stir in chilies. Pour hot sauce over salad. Toss lightly. Serve at once. Pass corn chips to sprinkle atop. Makes 6 servings.
  Note: If desired, cheese sauce may be made ahead and served cold. Increase milk in sauce to ¾ cup. Chill till serving time. If sauce is too thick, stir in a little milk.

POPEYE'S HASH PIE

Total cooking time: 21 minutes 30 seconds

5	14	2	0:30					

  1 10-ounce package frozen chopped spinach
  2 beaten eggs
  1 10¾-ounce can condensed cream of mushroom soup
  ¼ cup all-purpose flour
  1 teaspoon prepared mustard
  1 tablespoon prepared horseradish
  1 15-ounce can corned beef hash
  1 9-inch baked pastry shell (crimp edges high)
  ½ cup (2 ounces) shredded process American cheese
  1 tablespoon chopped pimiento

Place frozen spinach in 10×6×1½-inch baking dish. Cook, covered with waxed paper, at **HIGH** for 5 minutes, breaking up and stirring once. Drain spinach very well, pressing out excess water. In bowl, combine eggs, soup, flour, mustard, and horseradish; stir in spinach.
  Spread hash in baked shell; spoon spinach mixture over. Cook, uncovered, at **MEDIUM HIGH (7)** for 14 minutes, giving a quarter turn after 7 minutes. Cover with waxed paper. Give a quarter turn and continue to cook at **MEDIUM HIGH (7)** for 2 minutes. Combine cheese and pimiento; sprinkle atop pie. Cook, uncovered, at **MEDIUM HIGH (7)** for 30 seconds. Let stand 5 minutes before serving. Makes 6 servings.

MEXITACO TOSS

Total cooking time: 11 minutes

5	4	2						

  1 pound ground beef
  ¼ cup chopped onion
  1 tablespoon beef-flavor gravy base
  ½ teaspoon chili powder
  ¼ teaspoon paprika
  ⅔ cup water
  1 tablespoon cornstarch
  1 tablespoon cold water
        • • •
  1 medium head lettuce, torn (4 cups)
  1 large tomato, cut in wedges
  1 small onion, thinly sliced and separated
     into rings
  1 cup (4 ounces) shredded sharp natural
     cheddar cheese
  ½ cup sliced ripe olives
  ¼ cup green pepper strips
  1 6-ounce package corn chips, coarsely crushed

In casserole or baking dish, crumble ground beef. Add chopped onion. Cook, uncovered, at **HIGH** for 5 minutes, stirring 3 times. Spoon off excess fat. Add gravy base, chili powder, paprika, and ⅔ cup water; cook, uncovered, at **HIGH** for 4 minutes. Combine cornstarch and cold water; stir into meat mixture. Cook, uncovered, at **HIGH** 2 minutes, till mixture thickens and boils, stirring once.
  In large salad bowl, combine lettuce, tomato, sliced onion, cheese, olives, and green pepper; spoon on hot meat sauce. Top with corn chips and toss. Serve immediately. Makes 4 to 6 servings.

HOT BANANA SPLITS

Total cooking time: 5 minutes 25 seconds

0:25	2:30	2:30						

  2 tablespoons butter or margarine
  ⅔ cup packed brown sugar
  ¼ cup milk
  ¼ cup chopped walnuts
  4 medium bananas
    Strawberry ice cream
    Vanilla ice cream

In 8×8×2-inch baking dish, melt butter at **HIGH** for 25 to 30 seconds. Stir in brown sugar and milk. Heat at **HIGH** for 2½ minutes, till sugar dissolves and mixture is bubbly. Stir in nuts. Meanwhile, peel bananas; halve crosswise and lengthwise. Place bananas in baking dish, turning over in sauce to coat each piece. Cook, uncovered, at **HIGH** for 2½ minutes till fruit is warm, moving corner pieces to center after 1½ minutes.
  Spoon bananas into dishes. Top with one small scoop each of strawberry and vanilla ice cream. Garnish with maraschino cherry, if desired. Makes 4 to 6 servings.

HAWAIIAN FRANK CASSEROLE

Total cooking time: 14 minutes

4	10						

  1 20-ounce can pineapple chunks
  1 18-ounce can sweet potatoes, halved
  1 pound (8 to 10) frankfurters, halved crosswise
  ¼ cup packed brown sugar
  2 tablespoons cornstarch
  ½ cup orange juice
  2 tablespoons chili sauce
  3 tablespoons vinegar
  ½ teaspoon grated orange peel

Drain pineapple, reserving syrup. Arrange pineapple, sweet potatoes, and franks in 2-quart casserole. In 4-cup glass measure, combine brown sugar and cornstarch. Stir in reserved pineapple syrup, the orange juice, and chili sauce. Cook, uncovered, at **HIGH** for 4 minutes, stirring after each minute. Stir in vinegar and peel. Pour over casserole. Cook, covered, at **HIGH** for 10 minutes or till hot, stirring twice. Makes 6 servings.

SCRUMPTIOUS BAKED CHICKEN

Total cooking time: 25 minutes

6	10	4	5				

  6 slices bacon
  3 large chicken breasts, boned, skinned, and halved
    lengthwise
  1 3½-ounce package smoked sliced beef
  1 10¾-ounce can condensed cream of mushroom soup
  1 cup dairy sour cream
  2 tablespoons all-purpose flour

Place bacon on microwave roasting rack in a 12×7½×2-inch baking dish. Cook at **HIGH** for 6 to 7 minutes. Crumble and set aside. Remove rack. Pour off excess drippings. Place chicken in same baking dish. Cook, covered, at **MEDIUM HIGH (7)** for 10 minutes. Spoon off juices. Place pieces of beef under chicken. Cover to keep warm.

Combine soup, sour cream, and flour. Cook, uncovered, at **MEDIUM HIGH (7)** for 4 minutes, stirring once. Spoon over chicken. Cook, uncovered, at **MEDIUM HIGH (7)** for 5 minutes. Sprinkle bacon atop. Makes 6 servings.

CHEESE-TOPPED CHILI BUNS

Total cooking time: 3 minutes

3							

In 1-quart casserole, heat one 15-ounce can chili with beans, covered, at **HIGH** for 3 minutes, stirring once. Spread bottom of 6 split and toasted hamburger buns with ¼ cup chili mixture. Top with 1 tablespoon French onion sour cream dip and half slices of process American cheese. Top with burger lids. Makes 6 servings.

BURGUNDY-BERRIED HAM

Total cooking time: 16 minutes

4	12						

  ½ cup packed brown sugar
  1 8-ounce can (1 cup) whole cranberry sauce
  ¼ cup burgundy or dry red wine
  1 teaspoon prepared mustard
  1 3-pound canned ham, cut in ¼-inch slices

In 2-cup glass measure, combine brown sugar, cranberry sauce, wine, and mustard. Heat, uncovered, at **HIGH** for 4 minutes, till sugar is melted and mixture blended and heated through, stirring after 2 minutes. Arrange ham in 13×9×2-inch baking dish. Pour heated glaze atop. Cook, covered, at **MEDIUM HIGH (7)** for 12 minutes, giving dish half turn once. Makes 12 servings.

TEST KITCHEN TIPS

Indoor-outdoor Barbecues. Team the speed of the microwave oven with the flavor of meat cooked on an outdoor barbecue grill and you can have perfect meats every time. The recipe below shows how to begin a steak on the outdoor grill and finish it in the microwave. But you can reverse the order if you prefer. Or, try barbecuing an extra pound of hamburgers next time the grill is hot. Freeze them until some chilly rainy eve, then defrost and reheat for an indoor picnic. Chicken and ribs profit from precooking in the microwave, too—then there is no need to worry that the thick pieces aren't quite done, or that the skin will be overdone.

Perfect Sirloin Steak: Combine ½ cup clear French salad dressing with herbs and spices, ½ cup dry white wine, 2 tablespoons sliced green onion, 1 tablespoon Worcestershire sauce, and dash pepper; pour over a 2½- to 3½-pound beef sirloin steak (1½ inches thick) in a shallow baking dish. Cover; marinate several hours or overnight, turning at least once. Drain, reserving marinade. Broil steak over hot coals on barbecue grill for 10 minutes, turning once, or till nicely browned, brushing with marinade occasionally. Place steak in shallow baking dish; cook, covered, at **MEDIUM HIGH (7)** for 5 to 8 minutes for rare doneness, 8 to 10 minutes for medium. Brush again with marinade before serving. Makes 6 to 8 servings.

BEEF 'N MAC ITALIAN-STYLE

Total cooking time: 11 minutes 30 seconds

4	6	1:30					

- 1 16-ounce can stewed tomatoes, cut up
- 3 tablespoons all-purpose flour
- ¼ cup dry red wine
- ¼ cup (½ package) dry onion soup mix
- ¼ teaspoon dried oregano, crushed
- 2 cups cubed cooked beef
- 1 cup macaroni, cooked and drained
- ½ cup (2 ounces) shredded Monterey Jack cheese

Stir tomatoes into flour in 1½-quart casserole. Stir in wine, soup mix, oregano, and dash pepper. Cook, uncovered, at **HIGH** for 4 to 5 minutes, stirring after each minute or till bubbly. Stir in beef and macaroni. Cook, covered, at **MEDIUM HIGH (7)** for 6 minutes, stirring once. Top with cheese. Cook, uncovered, at **MEDIUM (5)** for 1½ to 2 minutes or till cheese melts. Makes 4 servings.

SAUCY CHICKEN DINNER

Total cooking time: 10 minutes

5	5						

- 1 envelope cheese sauce mix
- 1 envelope chicken gravy mix
- ¼ teaspoon onion salt
- 1 cup milk
- 1 10-ounce package frozen peas
- 2 cups cubed cooked chicken
- 1 3-ounce can chopped mushrooms, drained
- 1 tablespoon chopped pimiento
- Hot cooked noodles

In large bowl, combine sauce mix, gravy mix, onion salt, and dash pepper. Gradually stir in 1 cup water and milk. Cook, uncovered, at **HIGH** for 5 to 6 minutes, stirring after each minute. Stir in peas, chicken, mushrooms, and pimiento. Cook, uncovered, at **HIGH** for 5 minutes, stirring twice. Serve over noodles. Makes 6 servings.

SPEEDY PORK CHOPS

Total cooking time: 30 minutes

30							

- 6 pork chops, ½ inch thick
- 1 8-ounce can tomato sauce
- ½ cup chopped green pepper
- 1 3-ounce can sliced mushrooms, drained
- 1 envelope onion gravy mix

Trim excess fat from chops. Place chops in 12×7½×2-inch baking dish. Sprinkle with salt and pepper. Combine tomato sauce, green pepper, mushrooms, and gravy mix; pour over chops. Cook, covered, at **MEDIUM HIGH (7)** for 30 minutes, rearranging chops once. Makes 6 servings.

FROZEN RAVIOLI LASAGNA

Total cooking time: 50 minutes

5	35	10					

- 1 pound ground beef
- 1 8-ounce can pizza sauce
- 1 15-ounce can spinach, well-drained
- 1 cup cream-style cottage cheese with chives
- 1 15-ounce can ravioli in tomato sauce
- 3 tablespoons grated Parmesan cheese

In 1-quart casserole or mixing bowl, crumble ground beef. Cook, uncovered, at **HIGH** for 5 minutes, stirring three times. Spoon off excess fat. Stir in pizza sauce. In 10×6×1½-inch baking dish, spread drained spinach. Top with *half* the meat sauce, all the cottage cheese, all the ravioli in tomato sauce, then the remaining meat sauce. Cover tightly. Seal, label, and freeze.*

To cook frozen casserole: Remove foil, if used, and recover with waxed paper. Cook at **MEDIUM LOW (3)** for 35 minutes giving dish half turn after 20 minutes. Cook at **HIGH** for 10 to 12 minutes giving dish half turn once. Uncover; top with Parmesan cheese.

*Or cook unfrozen casserole, uncovered, at **HIGH** for 5 to 7 minutes. Top with Parmesan. Makes 4 servings.

FROZEN CHEESY HAM CASSEROLES

Total cooking time: 57 minutes

2	15	3	30	7			

- 1 8-ounce jar (1 cup) process cheese spread
- 2 10-ounce packages frozen chopped broccoli
- ½ cup chopped onion
- 4 tablespoons butter or margarine
- 2 10¾-ounce cans condensed cream of chicken soup
- ½ cup milk
- ½ teaspoon Worcestershire sauce
- 4 cups diced cooked ham (1⅓ pounds)
- 2 cups uncooked packaged precooked rice
- ½ cup rich round cracker crumbs (12 crackers)

Soften cheese spread in the jar (lid removed) at **LOW (1)** for 2 minutes or till soft enough to spread. In 2-quart casserole, cook broccoli, covered, at **HIGH** for 15 minutes, stirring twice. Drain and set aside. In same casserole, combine onion and butter; cook, uncovered, at **HIGH** for 3 minutes, till tender. Stir in cheese spread, then broccoli. Add remaining ingredients except crumbs and mix well. Turn into two 1½-quart casseroles. Cover tightly. Seal, label, and freeze.*

To cook frozen casserole: Remove foil if used. Cook, covered, at **MEDIUM LOW (3)** for 30 minutes, stirring and giving dish half turn after 15 minutes. Cook, covered, on **HIGH** for 7 minutes or till hot, stirring once. Top with ¼ *cup* of the crumbs.

*Or cook unfrozen casserole at **HIGH** for 8 minutes, stirring 3 times. Top with ¼ cup of the crumbs. Makes 2 casseroles, 4 to 5 servings each.

French Onion Sauce for Meat

TIMETABLE

1. Prepare Horseradish Sour Cream: Stir 1 teaspoon prepared horseradish into ½ cup dairy sour cream.
2. Cut cheese; cover.
3. Slice tomatoes and avocados; chill.
4. Set table.
5. Make French Onion Sauce.
6. Assemble beef sandwiches.

MENU

Deli Roast Beef on Kaiser Roll
French Onion Sauce   Horseradish Sour Cream
Dill Pickle Spears   Tomato and Avocado Wedges
Deli Potato Salad
Fresh Fruit and Cheese
Beer

NO-FUSS SAUCES

FRENCH ONION SAUCE FOR MEAT

Total cooking time: 9 minutes

6	3						

- 2 large onions, thinly sliced (3 cups)
- 2 tablespoons butter or margarine
- 2 tablespoons cornstarch
- 2 tablespoons cold water
- 1 10½-ounce can condensed beef broth
- ¼ teaspoon Worcestershire sauce
  Grated Parmesan cheese

In 1-quart casserole, combine onions and butter. Cook, covered, at **HIGH** for 6 to 7 minutes, till tender, stirring once. Combine cornstarch and water; add to onions with beef broth and Worcestershire. Cook, uncovered, at **HIGH** for 3 to 3½ minutes, till thickened and bubbly, stirring after each minute. Serve with sliced beef on French bread slices, oven-baked meatballs, meat loaf, or minute steaks. Pass Parmesan cheese. Makes 2 cups sauce.

CIDER MARINADE FOR MEAT

Total cooking time: 7 minutes

2	5						

- ½ cup apple cider or apple juice
- ¼ cup vinegar
- ¼ cup sliced green onion
- 2 tablespoons butter or margarine
- 2 tablespoons bottled steak sauce
- 2 tablespoons honey
- 1 teaspoon salt
- 1 teaspoon dried tarragon, crushed
- ¼ teaspoon pepper

In 2-cup glass measure, combine all ingredients. Cook, uncovered, at **HIGH** for 2 to 3 minutes, till mixture comes to boiling. Cook at **HIGH** for 5 minutes, stirring occasionally. Use as marinade for meat and chicken or as a barbecue brush-on during the last 10 to 15 minutes of grilling. Pass remainder of sauce to spoon over each serving. Makes about ¾ cup sauce.

ALMOND-CHEESE VEGETABLE SAUCE

Total cooking time: 2 minutes

2							

- 1 11-ounce can condensed cheddar cheese soup
- ½ teaspoon curry powder
- ¼ cup milk
- 2 tablespoons toasted slivered almonds

In 2-cup glass measure, gradually blend soup into curry powder. Gradually stir in milk. Cook, uncovered, at **HIGH** for 2 to 3 minutes, till hot, stirring twice. Serve over cooked cauliflower, broccoli, or asparagus; sprinkle with nuts. Makes 1½ cups sauce.

FRUITED BARBECUE SAUCE FOR MEAT

Remember this vivid barbecue sauce the next time you're grilling beef or pork ribs—

Total cooking time: 6 minutes

6							

- 1 12-ounce jar (1 cup) pineapple preserves
- ½ cup canned whole cranberry sauce
- ½ cup chili sauce
- ¼ cup vinegar

In 4-cup glass measure, combine all ingredients. Cook, uncovered, at **HIGH** for 6 minutes, stirring 2 times. Remove; beat with rotary beater to break up cranberries. Use as brush-on for meat or vegetables during last 15 minutes of grilling. Makes 2¼ cups sauce.

WINE SAUCE FOR FISH

Total cooking time: 6 minutes 30 seconds

5	1	0:30					

- 1 tablespoon cornstarch
  Dash salt
- ½ cup light cream
- ½ cup chicken broth
- ¼ cup dry white wine
  • • •
- 1 slightly beaten egg yolk
- ½ cup halved seedless green grapes

In 2-cup glass measure, combine cornstarch and salt. Blend in a little of the cream till smooth. Add remaining cream, chicken broth, and wine all at once. Cook, uncovered, at **MEDIUM (5)** for 5 to 5½ minutes or till mixture thickens and bubbles, stirring after each 30 seconds.

Gradually stir about ½ cup of the sauce into the beaten egg yolk; return mixture to glass measure. Cook, uncovered, at **MEDIUM (5)** for 1 minute more, stirring once. Add grapes. Heat at **HIGH** for 30 seconds till grapes are warm. Serve over baked or poached fish. Makes 1½ cups sauce.

HOT MUSTARD SAUCE FOR MEAT

Total cooking time: 2 minutes 30 seconds

1:30	1						

- 3 tablespoons dry onion soup mix
- ⅓ cup water
- 1 cup dairy sour cream
- 1 to 1½ teaspoons dry mustard

In 2-cup glass measure, soak onion soup in water for 5 minutes, till softened. Heat, uncovered, at **HIGH** for 1½ minutes, till boiling. Blend in sour cream and mustard. Heat, uncovered, at **MEDIUM HIGH (7)** for 1 to 1½ minutes or till hot, stirring every 30 seconds. Serve with sliced cooked beef or ham loaf. Makes 1⅓ cups sauce.

MINUTE-MINDED VEGETABLES

CHEESY POTATOES DELUXE

Total cooking time: 9 minutes

8	1							

  1 8-ounce carton Neufchatel cheese dip with bacon and horseradish
  1 cup cream-style cottage cheese
  ½ cup (2 ounces) shredded sharp process American cheese
  2 tablespoons snipped parsley
  ½ teaspoon salt
  6 cups cubed cooked potatoes

Combine dip, cottage cheese, *half* the shredded cheese, the parsley, and salt. Add potatoes; stir gently to coat. Turn into 12×7½×2-inch baking dish. Cook, covered, at **MEDIUM HIGH (7)** for 8 to 9 minutes, stirring once. Sprinkle with paprika. Top with remaining cheese. Cook, uncovered, at **MEDIUM HIGH (7)** for 1 minute. Makes 8 servings.

POTATO AND STUFFING BAKE

Total cooking time: 6 minutes

6								

    Instant mashed potatoes for 12 servings
  2 chicken bouillon cubes
  ½ cup hot water
  2 cups herb-seasoned stuffing mix
  1 beaten egg
  1 tablespoon snipped parsley
  ⅛ teaspoon pepper

Prepare instant potatoes according to package directions. In 2-quart casserole, dissolve bouillon cubes in the hot water. Stir in dry stuffing mix, egg, parsley, and pepper. Fold in mashed potatoes. Sprinkle with paprika, if desired. Cook, covered, at **HIGH** for 6 to 8 minutes, till heated through. Makes 8 to 10 servings.

QUICK GLAZED SWEET POTATOES

Total cooking time: 6 minutes

2	4							

  ¼ cup packed brown sugar
  1 tablespoon orange-flavored breakfast drink powder
  2 teaspoons cornstarch
  ½ cup cold water
  3 tablespoons butter or margarine
  1 18-ounce can vacuum pack sweet potatoes

In 1½-quart casserole, combine brown sugar, orange drink powder, cornstarch, and water. Cook, uncovered, at **HIGH** for about 2 minutes, till mixture thickens and bubbles, stirring after each minute. Stir in butter. Add potatoes, stirring to coat with mixture. Cook, uncovered, at **HIGH** for 4 minutes or till heated through, turning each potato over once. Makes 4 servings.

ZUCCHINI PARMESAN

Total cooking time: 10 minutes

10								

  6 cups sliced zucchini (about 1½ pounds)
  2 tablespoons butter or margarine
  ½ teaspoon celery salt
  3 tablespoons grated Parmesan cheese

In an 8×8×2-inch baking dish, combine zucchini, butter, and celery salt. Cover with waxed paper and cook at **HIGH** 10 to 12 minutes, stirring every 3 minutes. Sprinkle Parmesan on top. Makes 6 servings.

PEAS AND MUSHROOMS

Total cooking time: 7 minutes

2	3	2						

  2 tablespoons sliced green onion
  1 tablespoon butter or margarine
  1 10-ounce package frozen peas
  1 3-ounce can sliced mushrooms, drained

In 1-quart casserole, combine onion and butter. Cook, uncovered, at **HIGH** for 2 minutes till onion is tender. Add peas and ¼ teaspoon salt; cook, covered, at **HIGH** for 3 minutes, stirring once. Stir in mushrooms. Cook, covered, at **HIGH** 2 minutes. Makes 5 servings.

TOMATO-CORN BAKE

Total cooking time: 4 minutes

4								

  3 medium tomatoes
  1 8-ounce can whole kernel corn, drained
  ½ cup (2 ounces) shredded process Swiss cheese
  1 tablespoon sliced green onion

Cut tomatoes in half crosswise; remove seeds and most of pulp from center of each. Sprinkle cavities with salt. Combine corn, cheese, and onion; firmly pack 2 to 3 tablespoons mixture into each tomato shell. Place in 10×6×1½-inch baking dish. Cook, uncovered, at **HIGH** for 4 to 5 minutes, till heated through. Makes 6 servings.

HERBED CABBAGE-CARROT TOSS

Total cooking time: 6 minutes

6								

In 2-quart casserole, combine 3 cups shredded cabbage, 1 cup shredded carrot, 1 medium red onion, thinly sliced and halved, 2 tablespoons snipped parsley, 1 tablespoon butter, ½ teaspoon salt, and ⅛ teaspoon dried basil, crushed. Cook, covered, at **HIGH** for 6 to 7 minutes, till vegetables are tender-crisp, stirring once. Makes 4 servings.

BASIL CARROTS

Total cooking time: 10 minutes

10								

  3 cups thin diagonally sliced carrots (6 medium)
  1 tablespoon butter or margarine
  ¼ teaspoon dried basil, crushed

In 1-quart casserole or serving dish, cook carrots, covered, in ⅓ cup water at **HIGH** for 10 to 12 minutes or till tender, stirring twice. Drain. Stir in butter, ¼ teaspoon salt, and basil. Makes 6 servings.

TEST KITCHEN TIPS

  Sauce and gravy mixes can save the day when you need to dress up a meal in a hurry. It's wise to keep a selection on hand: white, cheese, hollandaise, or spaghetti sauce; mushroom, onion, chicken, or au jus gravy to name a few.
  A 2- or 4-cup glass measure makes an ideal container to measure, mix, and cook all in one. Be sure to allow for boiling and stirring room; choose a measure twice the volume of the mixture. *Wood, plastic, or rubber* spatulas, scrapers, or whisks may be left in the sauce during cooking. If time is a consideration, cook the sauce ahead, cover, and reheat it just before serving.
  Packaged Sauce and Gravy Mixes: In 2-cup glass measure, combine dry mix and 1 cup liquid as package directs. Cook, uncovered, at **HIGH** for 2½ minutes, till mixture thickens and boils, stirring after 1 minute, then every 30 seconds. Makes 1 cup.
  If package directions say to add ⅔ cup liquid, cook 2 minutes.
  If package directions say to add 2 cups liquid, use a 4-cup measure and cook 7 minutes.
  Packaged Spaghetti Sauce Mix: In 4-cup glass measure or 2-quart casserole, combine ingredients as package directs (usually tomato sauce or tomato paste, water, and butter or oil). For 2 to 2½ cups mixture, cook, uncovered, at **HIGH** for 6 to 7 minutes, till boiling, stirring after 3 minutes. Reduce setting to **MEDIUM (5)**; cook, covered, 10 minutes more, stirring once or twice. Makes 2 to 2½ cups.

PEPPY WAX BEANS

Total cooking time: 7 minutes

4	3							

  1 large onion, thinly sliced
  2 tablespoons butter or margarine
        • • •
  1 cup chopped tomato (1 large)
  ¼ teaspoon salt
  ¾ teaspoon chili powder
    Dash pepper
  1 16-ounce can cut wax beans, drained

In 1-quart casserole or serving dish, combine onion and butter. Cook, covered, at **HIGH** for 4 minutes, till onion is tender, stirring once. Stir in remaining ingredients; mix well. Cook, uncovered, at **HIGH** for 3 minutes, till heated through, stirring once. Serve in sauce dishes. Makes 4 or 5 servings.

CRANBERRIED BEETS

Total cooking time: 7 minutes

3	4							

  1 tablespoon sugar
  1 tablespoon cornstarch
  ⅛ teaspoon salt
  ¾ cup cranberry juice cocktail
        • • •
  1 16-ounce can sliced beets, drained
  ¼ teaspoon shredded orange peel

In 1-quart casserole, combine sugar, cornstarch, and salt. Stir in cranberry juice cocktail. Cook, uncovered, at **HIGH** for 3 minutes, till mixture is thickened and bubbly, stirring after each minute. Add beets and orange peel. Cook, uncovered, at **HIGH** for 4 to 5 minutes, till heated through. Makes 3 or 4 servings.

DEVILED GREEN BEANS

Total cooking time: 3 minutes 30 seconds

0:30	3							

  1 tablespoon butter or margarine, melted
  2 teaspoons prepared mustard
  ½ teaspoon Worcestershire sauce
    Dash salt
    Dash pepper
  1 16-ounce can cut green beans, drained
  2 tablespoons cornflake crumbs

In 1-quart casserole, melt butter at **HIGH** for 30 seconds. Stir in mustard, Worcestershire, salt, and pepper. Add beans and stir to coat. Heat, uncovered, at **HIGH** for 3 minutes, till heated through, stirring once. Sprinkle with crumbs before serving. Makes 4 servings.

Spicy Wine Fondue

TIMETABLE

1. Cut up fruit for fondue; chill. Slice zucchini.
2. Make wine fondue; set aside.
3. Make potato bake except for final heating.
4. Prepare chicken; cover to keep warm.
5. Set table while chicken cooks.
6. Cook potato bake; saute zucchini in skillet.
7. Bake biscuits while vegetables cook.
8. Reheat wine fondue.

MENU

Scrumptious Baked Chicken (page 146)

Potato and Stuffing Bake (page 150)

Sauteed Zucchini

Refrigerated Biscuits   Honey

Spicy Wine Fondue

Coffee

DESSERTS ON THE DOUBLE

SPICY WINE FONDUE

Total cooking time: 10 minutes

3	5	2					

- 1 cup cranberry juice cocktail
- ½ cup sugar
- ¾ teaspoon pumpkin pie spice
- Dash salt
- 3 tablespoons cornstarch
- 1 cup ruby port wine
- Fresh whole strawberries, honeydew melon cubes, fresh papaya cubes

In 1-quart ceramic fondue cooker, serving bowl, or 4-cup glass measure, combine cranberry cocktail, sugar, pumpkin pie spice, and salt. Heat, uncovered, at **HIGH** for 3 minutes. Cover; cook at **MEDIUM (5)** for 5 minutes more.

Stir together cornstarch and ¼ cup of the port. Add to cranberry mixture along with remaining port. Cook, uncovered, at **HIGH** for 2 to 3 minutes, stirring once each minute, till mixture thickens and bubbles. Serve with fruit dippers. Return to microwave oven to reheat if mixture cools. Makes 2 cups.

BUTTERED RUM SUNDAES

Total cooking time: 7 minutes

4	3						

- 4 tablespoons butter or margarine
- 2 tablespoons light corn syrup
- 1 package (2-layer-size) creamy white frosting mix
- ½ of 6-ounce can (⅓ cup) evaporated milk
- ¼ cup rum
- ½ cup chopped pecans
- Vanilla or chocolate ice cream

Place butter in 2-quart bowl. Cook at **HIGH** for 4 to 4½ minutes or till browned. Blend in corn syrup and about *half* the frosting mix. Add remaining frosting mix. Gradually stir in evaporated milk. Cook at **HIGH** for 3 minutes, stirring twice, till frosting mix is dissolved and mixture is golden. Add rum and nuts. Serve warm over vanilla or chocolate ice cream. Makes about 2 cups.

To reheat sauce: In 2-cup glass measure, thin 1 cup sauce with 1 tablespoon more milk or rum. Cook, uncovered, at **MEDIUM HIGH (7)** for 1½ minutes.

WHIPPED CHEESE TOPPER

Total cooking time: 3 minutes

3							

Place one 3-ounce package cream cheese and ½ cup shredded natural cheddar cheese side by side in small mixer bowl; add 1 tablespoon milk. Heat, uncovered, at **LOW (1)** for 3 minutes, till softened. Beat with electric mixer till fluffy. Spoon atop baked apples. Makes 6 servings.

DOUBLE CHOCOLATE SQUARES

Total cooking time: 14 minutes

14							

- 2 cups packaged biscuit mix
- 1 4½- or 4¼-ounce package *instant* chocolate pudding mix
- 2 beaten eggs
- ½ cup milk
- ⅓ cup cooking oil
- 1 6-ounce package (1 cup) semisweet chocolate pieces
- • • •
- Vanilla ice cream

In mixing bowl, rub biscuit mix between fingers to make fine, even crumbs. Stir in pudding mix, eggs, milk, and oil. Stir in chocolate pieces. Place inverted "shot" glass in center of greased and waxed-paper-lined 12×7½×2-inch baking dish; spread dough in dish.

Cook, uncovered, at **MEDIUM (5)** for 14 to 15 minutes, giving dish quarter turns every 5 minutes, till wooden pick comes out clean. Remove glass. Cool 5 minutes in dish; invert and remove from dish. Cut in squares and serve with ice cream. Makes 8 servings.

VELVET CUSTARD SAUCE

Total cooking time: 6 minutes

3	3						

- 1 3¼-ounce package *regular* vanilla pudding mix
- 2½ cups milk
- 3 tablespoons dry sherry
- ½ teaspoon vanilla
- Fresh or canned fruit

In 4-cup glass measure, combine pudding mix and milk. Cook, uncovered, at **HIGH** for 3 minutes. Cook at **HIGH**, covered, for 3 minutes, stirring after each minute. Stir in sherry and vanilla. Cover with waxed paper; chill. Stir every 30 minutes while cooling. Serve over fresh or canned fruits. Makes 2½ cups.

CARAMEL APPLE FONDUE

Total cooking time: 6 minutes

6							

- 1 12-ounce jar caramel ice cream topping
- 1 18-ounce can butterscotch pudding
- ⅓ cup rum
- Apple wedges
- Large marshmallows

In ceramic fondue pot or mixing bowl, combine topping, pudding, and rum. Cover; heat at **HIGH** for 6 minutes, stirring every 2 minutes. Transfer to fondue burner or turn into fondue pot. Spear apple or marshmallow with fondue fork; dip in mixture. Makes 6 servings.

153

FOODS
FROM YOUR FREEZER

Your freezer + microwave oven = fast, carefree cooking.
With a few frozen basic recipes on hand you
can make a steaming bowl of Booya (recipe on page 164),
Saucy Meatball Sandwiches (recipe on page 161),
and home-style Creamy Chicken Pot Pie (recipe on page
165) at a moment's notice. Plus you can use cool
microwave cooking on those hot summer days to blanch
vegetables and make delicious freezer jams too!

MICRO MENU PLANNER

MAIN DISHES

VEGETABLES

BREADS

DESSERTS

SOUPS & SANDWICHES

FRUITS AND JAMS

FROZEN BASIC MIXTURES

BEVERAGES

FREEZE-EASY CASSEROLES

FROZEN CURRIED LAMB

Total cooking time: 1 hour 12 minutes

3	30	3	30	6			

- 2 tablespoons butter or margarine
- 1 cup chopped onion

• • •

- 2 pounds lean lamb, cut in ½-inch cubes
- 1 clove garlic, minced
- 1 to 1½ tablespoons curry powder
- 1½ teaspoons salt
- ½ teaspoon ground ginger
- 2 tomatoes, peeled and chopped
- 3 tablespoons all-purpose flour

In 2-quart casserole, combine butter and onion. Cook, covered, at **HIGH** for 3 to 5 minutes. Add meat, garlic, curry powder, salt, and ginger; mix well. Stir in tomatoes and ¼ cup water. Cook, covered, at **MEDIUM (5)** for 30 to 45 minutes, stirring occasionally, till tender. Blend flour and ⅓ cup cold water; stir into mixture. Cook at **HIGH** for 3 to 5 minutes, till thickened, stirring after each minute. Spoon into half gallon freezer container. Seal, label, and freeze.

To serve frozen curry: Dip container of curry into very hot water to loosen. Place block of frozen curry in 2-quart casserole. Cook at **MEDIUM LOW (3)** for 30 to 35 minutes, stirring and breaking up 3 to 4 times, till defrosted. Heat, covered, at **HIGH** for 6 to 10 minutes, till heated through. Serve with hot cooked rice. Pass condiments as desired: sliced green onion, coconut, chutney, raisins, peanuts. Makes 6 to 8 servings.

FROZEN SWISS STEAK STRIPS

Total cooking time: 1 hour 15 minutes

45	25	5					

- 2 pounds beef round steak, ½ inch thick
- ¼ cup all-purpose flour
- ¾ teaspoon salt
- ¼ teaspoon pepper
- 1 6-ounce can sliced or chopped mushrooms
- 1 15-ounce can tomato sauce with green peppers and onions and celery

Pound meat with mallet to tenderize. Cut into 3-inch-long strips, trimming fat off. Mix flour, salt, and pepper; sprinkle on meat to coat. In 2-quart casserole, combine meat, undrained mushrooms, and tomato sauce. Cook, covered, at **MEDIUM (5)** for 45 minutes, stirring once, till meat is tender. Turn into two 1-quart freezer containers (3 cups each). Seal, label, and freeze.

To serve frozen casserole: Dip freezer container in hot water to loosen; place block of frozen meat mixture in 1-quart casserole. Cook, uncovered, at **MEDIUM LOW (3)** for 25 to 30 minutes, turning block over and breaking up 3 times. Stir in ¼ cup water. Heat, covered, at **HIGH** for 5 to 6 minutes, till heated through, stirring once. Serve with noodles or rice. Makes two 4-serving meals.

TEST KITCHEN TIPS

Freezer Tips. Many home-cooked or partially cooked food mixtures can be frozen successfully. For best results, season lightly because some flavors intensify during freezing.

Divide the food into family-size or individual-size portions. Package in non-foil containers for microwave thawing and cooking. Plastic and paper cartons without metal handles or trim can be placed directly in the microwave for defrosting, then the food transferred to a ceramic casserole for heating.

Allow headspace of about 2 inches between liquid foods and the top of the container. Wrap solid items tightly to remove as much air as possible.

To save freezer space and reuse dishes, line casseroles, dishes, or plates with plastic wrap or freezer paper, leaving long ends. Fill, seal, and place container in the freezer. When the food is solid, remove from the container; wrap and seal in moisture-vapor-proof material. Later, thaw and cook the unwrapped food in the same casserole or dish.

Label each package with contents, number of servings, date frozen (or date before which the food must be used), and any serving instructions.

Keep the temperature in your freezer at zero degrees or lower for maximum quality of food.

Use the food within recommended storage times. Breads and rolls, cakes, pastry, and pies keep well for 2 months. Cookies and cookie dough are safely frozen for 6 to 12 months. Casseroles, creamed dishes, meat pies, cooked meats, soups, and stews are generally fine for 2 to 4 months. You can keep spaghetti and meat balls in sauce for 3 months.

Remember that some foods don't freeze well because of flavor and texture changes. These include fried foods, boiled frostings, hard-cooked egg whites, green onions, radishes, cucumber, and salad greens. Mayonnaise and sour cream may separate.

For more frozen casserole recipes, see Frozen Ravioli Lasagna (recipe on page 147), Frozen Cheesy Ham Casserole (recipe on page 147), Ham Vegetable Bake (recipe on page 61), Jiffy Spaghetti and Meatballs (recipe on page 87). You'll also want to try our frozen basic mixtures to keep on hand in your freezer and make into a myriad of different dishes—Basic Pork Mixture (recipes on page 159), Basic Burger Dress-ups (recipes on page 160), Basic Oven Meatballs (recipes on page 161), and Basic Ground Beef (recipes on page 163).

Mom's Pork Stew

TIMETABLE

1. Prepare Versatile Frozen Pork Base; freeze.
2. Prepare Hot Fruit Compote except for adding bananas before final heating.
3. Prepare stew; cover to keep warm.
4. Set table while stew cooks.
5. Heat bread (about 1 minute at **HIGH**).
6. Add banana and finish heating compote just before serving with cookies for dessert.

MENU

Mom's Pork Stew

Whole Wheat Bread   Butter

Hot Fruit Compote (recipe page 91)

Peanut Butter Cookies

Coffee   Milk

VERSATILE FROZEN PORK BASE

QUICK PORK A LA STROGANOFF

Total cooking time: 23 minutes

20	3						

- 1 10½-ounce can condensed beef broth
- 3 tablespoons dry white wine
- 1 tablespoon catsup
- 1 package (2 cups) Versatile Frozen Pork Base
- ¼ cup all-purpose flour
- ½ cup dairy sour cream

Reserve ⅓ cup beef broth. In 2-quart casserole, mix remaining broth, wine, catsup, and frozen pork mixture. Cook, covered, at **MEDIUM HIGH (7)** for 20 minutes, stirring twice to break up frozen mixture. Meanwhile, blend flour and reserved broth; stir in sour cream and mix well. Blend ¾ cup of hot meat mixture into sour cream; return to casserole. Cook, covered, at **MEDIUM HIGH (7)** for 3 to 4 minutes, stirring after each minute, till thickened and bubbly. Serve over noodles. Makes 4 servings.

VERSATILE FROZEN PORK BASE

Total cooking time: 23 minutes

8	15						

- 2 pounds boneless pork shoulder, cut in ½-inch cubes
- 1 cup water
- 1 cup chopped onion
- 1 clove garlic, minced
- ¼ teaspoon salt

In 2-quart casserole, combine all ingredients. Cook, covered, at **HIGH** for 8 minutes, till mixture simmers. Stir. Cook, covered, at **MEDIUM (5)** for 15 minutes. Pour into two 2-cup freezer containers. Seal, label, and freeze. Makes two 2-cup portions.

BARBECUED PORK AND RICE

Total cooking time: 20 minutes

20							

- 2 tablespoons brown sugar
- 2 tablespoons all-purpose flour
- 1 8-ounce can tomato sauce
- 1 tablespoon lemon juice
- 1 teaspoon prepared mustard
- 1 teaspoon Worcestershire sauce
  Several dashes bottled hot pepper sauce
- 1 package (2 cups) Versatile Frozen Pork Base

In 2-quart casserole, mix brown sugar and flour. Stir in tomato sauce, lemon juice, mustard, Worcestershire, and hot pepper sauce. Add frozen pork base. Cook, covered, at **MEDIUM HIGH (7)** for 20 minutes, stirring twice to break up frozen mixture. Serve on rice. Makes 4 servings.

MOM'S PORK STEW

Total cooking time: 34 minutes

15	15	4					

- 1 package (2 cups) Versatile Frozen Pork Base
- 2 cups water
- 1 bay leaf
- 1½ teaspoons salt
- ½ teaspoon dried marjoram, crushed
- ½ teaspoon dried thyme, crushed
  Dash pepper
  • • •
- 4 medium carrots, peeled and thinly sliced
- 4 small potatoes, peeled and cut up
- ½ 10-ounce package (1 cup) frozen peas
- 1 3-ounce can sliced mushrooms, drained
- ¼ cup all-purpose flour
- ½ cup cold water
- ½ teaspoon kitchen bouquet

In 3-quart casserole, combine frozen pork base, the 2 cups water, bay leaf, salt, marjoram, thyme, and pepper. Cover and cook at **MEDIUM HIGH (7)** for 15 minutes, stirring twice to break up frozen pork mixture. Add vegetables. Cover and cook at **HIGH** for 15 minutes or till tender. Combine flour and remaining ½ cup water. Add to stew. Cook, uncovered, at **HIGH** for 4 to 5 minutes or till thickened and bubbly, stirring three times. Stir in kitchen bouquet. Makes 4 servings.

EASY ORIENTAL SUPPER

Total cooking time: 31 minutes

15	10	4	2				

- 1 13¾-ounce can chicken broth
- 1 package (2 cups) Versatile Frozen Pork Base
- 1½ cups diagonally sliced celery
- ½ of 8-ounce can water chestnuts, drained and sliced (½ cup)
- 1 3-ounce can sliced mushrooms, drained
  • • •
- 3 tablespoons cornstarch
- ¼ cup soy sauce
- 1 6-ounce package frozen Chinese pea pods
- 2 tablespoons toasted slivered almonds
  Hot cooked rice

In 2-quart casserole, combine broth and frozen pork base. Cook, covered, at **MEDIUM HIGH (7)** for 15 minutes, stirring twice to break up pork mixture. Add celery, water chestnuts, and mushrooms. Cook at **MEDIUM HIGH (7)** for 10 minutes. Combine cornstarch and soy sauce. Stir into pork mixture. Cook, uncovered, at **HIGH** for 4 to 5 minutes, stirring after each minute, till thickened and bubbly.

Meanwhile, rinse pea pods with hot tap water; stir into casserole. Cook, uncovered, at **HIGH** 2 minutes, stirring once. Sprinkle with toasted almonds. Serve with hot cooked rice. Makes 6 servings.

CREATE A BLUE RIBBON BURGER

MEXICAN BURGERS

Serve with corn chips, hot chili peppers, frosty mugs of beer, and fresh pineapple wedges—

Total cooking time: 11 minutes

5	4	2					

- 1 7¾-ounce can frozen avocado dip
- 1 tablespoon lemon juice
  Few drops bottled hot pepper sauce
- 1 small tomato, peeled, seeded, and chopped
  • • •
- ½ cup crushed corn chips
- ⅓ cup milk
- 1 teaspoon Worcestershire sauce
- ½ teaspoon onion salt
- 1 pound ground beef
  • • •
- 5 hamburger buns, split, toasted, and buttered

Thaw can of frozen avocado dip by running hot water over can. Remove one end and puncture other end; push out dip into small bowl. Cook, uncovered, at **MEDIUM LOW (3)** for 5 minutes. Add lemon juice, hot pepper sauce, and tomato.

In bowl, combine corn chips, milk, Worcestershire sauce, and onion salt; mix well. Add ground beef and mix till well combined. Shape into 5 patties about 4¼ inches in diameter. Place in 12×7½×2-inch baking dish. Cook, covered, at **HIGH** for 4 to 5 minutes. Turn patties over; spoon off juices. Continue cooking, covered, at **HIGH** 2 minutes longer. Serve burgers in toasted buns and top with avocado mixture. Makes 5 servings.

PIZZA IN A BURGER

Total cooking time: 7 minutes

5	2						

- ¼ cup grated Parmesan cheese
- ¼ cup chopped pitted ripe olives
- 2 tablespoons finely chopped onion
- ¼ teaspoon salt
- ½ teaspoon dried oregano, crushed
- ¼ cup catsup
  Dash pepper
- 1 pound ground beef
  • • •
- 4 slices (6 ounces) mozzarella cheese, cut in strips
  • • •
- 6 slices French bread, toasted

In bowl, combine Parmesan cheese, olives, onion, salt, oregano, catsup, and pepper. Add ground beef and mix well. Shape into 4 patties 4-inches in diameter. Place in 8×8×2-inch baking dish. Cook, covered, at **HIGH** for 5 minutes. Turn patties over; spoon off juices. Top with cheese and continue cooking, uncovered, at **HIGH** for 2 minutes. Serve on French bread. Makes 4 servings.

GOURMET STEAKBURGERS

Total cooking time: 3 minutes

3							

Cook *Basic Burgers* (below). Combine one 10½-ounce can mushroom gravy, 1½ teaspoons soy sauce, and ¼ cup toasted slivered almonds. Pour over burgers. Cook, covered, at **HIGH** for 3 to 4 minutes or till heated through. Serve mushroom sauce over burgers. Makes 4 servings.

BASIC BURGERS

Total cooking time: 10 minutes

6	4						

- 1 pound ground chuck shaped into 4 patties 4-inches in diameter

Place double thickness of waxed paper between burgers. Wrap in freezer bags or freezer wrap. Seal, label, and freeze. When ready to use: Separate patties and place in 8×8×2-inch baking dish. Cook, uncovered, at **MEDIUM LOW (3)** for 6 to 7 minutes, rearranging and giving dish half turn once (remove any patties that are thawed). Let stand 5 minutes before using.

To cook: Place 4 burgers in 8×8×2-inch baking dish. Cook, covered, at **HIGH** for 4 to 5 minutes, giving dish half turn once. (Or cook 2 patties, covered, at **HIGH** for 2½ to 3 minutes, giving dish half turn once.)

SAUERBRATEN BURGERS

Total cooking time: 16 minutes 30 seconds

6	5	4	1:30				

- 8 gingersnaps, crushed (½ cup)
- 1 8-ounce can tomato sauce
- ⅓ cup finely chopped onion
- ¼ cup raisins
- ¾ teaspoon salt
- 1½ pounds ground beef
- 2 tablespoons brown sugar
- 3 tablespoons vinegar
- 1 teaspoon prepared mustard

Set aside 2 tablespoons gingersnaps. In bowl, combine remaining gingersnaps, ¼ *cup* of the tomato sauce, the onion, raisins, and salt. Add ground beef; mix well. Shape into 6 patties about 4½ inches in diameter. Place in 13×9×2-inch baking dish. Cook, covered, at **HIGH** for 6 minutes; spoon off juices. Turn over and rearrange. Cook, covered, at **HIGH** for 5 minutes longer.

In small bowl, combine remaining tomato sauce, ¼ cup water, brown sugar, vinegar, mustard, and dash pepper. Pour over burgers. Cook, covered, at **HIGH** for 4 minutes. Remove burgers and keep warm. Pour sauce into small bowl. Stir in reserved gingersnap crumbs. Cook, uncovered, at **HIGH** for 1½ minutes, stirring twice. Pass sauce with burgers. Makes 6 servings.

4-WAY FROZEN MEATBALLS

ORIENTAL MEATBALL SUPPER

Total cooking time: 16 minutes

10	2	3	1			

⅓ recipe (24) frozen Basic Meatballs
2 cups water
3 teaspoons instant beef bouillon granules
½ cup sliced water chestnuts
¼ cup sliced green onion
3 tablespoons soy sauce
3 tablespoons cornstarch
⅓ cup cold water
1 6-ounce package frozen Chinese pea pods
2 medium tomatoes, cut in eighths
Hot cooked rice

In 2-quart casserole, combine meatballs, water, and bouillon granules. Cook, covered, at **MEDIUM HIGH (7)** for 10 minutes, stirring twice. Stir in water chestnuts, green onion, and soy sauce. Cook, covered with waxed paper, at **MEDIUM HIGH (7)** for 2 minutes.

Thoroughly blend cornstarch and the ⅓ cup cold water; stir into meatball mixture. Cook, uncovered, at **HIGH** for 3 to 4 minutes, stirring twice.

Pour hot water over pea pods to break up; stir into meatball mixture. Add tomato wedges. Cook at **HIGH** for 1 to 1½ minutes longer. Serve over rice. Makes 6 servings.

BASIC MEATBALLS

Total cooking time: 32 minutes

8	8	8	8			

3 eggs
½ cup milk
3 cups soft bread crumbs (4 slices)
½ cup finely chopped onion
2 teaspoons salt
3 pounds ground beef

In large bowl, beat eggs. Stir in milk, crumbs, onion, and salt. Add meat and mix well. Chill. With wet hands, shape meat mixture into 6 dozen (72) balls. Arrange 18 balls in 9-inch pie plate and cook, uncovered, at **MEDIUM (5)** for 8 minutes, turning meatballs over and rearranging twice. Repeat till all are cooked.

Place cooked meatballs on a baking pan; place in freezer just till frozen. Using 24 balls per package, wrap in moisture-vaporproof bags. Seal, label, and freeze. Makes 3 packages of 24 meatballs.

JIFFY SPAGHETTI AND MEATBALLS

See page 87 for this all-American favorite. It goes from freezer to table in less than 30 minutes. And it starts with *Basic Meatballs* like all the recipes on this page.

CHILI MEATBALL STEW

Total cooking time: 22 minutes

4	18					

1 cup chopped onion
¾ cup chopped green pepper
¼ cup water
• • •
⅓ recipe (24) frozen Basic Meatballs
1 16-ounce can tomatoes, cut up
1 16-ounce can red kidney beans, drained
1 8¾-ounce can whole kernel corn
1 8-ounce can tomato sauce
1 teaspoon salt
1 to 1½ teaspoons chili powder
1 bay leaf
• • •
½ cup (2 ounces) shredded natural cheddar cheese
½ cup crushed corn chips

In 2½-quart casserole, combine onion, green pepper, and water; cook, covered, at **HIGH** for 4 minutes. Add frozen meatballs, tomatoes, kidney beans, undrained corn, tomato sauce, salt, chili powder, and bay leaf.

Cook, covered, at **MEDIUM HIGH (7)** for 18 to 20 minutes, stirring 3 times, till meatballs are heated through. Remove bay leaf. Serve in bowls. Pass cheese and corn chips to sprinkle atop each serving. Makes 6 to 8 servings.

SAUCY MEATBALL SANDWICHES

Total cooking time: 10 minutes

3	7					

½ cup catsup
⅓ cup chili sauce
¼ cup water
2 tablespoons brown sugar
1 tablespoon Worcestershire sauce
1 tablespoon prepared mustard
1 teaspoon celery seed
¼ teaspoon salt
¼ teaspoon garlic powder
Few drops bottled hot pepper sauce
3 thin slices lemon
• • •
⅓ recipe (24) frozen Basic Meatballs
8 hard rolls or frankfurter buns, split and toasted
1 onion, sliced and separated into rings

In casserole, combine catsup, chili sauce, water, brown sugar, Worcestershire, mustard, celery seed, salt, garlic powder, hot pepper sauce, and lemon slices. Cook, uncovered at **HIGH** for 3 to 4 minutes, stirring once.

Stir in frozen meatballs. Cook, covered with waxed paper, at **HIGH** for 7 minutes, stirring once or till meatballs are heated through. Remove lemon slices. Serve meatballs and sauce on toasted rolls. Garnish with onion rings. Makes 8 sandwiches.

Savory Stuffed Peppers

TIMETABLE

1. Prepare cabbage salad except dressing; chill.
2. Prepare Quick Peach Crumble.
3. Cook pepper shells.
4. Set table while peppers cook.
5. Cook packaged rice on top of range.
6. Finish stuffing and cooking peppers.
7. Pour dressing on salad and heat rolls (page 36).
8. Reheat dessert, if desired.

MENU

Savory Stuffed Peppers

Packaged Beef-flavored Rice

Tossed Cabbage Salad

Crusty Rolls   Butter

Quick Peach Crumble (page 91)

START WITH BASIC GROUND BEEF

LAZY-DAY LASAGNA

Total cooking time: 20 minutes

10	10						

- 4 ounces lasagna noodles
- 1 15½-ounce jar spaghetti sauce with mushrooms
- 1 pint frozen Basic Ground Beef Mixture
- ½ teaspoon dried leaf oregano
- 1 cup cream-style cottage cheese
- 1 6-ounce package sliced mozzarella cheese

Cook noodles on top of range using package directions; drain. In 1½-quart casserole, combine spaghetti sauce, frozen beef mixture, and oregano. Cook, covered, at **MEDIUM HIGH (7)** for 10 minutes, stirring 3 times to break up meat. In greased 10×6×1½-inch baking dish, layer *half* the ingredients in this order: noodles, cottage cheese, mozzarella, and meat sauce. Repeat layers. Bake, covered, at **MEDIUM HIGH (7)** for 10 minutes, giving dish half turn once. Let stand 10 minutes. Makes 6 servings.

SPEEDY SPANISH RICE

Total cooking time: 11 minutes

5	3	3					

- 2 cups water
- 1 6-ounce can tomato paste
- ⅓ cup chili sauce
- 1 teaspoon sugar
- 1 teaspoon salt
- 1 pint frozen Basic Ground Beef Mixture
- 1¼ cups uncooked packaged precooked rice

In 2-quart casserole, combine water, tomato paste, chili sauce, sugar, salt, and dash pepper. Add frozen meat mixture. Cook, covered, at **MEDIUM HIGH (7)** for 5 minutes, stirring to break up meat. Cook at **MEDIUM HIGH (7)** for 3 minutes more till hot. Stir in rice. Cook, tightly covered, at **MEDIUM HIGH (7)** for 3 minutes, stirring twice. Let stand, covered, for 5 minutes. Fluff with fork. Makes 4 servings.

BEEFY BEAN BAKE

Total cooking time: 15 minutes

10	5						

- 1 28-ounce can pork and beans in tomato sauce
- ¼ cup catsup
- 1 tablespoon prepared mustard
- 1 teaspoon soy sauce
- 1 teaspoon Worcestershire sauce
- 1 pint frozen Basic Ground Beef Mixture

In 2-quart casserole, combine beans, catsup, mustard, soy, and Worcestershire. Add frozen meat mixture. Cook, covered, at **MEDIUM HIGH (7)** for 10 minutes, stirring three times. Cook, uncovered, at **MEDIUM HIGH (7)** for 5 minutes more. Serve in bowls. Makes 4 or 5 servings.

EASY BEEFWICHES

Total cooking time: 10 minutes

10							

- 1 10¾-ounce can condensed tomato soup
- 1 teaspoon Worcestershire sauce
  Dash pepper
- 2 tablespoons all-purpose flour
- 1 pint frozen Basic Ground Beef Mixture
- 4 to 6 hamburger buns, split and toasted

In 1½-quart casserole, combine soup, Worcestershire, and pepper. Stir in flour. Add frozen meat mixture. Cook, covered, at **MEDIUM HIGH (7)** for 10 minutes, stirring 3 times. Serve in buns. Makes 4 to 6 servings.

BASIC GROUND BEEF MIXTURE

Total cooking time: 9 minutes

9							

- 2 pounds ground beef
- 1 cup chopped celery
- 1 cup chopped onion
- ½ cup chopped green pepper

In large bowl, combine ground beef, celery, onion, and green pepper. Cook, uncovered, at **HIGH** for 9 minutes, stirring 4 times. Drain off excess fat. Spoon into three 1-pint freezer containers. Seal, label, and freeze. Makes 3 pints.

SAVORY STUFFED PEPPERS

Total cooking time: 23 minutes

10	5	8					

- 1 pint frozen Basic Ground Beef Mixture
- 1 8-ounce can tomato sauce
- ½ teaspoon Worcestershire sauce
- ½ teaspoon salt
- 1 12-ounce can whole kernel corn, drained
- 1 cup (4 ounces) shredded sharp process American cheese
- 4 large green peppers

In 2-quart casserole, combine frozen beef mixture, *half* the tomato sauce, the Worcestershire, and salt. Cook, covered, at **MEDIUM HIGH (7)** for 10 minutes, stirring once to break up frozen mixture. Add corn and cheese and set aside.

Halve peppers lengthwise; remove seeds and membranes. Place peppers cut side down in 13×9×2-inch baking dish. Cook, covered with waxed paper, at **HIGH** for 5 minutes. Drain; turn cut side up. Sprinkle insides lightly with salt. Fill with ground beef mixture; spoon on remaining tomato sauce, using about 1 tablespoon for each. Cook, uncovered, at **HIGH** for 8 minutes, giving dish half turn after 4 minutes. Makes 4 servings.

HANDY BASIC BEEF CUBES

BARBECUED BEEF SANDWICHES

Total cooking time: 13 minutes

7	6						

- 1 package (2 cups) Frozen Basic Beef Base
- ½ cup extra hot catsup
- 1 tablespoon Worcestershire sauce
- 1 teaspoon Dijon-style mustard
  Dash bottled hot pepper sauce
- 2 teaspoons cornstarch
- 1 teaspoon celery seed
- ½ teaspoon sugar
- 6 onion buns

In 2-quart casserole, cook frozen beef base, covered, at **MEDIUM HIGH (7)** for 7 to 8 minutes or till thawed. Break up with fork, if necessary. Combine remaining ingredients except buns in 2-cup glass measure; mix well. Stir into beef. Cook, covered, at **MEDIUM HIGH (7)** for 6 to 7 minutes, stirring 3 times. Serve on buns. Makes 6.

FROZEN BASIC BEEF BASE

Total cooking time: 1 hour 8 minutes

8	60						

- 2 pounds boneless beef chuck, cut in ½-inch cubes
- 1 cup water
- 1 teaspoon beef bouillon granules
- 1 cup chopped onion
- ¼ teaspoon garlic salt

In 2-quart casserole, mix all ingredients. Cook, covered, at **HIGH** for 8 minutes, till mixture simmers. Stir. Cook, covered, at **MEDIUM (5)** for 1 to 1¼ hours or till tender. Pour into two 2-cup freezer containers. Seal, label, and freeze. Makes two pints.

EASY BEEF STEW

Total cooking time: 26 minutes

15	8	3					

- 1 package (2 cups) Frozen Basic Beef Base
- 1 10½-ounce can mushroom gravy
- 2 tablespoons dry onion soup mix
- 1 teaspoon prepared horseradish
- 1 10-ounce package frozen Danish-style vegetables
- 1 tablespoon cornstarch

In 2-quart casserole, combine beef base and gravy. Cook, covered, at **MEDIUM HIGH (7)** for 15 minutes, stirring twice to break up frozen beef. Stir in soup mix, horseradish, and vegetables. Cook, covered, at **HIGH** for 8 minutes, stirring twice to blend in sauce cubes. Combine cornstarch and 2 tablespoons cold water. Stir into stew. Cook at **HIGH** for 3 minutes or till bubbly, stirring each minute. Serves 4.

BEEFY "PIZZA" PIE

Total cooking time: 16 minutes

10	5	1					

- 2 tablespoons all-purpose flour
- 1 8-ounce can (1 cup) pizza sauce
- 1 package (2 cups) Frozen Basic Beef Base
- 1 4-ounce can sliced mushrooms, drained
  Packaged instant mashed potato buds (6 servings)
- 1 beaten egg
- 2 tablespoons grated Parmesan cheese
- ½ teaspoon dried oregano, crushed
- 3 slices mozzarella cheese, halved diagonally

In 2-quart casserole, combine flour and ¼ cup of the sauce. Stir in remaining sauce; add frozen beef and mushrooms. Cook, covered, at **MEDIUM HIGH (7)** for 10 to 12 minutes; break up frozen beef with fork after 7 minutes.

Prepare mashed potatoes according to package directions, *reducing water called for in directions by ½ cup*. Beat in egg, Parmesan, and oregano. Spoon potatoes into 9-inch pie plate forming a "crust." Spoon hot beef mixture into crust. Cook, covered, at **HIGH** for 5 minutes or till heated through. Top with cheese triangles. Cook, uncovered, at **HIGH** for 1 minute or till cheese melts. Sprinkle with snipped parsley. Makes 6 servings.

BOOYA

Total cooking time: 1 hour 7 minutes

7	45	15					

- 1 package (2 cups) Frozen Basic Beef Base
- 3 cups water
- 1 tablespoon salt
- 1 teaspoon paprika
- 1 teaspoon dried oregano, crushed
- ½ teaspoon dried savory, crushed
- 1 cup parsley sprigs
- 1 large onion, sliced
- 1 cup chopped red cabbage
- 1 cup chopped carrot
- 1 cup chopped rutabaga
- 1 cup chopped celery
- ¼ cup chopped green pepper
- 1 28-ounce can tomatoes, cut up

• • •

- 1 16-ounce can cut green beans
- 1 8-ounce can peas
- 1 8-ounce can whole kernel corn

In 4- or 5-quart casserole, combine frozen beef base and water. Cook, covered, at **MEDIUM HIGH (7)** for 7 to 8 minutes; break up frozen beef with fork. Stir in remaining ingredients except beans, peas, and corn. Cook, covered, at **HIGH** for 45 to 50 minutes or till vegetables are almost tender. Stir in undrained green beans, peas, and corn. Cook, covered, at **MEDIUM (5)** for 15 minutes. Makes about 3 quarts.

TASTY FROZEN CHICKEN BASE

CREAMY CHICKEN POT PIE

Total cooking time: 34 minutes

7	15	4	2	3	3		

1 10-ounce package frozen peas and carrots
1 package Frozen Chicken Base
½ cup chopped onion
6 tablespoons butter or margarine
⅓ cup all-purpose flour
1 teaspoon salt
½ cup milk
1 cup dairy sour cream
¼ cup chopped pimiento
  Packaged instant mashed potato buds (4 servings)
1 cup milk
1 beaten egg
1 cup herb-seasoned stuffing mix

Cut slit in top of vegetable carton; cook at **HIGH** for 7 minutes; set aside. Place frozen chicken in 3-quart casserole. Cook, covered, at **MEDIUM HIGH (7)** for 15 minutes; break up with fork, if necessary. Set aside.

In small bowl, combine onion and butter; cook, uncovered, at **HIGH** for 4 minutes or till tender. Stir in flour and salt. Add onion mixture and the ½ cup milk to chicken; mix well. Cook, uncovered, at **HIGH** for 2 to 3 minutes or till bubbly, stirring after each minute. Stir in sour cream, pimiento, and peas and carrots. Cook, covered, at **HIGH** for 3 to 4 minutes or till bubbly.

Prepare mashed potatoes according to package directions *except use the 1 cup milk instead of the amount called for on package.* Beat in egg. Stir in stuffing mix. (Potato mixture will be quite wet.) Drop by spoonfuls onto bubbly chicken mixture. Sprinkle with paprika. Cook, uncovered, at **HIGH** for 3 to 5 minutes or till potatoes are hot and set. Makes 6 servings.

FROZEN CHICKEN BASE

Total cooking time: 35 minutes

35						

4 pounds chicken breasts (8 halves)
2 parsley sprigs
4 celery branches with leaves
1 carrot, peeled and quartered
1 small onion, cut up
2 teaspoons salt
¼ teaspoon pepper
3 cups water

In 4- or 5-quart casserole, combine all ingredients. Cook, covered, at **HIGH** for 35 to 45 minutes or till tender, turning chicken over and rearranging once. Strain broth and refrigerate. Remove chicken from bones; cube. In three 3-cup freezer containers, pack 2 cups chicken and 1⅓ cups broth. Seal, label, and freeze. Makes 3 packages.

CHICKEN AND DUMPLINGS OLÉ

Total cooking time: 55 minutes 45 seconds

15	30	10	0:45				

1 package Frozen Chicken Base
2 cups vegetable juice cocktail
1 10-ounce package frozen cut green beans
1 cup diced pared potato
½ cup sliced celery
½ cup chopped onion
1½ teaspoons salt
1 to 2 teaspoons chili powder
6 drops bottled hot pepper sauce
1 cup packaged biscuit mix
½ cup yellow cornmeal
1 cup (4 ounces) shredded process American cheese
2 tablespoons snipped parsley
⅔ cup milk

In 3-quart casserole, combine Frozen Chicken Base and the vegetable juice cocktail. Cook, covered, at **MEDIUM HIGH (7)** for 15 minutes; break up frozen chicken mixture with fork, if necessary. Add beans, potatoes, celery, onion, salt, chili powder, and pepper sauce. Cook, covered, at **HIGH** for 30 to 35 minutes or till vegetables are tender.

Meanwhile, in mixing bowl, combine biscuit mix, cornmeal, *half* the cheese, and the parsley. Add milk; stir just till moistened. Drop dough in 6 portions onto hot stew mixture. Cook, covered, at **MEDIUM (5)** for 10 to 12 minutes or till dumplings are no longer doughy. Sprinkle dumplings with remaining cheese. Cook at **HIGH** for 45 seconds or till cheese melts. Makes 6 servings.

BRUNSWICK STEW

Total cooking time: 55 minutes

15	40						

1 package Frozen Chicken Base
1 13¾-ounce can chicken broth
1 cup water
1 10-ounce package frozen cut okra
1 10-ounce package frozen baby lima beans
1 16-ounce can tomatoes, cut up
2 cups diced pared potatoes
½ cup chopped onion
1½ teaspoons salt
½ teaspoon dried marjoram, crushed
½ teaspoon dried rosemary, crushed
¼ teaspoon pepper
1 bay leaf

In 4- or 5-quart casserole, combine Frozen Chicken Base, broth, and water. Cook, covered, at **MEDIUM HIGH (7)** for 15 minutes; break up frozen chicken mixture with fork, if necessary. Add okra, limas, tomatoes, potatoes, onion, and seasonings. Cook, covered, at **HIGH** for 40 to 45 minutes or till vegetables are tender, stirring once. Remove bay leaf. Makes 8 servings.

Freezer Peach Jam, Frozen Strawberry Jam, Freezer Pineapple Conserve

FREEZER RASPBERRY JAM

Total cooking time: 3 minutes

2	1							

1½ **quarts (6 cups) fresh red raspberries**
5¼ **cups sugar**
¾ **cup water**
1 **1¾-ounce package powdered fruit pectin**

Crush berries to make 3 cups pulp (add water if necessary to make 3 cups). Place in large bowl. Stir in sugar; mix well. In 1½-quart bowl, combine water and pectin. Cook at **HIGH** for 2 to 2½ minutes or till boiling. Stir well. Cook at **HIGH** for 1 minute. Stir into fruit mixture. Continue stirring for 3 minutes. Quickly ladle into freezer containers. Cover and let stand 24 hours or till set. Store up to 3 weeks in refrigerator or 1 year in freezer. Makes seven ½-pints.

FREEZING FRUITS AND JAMS

FREEZER PEACH JAM

Total cooking time: 3 minutes

2	1						

  2 pounds ripe, fresh peaches, peeled
  2 tablespoons lemon juice
  5½ cups sugar

• • •

  ¾ cup water
  1 1¾-ounce package powdered fruit pectin

Pit and grind peaches. Treat peaches with ascorbic acid color keeper to prevent darkening. Measure 2½ cups peach pulp (add water if necessary to make the 2½ cups). Place in large bowl. Add lemon juice. Stir in sugar; mix well.

In 1½-quart bowl, combine water and pectin. Cook at **HIGH** for 2 to 2½ minutes or till boiling. Stir well. Cook at **HIGH** for 1 minute. Stir into fruit mixture. Continue stirring for 3 minutes. Quickly ladle into freezer containers. Cover and let stand 24 hours or till set. Store up to 3 weeks in refrigerator or 1 year in freezer. Makes seven ½-pints.

FROZEN STRAWBERRY JAM

Total cooking time: 6 minutes

2	4						

  2 10-ounce packages frozen strawberries
  3½ cups sugar
  ½ of 6-ounce bottle liquid fruit pectin

Remove one of metal ends from strawberry cartons. Place opened packages in microwave oven with open side up. Cook, uncovered, at **MEDIUM LOW (3)** for 2 minutes. Empty fruit into large bowl. Cook, uncovered, at **MEDIUM LOW (3)** for 4 to 5 minutes, breaking fruit apart with fork after 2 minutes. Mash strawberries. Stir in sugar; mix well. Let stand 20 minutes, stirring occasionally.

When sugar has dissolved, add pectin. Stir for 3 minutes. Quickly ladle into freezer containers. Cover and let stand 24 hours or till set. Store up to 3 weeks in refrigerator or 1 year in freezer. Makes four ½-pint containers.

SYRUP FOR FREEZING FRUITS

In 2-quart glass measure or bowl, combine sugar and water according to chart. Heat at **HIGH** for time indicated in chart until mixture boils, stirring occasionally to dissolve sugar. Chill. Use thin syrup for sweet fruit, heavy syrup for sour fruit, and medium syrup for other fruit.

Type of Syrup	Sugar (cups)	Water (cups)	Time at **HIGH**	Yield (cups)
Thin	2	4	13 minutes	5
Medium	3	4	14 minutes	5½
Heavy	4¾	4	15½ minutes	6½

FREEZER PINEAPPLE CONSERVE

Total cooking time: 3 minutes

2	1						

  1 large fresh pineapple
  1 teaspoon grated orange peel
  ½ cup orange juice
    Yellow food coloring
  5 cups sugar
  ½ cup chopped walnuts
  ½ cup flaked coconut

• • •

  ¾ cup water
  1 1¾-ounce package powdered fruit pectin

Remove pineapple crown. Wash and peel pineapple; remove eyes and core. Cut into pieces. Place pineapple, a few pieces at a time, in blender container; cover and blend on low speed till finely chopped (not pureed). Measure 2 cups chopped pineapple. In large bowl, combine pineapple, peel, orange juice, and several drops yellow food coloring. Stir in sugar, nuts, and coconut.

In 1½-quart bowl, combine water and pectin. Cook at **HIGH** for 2 to 2½ minutes or till boiling. Stir well. Cook at **HIGH** for 1 minute. Stir into fruit mixture. Continue stirring for 3 minutes. Quickly ladle into freezer containers. Cover and let stand 24 hours or till set. Store up to 3 weeks in refrigerator or 1 year in freezer. Makes six ½-pints.

BRANDIED PEACHES

Total cooking time: 22 minutes

7	5	10					

  2 cups sugar
  2 cups water
  2 inches stick cinnamon, broken in pieces

• • •

  6 to 9 small fresh peaches, peeled
  1 cup brandy

In deep 3-quart casserole, combine sugar, water, and cinnamon. Heat, uncovered, at **HIGH** for 7 to 9 minutes, till mixture boils, stirring once. Boil at **HIGH** for 5 minutes more. Add whole peaches (halve large peaches) and cook, loosely covered, at **HIGH** for 10 minutes, turning peaches over in syrup twice, till they can be easily pierced with a fork. Chill fruit and syrup.

Measure syrup; add ⅓ cup brandy for each cup syrup; stir well. Pack peaches into freezer containers. Fill with brandied syrup leaving ½-inch headspace. Seal. Store up to 1 month in refrigerator or 6 months in freezer. Makes 3 to 4 pints.

Note: If desired, thicken brandied peach syrup (1¼ cups from 1 jar) to make sauce for cakes or ice cream. In 4-cup glass measure, blend 1 tablespoon cornstarch and ¼ cup of the syrup; stir in remaining 1 cup syrup. Cook, uncovered, at **HIGH** for 3 minutes, till thickened and bubbly, stirring after each minute. Add a drop or two of red food coloring.

BLANCHING VEGETABLES FOR FREEZING

1. Prepare vegetables using the chart below.
2. Use only the amount of vegetable specified.
3. Add water as indicated. Do not add salt.
4. Cover all vegetables during cooking except spinach.
5. Set the Cook Power control at **HIGH.**
6. Cook for the minimum time specified in chart, stirring after *half* the time.
7. Check after the minimum cooking time—vegetable should be evenly heated with bright color throughout.
8. Continue cooking for maximum time, if needed.
9. Plunge into ice water at once. Chill for the same amount of time vegetable was cooked.
10. Drain well. Pat dry with paper toweling.
11. Package in moisture-vaporproof ½-pint or 1-pint freezer containers or freezer weight plastic bags.
12. Seal. Label with contents and date.
13. Freeze immediately at 0° or below. Spread packages out to freeze quickly, stack after solidly frozen.
14. Store at 0° or below for 8 to 12 months.
15. Cook using the chart on pages 179 to 183 as guide.

VEGETABLE	AMOUNT	WEIGHT	METHOD	TIME AT **HIGH**
Asparagus fresh, spears	30 (2 cups)	1 pound	Wash; cut off tough end. Cut spears into 1- to 2-inch lengths. Cook in 2-quart covered casserole with ¼ cup water. Rearrange once.	2½ to 3½ minutes
Beans fresh green or wax	3 cups	1 pound	Wash; remove ends and cut in 1- to 2-inch pieces. Cook in covered 1½-quart casserole with ½ cup water. Rearrange once.	3½ to 5½ minutes
Broccoli fresh, spears		1½ pounds	Wash; remove outer leaves and tough parts of stalks. Split lengthwise into 1-inch stalks. Cook in 2-quart covered casserole with ½ cup water. Turn or rearrange once.	3 to 5 minutes
Carrots fresh, sliced	6 to 8	1 pound	Wash and pare; slice ½ inch thick. Cook in 1½-quart covered casserole with ¼ cup water. Stir once.	3½ to 5½ minutes
Cauliflower fresh, buds	1	1 pound	Wash; remove outer leaves. Cut into flowerets. Cook in covered 2-quart casserole with ½ cup water.	3 to 5 minutes
Corn on the cob fresh	4 ears	1½ pounds	Cut corn from cob. Cook in covered 1-quart casserole with ¼ cup water, stirring once.	4 to 5 minutes
Peas fresh green, shelled	2 cups	2 pounds	Wash. Cook in 1-quart covered casserole with ¼ cup water.	3 to 4½ minutes
Spinach fresh	12 cups	1 pound	Wash and trim; cook in 2-quart casserole. Stir once.	2 to 3 minutes
Squash, summer fresh zucchini or yellow crookneck	2 medium (4 cups)	8 ounces each	Wash; slice ½ inch thick. Cook in 1½-quart covered casserole with ¼ cup water. Stir once.	2½ to 4 minutes
Turnips	4 medium	1 pound	Pare and cube. Cook in covered 1½-quart casserole with ¼ cup water. Stir once.	2½ to 4 minutes

Your microwave oven and freezer are an almost unbeatable team. Together they help you tackle everything from orange juice at sunup to cheesecake pie at sundown.

Included here are many frozen convenience foods grouped by subjects: Beverages; Main Dishes; Accompaniments; Breads; Desserts. Directions for using some frozen products are found throughout the book.

If the frozen product you have isn't listed, look for a similar item and use that general method and timing. Check doneness at the shortest suggested time, then add more time if needed. Also, read the label; many frozen foods now include microwave cooking directions.

Check pages 157 to 165 for preparing main dishes from scratch for freezer-to-table cooking. Remember to package any home-frozen food in serving-size quantities and correct packaging material for easy microwave thawing and heating.

We also tell you how to make your own frozen TV-type dinners on page 134.

BEVERAGES

FROZEN JUICE CONCENTRATE

6-ounce can

Remove metal top from the can. Heat can at **HIGH** for 30 seconds to soften concentrate. Empty into bowl or pitcher and heat again at **HIGH** for 30 seconds. Add water as directed and stir before serving.

If can is metal instead of paper: remove the concentrate from the can and warm in bowl or pitcher for 1 minute at **HIGH**.

For 12-ounce can: Heat opened can 30 seconds at **HIGH**; turn into bowl and heat 1 to 1½ minutes.

For 16-ounce can: Heat opened can 1 minute at **HIGH**; turn into bowl and heat 2 minutes.

FROZEN NONDAIRY COFFEE CREAMER

16-ounce carton

Place opened carton in microwave oven. Cook at **MEDIUM LOW (3)** for 5 minutes; shake and cook 4 minutes more at **MEDIUM LOW (3)**.

MAIN DISHES

FROZEN CHICKEN (fried or battered and cooked)

16-ounce package

Remove chicken pieces from container; place on microwave roasting rack in baking dish. Cook, uncovered, at **MEDIUM LOW (3)** for 6 minutes, till thawed, turning pieces and rearranging once. Cook, uncovered, at **MEDIUM HIGH (7)** for 4 minutes, till hot through, turning chicken over and rearranging once.

FROZEN EGG SUBSTITUTE

8-ounce carton

To thaw: Place opened carton in microwave oven. Cook at **LOW (1)** for 7 minutes; shake and cook at **LOW (1)** for 4 minutes more. Shake again and cook 4 minutes. Let stand 5 minutes. If necessary, break up chunks. For cooking instructions see page 48.

FROZEN ENTREE (in foil tray)

12-ounce package

Uncover foil tray; return foil tray to carton. Cook at **MEDIUM LOW (3)** for 6 minutes; stir and cook at **MEDIUM HIGH (7)** for 8 minutes, giving half turn once.

FROZEN ENTREE (in pouch)

10-ounce package

Place pouch on plate. Puncture top 2 or 3 times with fork. Heat at **HIGH** for 7 to 8 minutes, till hot.

FROZEN BREADED FISH STICKS AND BREADED FISH PORTIONS

Follow directions included with your browning dish.

FROZEN LOW CALORIE DINNER

18-ounce package

Uncover foil tray; return foil tray to carton. Cook at **MEDIUM HIGH (7)** for 15 minutes, giving tray half turn once.

FROZEN MACARONI AND CHEESE

8-ounce package

Uncover foil pan. Cook, uncovered, at **HIGH** for 9 minutes, stirring mixture after about 5 minutes.

For 20-ounce package: Same as above except cook at **HIGH** 12 minutes, stirring after 8 minutes.

FROZEN MEAT AND GRAVY (in pouch)

5-ounce package

Place pouch on plate. Puncture top with fork 2 or 3 times. Cook at **MEDIUM LOW (3)** for 3 to 4 minutes. Then cook at **MEDIUM HIGH (7)** for 2 to 2½ minutes.

FROZEN MEXICAN ENTREE (in foil tray)

22-ounce package

Uncover foil tray; return foil tray to carton. Cook at **MEDIUM LOW (3)** for 10 minutes; separate food if necessary. Cook at **MEDIUM HIGH (7)** for 12 minutes, giving tray half turn once.

FROZEN SANDWICHES

9-ounce package (2 sandwiches)

Place sandwiches on plate. Heat, uncovered, at **MEDIUM LOW (3)** for 5½ to 6 minutes for 2 sandwiches; 4 minutes for 1 sandwich.

FROZEN SOUP (in pouch)

8-ounce package

Place pouch on plate or in serving bowl; puncture top with fork 2 or 3 times. Cook at **HIGH** for 6 to 7 minutes, till mixture is heated through. Serve in bowl.

FROZEN STUFFED CABBAGE ROLLS

14-ounce package

Uncover foil pan; return foil pan to carton. Cook at **MEDIUM LOW (3)** for 18 minutes, giving pan half turn once. Cook at **MEDIUM HIGH (7)** for 7 to 8 minutes.

FROZEN STUFFED SHELLS

16- to 17-ounce package

Uncover foil pan; return foil pan to carton. Cook at **MEDIUM LOW (3)** for 8 to 10 minutes, giving pan half turn once, and stirring sauce at edges. Cook at **MEDIUM HIGH (7)** for 9 to 10 minutes, gently separating pieces after 5 minutes.

FROZEN TURKEY ROAST

3-pound package

To thaw, remove metal closure from end of package; leave roast in plastic wrapping (or remove from foil pan). Place in 12×7½×2-inch baking dish. Cook, uncovered, at **MEDIUM LOW (3)** for 15 minutes. Turn turkey roast over and cook, uncovered, at **MEDIUM LOW (3)** for 15 minutes more. Let stand 10 minutes to complete thawing.

To cook, place thawed roast, skin side up, on microwave roasting rack or inverted saucers in 12×7½×2-inch baking dish. Cook, uncovered, at **HIGH** for 36 to 38 minutes, (till meat thermometer registers 180°) giving dish a half turn once. Let stand 15 minutes before serving.

Do not use conventional meat thermometer in microwave oven during cooking.

FROZEN TV-TYPE HOMEMADE DINNERS
(see page 134)

FROZEN WELSH RAREBIT

10-ounce package

Uncover foil tray; return foil tray to carton. Cook at **HIGH** for 6 to 7 minutes, stirring twice.

ACCOMPANIMENTS

FROZEN BAKED STUFFED POTATOES

12-ounce package

Place potatoes on serving plate; cover with waxed paper. Cook at **HIGH** 6 to 7 minutes, turning plate once.

FROZEN FRENCH FRIED POTATOES

16-ounce package

Place on paper-towel-lined plate or paper plate. Cook, uncovered, at **HIGH** for 6 minutes, till hot. Potatoes will not be crisp.

FROZEN FRIED POTATO NUGGETS

8-ounce package

Place on paper-towel-lined plate or paper plate. Cook, uncovered, at **HIGH** for 3 to 4 minutes, till hot. Nuggets will not be crisp.
For 16-ounce package: Same except cook 7 minutes.

FROZEN RICE (in pouch)

12-ounce package

Place pouch in bowl. Puncture top with fork 2 or 3 times. Cook at **HIGH** for 7 to 8 minutes, stirring or rearranging contents once.

FROZEN VEGETABLES (see pages 179 to 183)

FROZEN VEGETABLES WITH SAUCE CUBES

8- to 10-ounce package

Place in 1-quart casserole; add water called for on package. Cook, covered, at **HIGH** for 5 to 5½ minutes, till sauce is thickened, stirring after 2 minutes.

FROZEN VEGETABLES (in foil casserole)

12-ounce package

Uncover foil tray; return foil tray to carton. Cook at **MEDIUM HIGH (7)** for 11 to 12 minutes or till heated through, giving tray half turn once.

FROZEN VEGETABLES WITH SAUCE (in pouch)

9- to 10-ounce package

Place pouch in bowl. Puncture top 2 or 3 times with fork to vent. Cook at **HIGH** for 6 to 8 minutes, stirring or rearranging contents once.

BREADS

FROZEN BREAD DOUGH (see page 77)

FROZEN BREAD, DINNER ROLLS, SWEET ROLLS, HAMBURGER BUNS, FRANKFURTER BUNS, DOUGHNUTS (see page 36)

FROZEN PANCAKE BATTER

17-ounce carton

Place opened carton in microwave oven. Cook at **MEDIUM LOW (3)** for 6 minutes; shake and cook 2 to 3 minutes more at **MEDIUM LOW (3)**. Let stand 5 minutes. If necessary, break up chunks.

FROZEN HOMEMADE PANCAKES (see page 141)

THAWING AND HEATING FROZEN CONVENIENCE BREADS

Remove cover from foil packages; place other breads on paper towel. Heat, uncovered, at **MEDIUM LOW (3)**. Breads may become dry, hard, or tough if overheated.

Frozen Baked Product	Amount	Time To Thaw at **MEDIUM LOW (3)**
Bagels	1	55 to 60 sec.
	2	1¼ to 1½ min.
	4	2 to 2¼ min.
Mini-doughnuts	2	30 to 40 sec.
	4	1 to 1¼ min.
	6	1¼ to 1½ min.
Muffin rounds or Corn rounds	1	25 to 30 sec.
	2	45 to 50 sec.
	4	1¼ to 1½ min.
Caramel rolls	10½-oz.	3 to 3¼ min.*
Danish coffee cake	13-oz.	5 min.*
Round coffee cake	9½-oz.	3 min.*
Cinnamon rolls	8¼-oz.	2 to 2¼ min.

*Give foil pan a half turn once.

DESSERTS

FROZEN BROWNIES

13-ounce package

Uncover foil tray. Cook brownies, uncovered, at **LOW (1)** for 4 minutes, turning tray once. Let stand 5 to 10 minutes before serving.

FROZEN CAKE (frosted 3-layer)

17-ounce package

Remove from package; place on plate. Heat, uncovered, at **LOW (1)** for 4 minutes.

For 12-ounce one-layer frosted cake: Same as above except heat for 3 minutes.

FROZEN CHEESECAKE

17-ounce package

Uncover foil tray. Heat cheesecake, uncovered, at **LOW (1)** for 4 minutes.

FROZEN FRUIT (see also page 82)

16-ounce package unsweetened fruit

Pour fruit into bowl. Heat, uncovered, at **MEDIUM LOW (3)** for 6 to 7 minutes, breaking apart after 3 minutes.

FROZEN PIE (2-crust unbaked)

26-ounce package

Remove pie from package. Heat, uncovered, at **HIGH** for 10 minutes. Place on baking sheet; bake in *conventional oven* at 450° F for 15 minutes, till crust is evenly browned.

For 37-ounce package: Same except cook, uncovered, at **HIGH** for 12 to 13 minutes; then bake in *conventional oven* at 450° F for 15 minutes.

FROZEN POUND CAKE

10¾-ounce package

Uncover foil tray. Heat cake, uncovered, at **LOW (1)** for 5 minutes; let stand about 10 minutes before serving.

FROZEN WHIPPED DESSERT TOPPING

4½-ounce carton

Place unopened carton in microwave oven. Heat at **MEDIUM LOW (3)** for 1 minute.

For 9-ounce carton: Same except heat 1½ minutes.

NEPTUNE'S HADDOCK DELIGHT

Tartar sauce and dillweed add spunk—

Total cooking time: 8 minutes

7	1							

1 8¾-ounce package frozen haddock dinner
2 tablespoons tartar sauce
⅛ teaspoon dried dillweed
1 small slice Swiss cheese

Remove foil top from frozen dinner. Place dinner back in carton. Cook at **MEDIUM HIGH (7)** for 7 to 8 minutes or till heated through, giving a half turn once. Spread haddock with tartar sauce; sprinkle with dillweed. Place cheese atop fish. Cook, uncovered, at **HIGH** for 1 to 1½ minutes or till cheese melts. Makes 1 serving.

HAM DINNER SUPREME

Total cooking time: 8 minutes 30 seconds

7	1:30							

1 10¼-ounce package frozen ham dinner
2 tablespoons canned whole cranberry sauce
1 canned pineapple slice
1 tablespoon finely chopped celery
6 to 8 miniature marshmallows

Remove foil top from dinner. Spread ham with cranberry sauce; top with pineapple slice. Sprinkle celery over peas. Cover. Cook at **MEDIUM HIGH (7)** for 7 to 8 minutes or till heated through, giving a half turn once. Place marshmallows on sweet potatoes. Cook, uncovered, at **MEDIUM HIGH (7)** for 1½ to 2 minutes or till marshmallows begin to melt. Makes 1 serving.

SAVORY MACARONI AND CHEESE

Total cooking time: 11 minutes 30 seconds

0:30	9	2						

1 tablespoon butter or margarine
2 tablespoons dried bread crumbs
1 tablespoon snipped parsley
Dash dried mixed herbs
• • •
1 12¼-ounce package frozen macaroni and cheese dinner
2 tomato slices

In small bowl, cook butter at **HIGH** for 30 seconds. Stir in crumbs, parsley, and herbs; set aside. Remove foil from frozen dinner. Place dinner back in carton. Cook at **MEDIUM HIGH (7)** for 9 minutes, giving half turn once. Top macaroni with tomato slices; sprinkle with crumbs. Cook, uncovered, at **MEDIUM HIGH (7)** for 2 minutes or till heated through. Makes 1 serving.

ITALIAN VEAL PARMIGIANO

Total cooking time: 8 minutes

7	1							

1 12¼-ounce package frozen veal parmigiano dinner
1 2-ounce can sliced mushrooms, drained
1 tablespoon chopped pimiento-stuffed green olives
Ground cinnamon
1 small slice mozzarella cheese

Remove foil top from frozen dinner. Spoon mushrooms over veal. Top peas with chopped olives. Sprinkle apple slices with cinnamon. Place dinner back in carton. Cook at **MEDIUM HIGH (7)** for 7 to 8 minutes or till heated through, giving a half turn once. Place cheese over veal. Cook, uncovered, at **HIGH** for 1 minute or till cheese melts. Makes 1 serving.

SPECIAL MEAT LOAF DINNER

Total cooking time: 11 minutes

2	8	1						

2 slices bacon
1 10¾-ounce package frozen meat loaf dinner (with brownie)
Semisweet chocolate pieces
Chopped nuts
Canned French fried onions

On paper plate, layer bacon and paper towels. Cook at **HIGH** for 2 minutes or till crisp. Crumble bacon and set aside. Remove foil top from dinner. Remove brownie; set aside. Place dinner back in carton. Cook at **MEDIUM HIGH (7)** for 8 to 9 minutes or till heated through, giving a half turn once. Replace brownie. Top brownie with semisweet chocolate pieces and nuts. Sprinkle bacon over meat loaf and onions over beans. Cook, uncovered, at **HIGH** for 1 to 1½ minutes or till chocolate melts. Makes 1 serving.

EASY PEPPER SWISS STEAK

Total cooking time: 9 minutes

8	1							

1 10-ounce package frozen Swiss steak dinner
¼ green pepper, cut in strips
1 onion slice, separated in rings
Garlic salt
2 small tomato wedges

Remove foil top from dinner. Top steak with green pepper strips and onion rings. Sprinkle lightly with garlic salt. Place dinner back in carton. Cook at **MEDIUM HIGH (7)** for 8 to 10 minutes or till heated through, giving a half turn once. Add tomato wedges. Cook, uncovered, at **HIGH** for 1 minute. Makes 1 serving.

CHARTS INDEX

REHEATING RENEWS FLAVOR

Dad's stuck in a traffic jam, Junior is still at his guitar lesson, Mom's working late—some days it's just impossible to eat together. At times like this, your microwave oven can be your short-order cook. Simply plan to cook as usual, separating out the single portion for the latecomer. Then cover and refrigerate. Dad, Junior, or Mom can reheat that portion when they arrive. Or maybe it's just you for lunch, and you'd like to heat up what's left of last night's dinner.

The chart here tells how to warm up small amounts of already-cooked foods. If your leftover choice isn't on the chart, choose a similar item and use that timing. All are reheated, covered, at the **MEDIUM HIGH (7)** setting because the food is already cooked and only needs heating.

Timing for all meats, main dishes, and side dishes is based on storage at refrigerator temperature; desserts and breads at room temperature.

If you'd like to warm beef stroganoff or macaroni and cheese, you might want to lower the setting to **MEDIUM (5)** to be sure the sour cream and cheese warm more slowly. Frosted cakes or sweet rolls may also be better at a lower setting so the icing won't melt.

KEEP LEFTOVERS FRESH

Whether you have a half-cup of gravy or half a roast left from dinner, the treatment is the same.

Cool the food quickly—don't let it stand at room temperature.

Wrap it well in a tightly-closed container. If you can use the food within the next few days, use refrigerator-to-microwave oven containers rather than foil. To preserve moisture, keep the roast in one large piece for storage rather than slicing it. Store poultry, gravy, and stuffing separately. If the amount of food is more than you can use shortly, wrap it in meal-size portions in freezer paper or bags and freeze.

Use the refrigerated food within two to three days.

Never refreeze uncooked portions of food. See page 157 for more freezer tips.

DISGUISE THE REST OF THE ROAST

All it takes is a little ingenuity to put new faces on leftovers. Remember that every bite of food you use helps stretch the food budget a little farther.

Beef leftovers can make a marvelous chef's salad, hot sandwich, stew, or hash. Use ham for a casserole, ham loaf, kabobs, split pea soup, or creamed ham with hard-cooked eggs. Lamb might lend itself to curry, shepherd's pie, or spaghetti; chicken and turkey leftovers could become Southern pot pie, meaty stuffing, corn chowder, or stir-fry with cooked rice.

Dabs of vegetables might dress up pancakes, canned soup, or scrambled eggs; cooked potatoes are good for hash, potato cakes, or cheesy au gratin dish.

Turn to page 134 for directions for making your own frozen TV-type individual dinners. And page 99 tells how to make cold coffee into an exotic dessert.

FOOD	AMOUNT	TIME AT MEDIUM HIGH (7)
Dinner:		
Meat, potato, and vegetable	1 serving each on dinner plate	2½ to 3 minutes
Meats:		
Chicken	4-ounce piece	2 minutes
Sliced beef, pork, ham, or turkey	2-ounce slice	1 to 1¼ minutes
Hamburger (without bun)	1 patty	1 minute
Pork chop	1	1½ minutes
Main Dishes:		
Meat-vegetable casserole	1 cup	3½ to 4 minutes
Chili	1 cup	3½ to 4 minutes
Spaghetti sauce	1 cup	4 minutes
Beef stew	1 cup	3½ to 4 minutes
Side Dishes:		
Vegetables, rice or noodles, cooked	1 cup	3 to 4 minutes
Mashed potatoes	1 cup	4½ to 5 minutes
Baked beans	1 cup	3 minutes
Desserts:		
Pie	1 wedge	30 seconds
Cake, unfrosted	1 square	30 seconds
Breads:		
Sweet roll	1	20 to 30 seconds
Bread (homemade, sliced) or doughnut	1	10 to 15 seconds
Dinner roll, muffin, or coffee cake	1 piece	15 to 20 seconds

CAKE MIX MAGIC

Choose your favorite one- or two-layer mix and prepare the batter as usual. Select the appropriate baking dish from the chart; you need not grease and flour it. Grease and sugar tube and fluted cake dishes for easier cake removal. If you intend to turn out a cake for layering, line the bottom of the dish with waxed paper, cut to fit.

Fill the dish about half full, using the amount of batter indicated in the chart. *Don't use more*—microwave cakes rise higher than those baked conventionally. Any extra batter can be used for cupcakes. Bake one layer at a time. Judge doneness by inserting a wooden pick near the center—pick should come out clean. Some standing time may be needed to dry the top completely. Cool layer or tube cakes on a flat surface 10 minutes, then *invert* on wire rack. Cool other cakes on a flat surface 10 minutes, then on wire rack.

Expect the cake's surface to be unbrowned and somewhat uneven; results may vary with brand of cake mix.

PRODUCT	BAKING DISH SIZE	SETTING	TIME	TIPS
Cake one-layer mix	8×1½-inch (round)	**MEDIUM (5)** then **HIGH**	6 to 7 minutes then 1 minute	Use all 2¼ cups batter. After 4 minutes, give dish half turn.
two-layer mix	two dishes, each 8×1½-inch (round)	**MEDIUM (5)** then **HIGH**	6 to 7 minutes then 1 minute	Divide batter between 2 dishes, using 2½ to 2¾ cups for each. Cook one at a time. After 4 minutes, give dish half turn.
two-layer mix	12×7½×2-inch	**MEDIUM (5)** then **HIGH**	13 minutes then 2½ minutes	Use scant 4 cups batter. After 7 minutes, give dish half turn. Use remaining batter for cupcakes.
two-layer mix	tube or fluted dish	**MEDIUM (5)** then **HIGH**	10 minutes then 4 to 5 minutes	Use all batter. After 5 minutes, give dish half turn.
Cupcakes or Muffins	1 in paper bake cup in 6-ounce custard cup	**HIGH**	30 to 35 seconds	Use 2 tablespoons batter for each.
	2	**HIGH**	45 to 50 seconds	Use 2 tablespoons batter for each.
	4 in custard cup as above or microwave muffin dish	**HIGH**	1 minute 25 seconds	Use 2 tablespoons batter for each. Rearrange custard cups or give muffin dish half turn after 40 seconds.
	6 in custard cup as above or microwave muffin dish	**HIGH**	2 minutes 25 seconds	Use 2 tablespoons batter for each. Rearrange custard cups or give muffin dish half turn after 1 minute 10 seconds.
Snack-type cake 14- to 15-ounce mix	8×8×2-inch	**MEDIUM (5)** then **HIGH**	8 minutes then 2½ minutes	Place custard cup in center of dish before adding batter. Use all of batter. After 4 minutes, give dish half turn. Let stand 10 minutes to cool.
Pound cake 16- to 17-ounce mix	two dishes, each 9×5×3-inch or 8½×4½×2½-inch	**MEDIUM (5)**	7 to 8 minutes	Divide batter between 2 dishes. Cook one at a time. After 3 and 5 minutes, give dish quarter turns. Let stand 10 minutes to cool.
Gingerbread 14-ounce mix	8×8×2-inch	**MEDIUM (5)** then **HIGH**	5 minutes then 2 to 2½ minutes	Use all of batter. After 3 minutes, give dish half turn.
Brownie mix 23-ounce pkg.	two dishes, each 8×1½-inch (round)	**MEDIUM (5)**	8½ minutes	Divide batter between 2 dishes. Cook one at a time. After 3 minutes and 5 minutes, give dish quarter turns.
8-ounce pkg.	9×5×3-inch or 8½×4½×2½-inch	**MEDIUM (5)**	7½ minutes	Use all of batter. After 3 and 5 minutes, give dish quarter turns.

Microwave ovens and convenience foods can make our lives easier. Many shortcut food products have been included throughout this book in chapters where they are helpful.

In this chapter canned and packaged mixes are grouped in sections by subject: Appetizers and Beverages; Main Dishes; Accompaniments; Sauces; Breads; Desserts.

If the convenience food you have isn't listed, look for a similar one and use that general method and timing. (Always check doneness at the shortest time stated, then add more cooking time as needed.) If a product similar to the one you want to use is not listed, it may not be suitable for microwave cooking.

APPETIZERS AND BEVERAGES

CHEESE FONDUE

14-ounce package

Remove from foil package; place in 1-quart casserole or serving dish. Cook, uncovered, at **MEDIUM HIGH (7)** for 4 minutes 15 seconds, stirring after each minute for the first 2 minutes, then every 45 seconds. Serve warm.

COCOA (see page 48)

INSTANT COFFEE AND TEA (see page 34)

MAIN DISHES

ADD HAMBURGER DINNER MIX

8- or 14-ounce package

Place meat in 2-quart casserole. Cook, uncovered, at **HIGH** for 5 minutes, stirring 3 times. Drain off fat. Add mix and ingredients as package directs (subtract ½ cup liquid, if desired). Cook, covered, at **MEDIUM (5)** for 15 to 20 minutes, stirring twice.

ADD TUNA DINNER MIX

8-ounce package

Prepare mix *using oven method*, combining ingredients in 2-quart casserole (subtract ¼ cup liquid, if desired). Cook, covered, at **MEDIUM (5)** for 15 to 20 minutes, stirring twice. Cook, covered, at **HIGH** for 3 minutes.

CANNED MEAT-VEGETABLE CASSEROLE MIXTURES

8-ounce can

Spoon into small serving bowl. Cook, covered, at **HIGH** for 2 minutes, till heated through, stirring once.

For 16-ounce can: Same as above except cook, covered, at **HIGH** for 4 minutes, stirring once.

MACARONI AND CHEESE MIX

7¼-ounce package

Cook macaroni *conventionally*. Drain; place in 1½-quart casserole. Add ingredients as package directs. Cook, covered, at **HIGH** for 3 to 4 minutes, stirring once.

For a 14-ounce package: Same as above except use 2-quart casserole; cook at **HIGH** 2 minutes.

ORIENTAL (DIVIDER PACK) DINNER

2 cans (28 ounces total)

In 1½-quart casserole, heat contents of small can, uncovered, at **HIGH** for 3 minutes, stirring once. Drain vegetables from large can; add to casserole and cook, uncovered, at **HIGH** for 4 minutes, stirring once.

PEPPER STEAK DINNER MIX

16-ounce package

In 2-quart casserole, cook meat, uncovered, at **HIGH** for 5 minutes, stirring 3 times. Drain off fat. Stir together sauce mix and water as package directs; add to casserole with drained vegetables. Cook, uncovered, at **HIGH** for 8 minutes, till thickened, stirring after 3 minutes, then after each minute.

SPAGHETTI DINNER MIX

8-ounce package

Cook spaghetti *conventionally*. In 4-cup glass measure, combine sauce and ingredients as directed on package. Cook, covered, at **HIGH** for 3 minutes, till boiling. Cook at **MEDIUM (5)** for 5 minutes. Serve over spaghetti.

For 19½-ounce package: Prepare as above except pour sauce from can into 4-cup glass measure; heat, uncovered, at **HIGH** for 2½ to 3 minutes. Serve over spaghetti; sprinkle with cheese.

VIENNA SAUSAGES

5-ounce can

Remove sausages from can; place on paper plate. Cook, uncovered, at **MEDIUM HIGH (7)** for 45 seconds.

ACCOMPANIMENTS

CREAMED POTATOES MIX

4¾-ounce package

In 2-quart casserole, heat 1¼ cups water at **HIGH**, uncovered, for 3 minutes. Add 2 cups milk and sauce mix and potatoes from package. Cook, covered, at **MEDIUM (5)** for 20 minutes, stirring 3 times. Let stand, covered, 5 minutes.

INSTANT MASHED POTATOES

packaged instant mashed potatoes

In 4-cup glass measure or 1½-quart bowl, combine ingredients (usually water, milk, butter, and salt) as package directs. Cook, covered, at **HIGH** till mixture is boiling. Stir in instant potatoes. Let stand before serving, if package directs.

SCALLOPED POTATOES MIX

5½-ounce package

In 2-quart casserole, heat 2½ cups water, uncovered, at **HIGH** for 5 minutes. Add milk and butter as package directs; stir in sauce mix and potatoes from package. Cook, covered, at **MEDIUM (5)** for 20 minutes, stirring 3 times, till potatoes are tender.

NOODLES ROMANOFF MIX

5½-ounce package

In 2-quart casserole, combine noodles and sauce mix from package with 1½ cups water and ½ cup milk. Cook, covered, at **MEDIUM (5)** for 18 minutes, stirring mixture 3 times, till noodles are tender. Let stand, covered, for about 5 minutes before serving.

QUICK-COOKING RICE

packaged precooked rice (minute type rice)

In 1-quart casserole, combine water and salt as package directs. Cook, uncovered, at **HIGH** till boiling. Stir in rice. Let stand, covered, for 5 minutes. Fluff rice mixture with a fork before serving.

SEASONED REGULAR RICE MIX

5½-ounce package

In 2-quart casserole, combine rice and additions as package directs. Cook, covered, at **HIGH** for 6 minutes, till boiling, stirring once. Cook, covered, at **MEDIUM (5)** for 12 minutes, stirring twice. Let stand, covered, for 5 minutes.
For 8-ounce package rice with vermicelli: Same as above.

SEASONED QUICK-COOKING RICE MIX

6-ounce package (minute type rice)

In 1½-quart casserole, combine rice and seasonings from package. Stir in additions as directed on package. Cook, uncovered, at **HIGH** for 6½ to 7 minutes, till boiling. Let stand, covered, 10 minutes before serving.

SOUP, CANNED AND PACKAGED (see page 52)

STUFFING MIX (15-minute)

5-, 6-, or 7-ounce package

In 1½-quart casserole, combine water and butter with seasoning packet as package directs. Cook, covered, at **HIGH** for 4 to 4½ minutes, till boiling. Cook, covered, at **MEDIUM (5)** for 3 minutes. Stir in stuffing crumbs and let stand, covered, 5 minutes. Fluff with fork.

CANNED VEGETABLES

8-ounce can

Pour undrained vegetables from can into bowl. Cook, covered with waxed paper, at **HIGH** for 2 minutes. Drain.
For 12-ounce can: Same as above except cook 2½ to 3 minutes, stirring once.
For 16-ounce can: Same as above except cook 3½ minutes, stirring once.

SAUCES AND GRAVIES

CANNED GRAVY

10½-ounce can

Pour gravy into serving bowl. Heat, uncovered, at **HIGH** for 4 minutes, till hot, stirring once.

CANNED SAUCE

10¼- to 11-ounce can

Pour sauce into serving bowl. Heat, uncovered, at **HIGH** for 4 minutes, till hot, stirring once.

GRAVY MIX (see page 151)

SAUCE MIX (see page 151)

SPAGHETTI SAUCE MIX

1 envelope

In 4-cup glass measure or 2-quart casserole, combine ingredients as package directs (usually tomato sauce or tomato paste, water, and butter or oil). For 2 to 2½ cups mixture, cook, uncovered, at **HIGH** for 6 to 7 minutes, till boiling, stirring after 3 minutes. Cook at **MEDIUM (5)**, covered, 10 minutes more, stirring once or twice.

BREADS

BREADS, DINNER ROLLS, SWEET ROLLS, HAMBURGER BUNS, FRANKFURTER BUNS, DOUGHNUTS (see page 36)

COFFEE CAKE MIX

10½-ounce package

Prepare batter as package directs. Spoon into ungreased 8×1½-inch round baking dish. Cook, uncovered, at **MEDIUM (5)** for 9 minutes, giving dish half turn after 5 minutes.

For 14-ounce package: Prepare batter as directed; pour into 8×8×2-inch baking dish. Cook, uncovered, at **MEDIUM (5)** for 12 minutes, then at **HIGH** for 1½ minutes, giving dish quarter turns twice. Let stand 15 minutes.

CORN BREAD MIX

8½-ounce package

Prepare batter as package directs. Spoon into ungreased 8×8×2-inch baking dish. Cook, uncovered, at **MEDIUM (5)** for 7 minutes, giving dish half turn once.

For 10-ounce package: Same except use 8×1½-inch round baking dish; cook at **MEDIUM (5)** for 8 minutes.

For 15-ounce package: Same except use 8×8×2-inch baking dish and cook at **MEDIUM (5)** for 10 minutes.

HOT ROLL MIX (see page 77)

NUT BREAD MIX

15½-ounce package

Prepare batter as package directs. Spoon into waxed paper-lined 9×5×3-inch loaf dish. Cook, uncovered, at **MEDIUM (5)** for 12 minutes; then cook at **HIGH** for 2 minutes, giving dish half turn once. Let stand 10 minutes.

DESSERTS

BROWNIE MIX (see page 175)

CAKE MIX, POUND CAKE MIX, CUPCAKES (see page 175)

FRUIT-FLAVORED GELATIN (see page 34)

FUDGE MIX

10½-ounce package

In 4-cup glass measure, combine water and butter as package directs. Cook, uncovered, at **HIGH** for 1 to 1½ minutes, till butter melts. Stir in dry ingredients till mixture is moistened. Heat, uncovered, at **MEDIUM (5)** for 2 minutes, stirring twice. Cool in buttered dish.

GINGERBREAD (see page 175)

PIE CRUST MIX OR STICKS (see page 117)

PUDDING MIX (regular)

3- to 4-ounce package

In 4-cup glass measure, combine mix and milk as package directs. Cook, uncovered, at **HIGH** for 6 minutes, stirring every 2 minutes, till thickened and bubbly. Cool.

COOKING STIR FRIED VEGETABLES

Asparagus: Preheat browning dish at **HIGH** for 5 minutes. Add 1 tablespoon cooking oil. Stir in 3 cups cut fresh asparagus (about 1 pound). Cook, covered, at **HIGH** for 3 minutes. Stir. Cook, covered, at **HIGH** for 2 minutes. Stir in 1 tablespoon butter or margarine. Season to taste with salt and pepper.

Mushrooms: Preheat browning dish at **HIGH** for 5 minutes. Add 1 teaspoon cooking oil. Stir in 1 cup fresh mushroom slices. Cook, covered, at **HIGH** for 45 seconds. Stir. Cook at **HIGH** 30 seconds. Stir in 1 tablespoon butter or margarine. Season to taste with salt and pepper.

Onion slices: Preheat browning dish at **HIGH** for 4 minutes. Add 1 teaspoon cooking oil. Stir in ½ cup onion slices. Cook, covered, at **HIGH** for 1½ minutes. Stir. Cook, covered, at **HIGH** for 45 seconds. Stir in 1 tablespoon butter or margarine. Season to taste with salt and pepper.

Frozen stir-fried Japanese- or Chinese-style vegetables: Preheat browning dish at **HIGH** for 4 minutes. Add 2 tablespoons cooking oil. Add vegetables from one 10-ounce package frozen Japanese- or Chinese-style vegetables (reserve the seasoning packet). Cook, covered, at **HIGH** for 3 minutes. Stir in the seasonings from the seasoning packet and the water called for on the package. Cook, covered, at **HIGH** for 2 minutes.

Zucchini: Preheat browning dish at **HIGH** for 4 minutes. Add 1 tablespoon cooking oil. Add 2 cups (about 8 ounces) sliced zucchini. Cook, covered, at **HIGH** for 3 minutes. Stir. Cook, covered, at **HIGH** for 2 minutes or till tender. Season to taste with salt, pepper, and a sprinkling of dried dillweed.

Pea Pods: Preheat browning dish at **HIGH** for 4 minutes. Add 1 tablespoon cooking oil. Add one 6-ounce package frozen pea pods. Cook, covered, at **HIGH** for 2 minutes. Stir. Cook, covered, at **HIGH** for 1 minute.

COOKING FRESH AND FROZEN VEGETABLES

Use the **HIGH** setting for all vegetables in the chart except dried lima, navy, and pinto beans.

Check the chart for directions; most vegetables are cooked covered with a casserole lid or waxed paper. Uncover carefully to avoid steam burns. Chart times are for vegetables cooked tender-crisp; if you prefer softer vegetables, cook them longer.

Pierce skins of potatoes, sweet potatoes, and winter squash with a fork before cooking to vent steam during cooking. Arrange stalks of fresh vegetables toward outside of the dish, tender parts toward center.

Many frozen vegetables can be cooked right in the carton or pouch. Before cooking, loosen the paper on the carton or cut several slits in carton. Prick the plastic pouch on top once or twice to vent the steam during cooking. Remove vegetables from foil packages and transfer to a glass cooking dish.

Turn to page 170 for preparing frozen convenience vegetables: baked stuffed potatoes, French fries, fried potato nuggets, and vegetable combinations with sauce cube concentrate, or those in foil casseroles or cooking pouches with sauce. Canned vegetables are on page 177.

Be careful not to overcook vegetables—they will become mushy if they are cooked too long. And remember to remove vegetables from the microwave oven when they are a little less done than you would cook them conventionally. Why? Because vegetables will continue to cook after you remove them from the microwave oven during the standing time. Leave the vegetables covered for 5 minutes to finish cooking. In the case of baked potatoes, remove them from the microwave oven when still slightly firm, then wrap in foil and let stand for 5 minutes to finish cooking. So plan your dinner so that the vegetables are done 5 minutes ahead of mealtime.

VEGETABLE	AMOUNT	WEIGHT	METHOD	TIME AT **HIGH**
Artichokes fresh, whole	1	10 ounce	Wash; remove stem and cut 1 inch from top. Brush cut edges with lemon juice. Cook in covered 2-quart casserole or wrap in waxed paper.	4 to 5 minutes
	2	SAME	SAME AS ABOVE	6 to 7 minutes
frozen hearts		9 ounces	Cook in 1-quart covered casserole with 2 tablespoons water. Stir once.	5 to 6 minutes
Asparagus fresh, spears	12–15 (1 cup)	8 ounces	Wash; cut off tough end. Leave whole or cut spears into 3- to 4-inch lengths. Cook in 1-quart covered casserole with ¼ cup water. Rearrange once.	3 to 4 minutes
	30 (2 cups)	1 pound	Same except use 2-quart casserole.	7 to 8 minutes
frozen, cut or whole	1½ cups	10 ounces	Cook in 1- or 1½-quart covered casserole. Rearrange or stir once.	8 to 10 minutes
Beans fresh green or wax	3 cups	1 pound	Wash; remove ends and cut in 1- to 2-inch pieces or leave whole. Place in 1½-quart casserole with water to cover. Cook, covered, rearranging once.	16 to 17 minutes
	4 cups		SAME AS ABOVE	19 to 20 minutes
frozen green or wax French-style or cut	1⅔ cups	9 ounces	Cook in 1-quart covered casserole with 2 tablespoons water. Stir once.	10 to 12 minutes
frozen Italian green	1½ cups	9 ounces	Cook in 1-quart covered casserole with 2 tablespoons water. Stir once.	6 to 8 minutes
frozen lima beans, baby or large	1½ to 1¾ cups	10 ounces	Cook in 1-quart covered casserole with ¼ cup water. Stir once.	9 to 10 minutes

COOKING FRESH AND FROZEN VEGETABLES

VEGETABLE	AMOUNT	WEIGHT	METHOD	TIME AT **HIGH**
Beans (continued)				
dried lima beans	1 cup	8 ounces	Rinse and presoak beans overnight in 3 cups water. Drain. Bring 1 quart water to boiling; add to beans in 3- to 5-quart casserole. Cook, covered, at **MEDIUM (5)**. Stir once.	45 minutes at **MEDIUM (5)**
navy beans	1 cup	8 ounces	Same as above for lima beans	60 minutes at **MEDIUM (5)**
pinto beans	1 cup	8 ounces	Same as above for lima beans	45 minutes at **MEDIUM (5)**
Beets				
fresh whole	6 medium (2 cups)	1 pound	Cut off all but 1 inch of stem and root. Wash; don't pare. Cook in 2-quart covered casserole with ½ cup water. Stir once. Peel when done.	18 to 20 minutes
fresh beet greens	4 cups	1 pound	Wash. Cut stems into 2-inch lengths. Cook in covered 2-quart casserole.	7 to 8 minutes
fresh, sliced or diced	6 medium (3 cups)	1 pound without leaves (1½ pounds with leaves)	Cut off all but 1 inch of stem and root; wash and pare. Slice or cube. Cook in 1½-quart covered casserole with ¼ cup water. Stir once.	11 to 12 minutes
Broccoli				
fresh, whole		1 pound	Wash; remove outer leaves and tough parts of stalks. Split stalk almost to bud. Cook whole in 2-quart covered casserole with ¼ cup water. Turn or rearrange once.	7 to 9 minutes
fresh, cut	4 to 5 cups	1½ pounds	Same as above except cut in 1½- to 2-inch pieces. Use 1½-quart covered casserole with ¼ cup water and stir once.	10 to 12 minutes
frozen, whole or chopped		10 ounces	Cook in covered 1½-quart casserole with 2 to 3 tablespoons water. Stir or rearrange once.	8 minutes
Brussels sprouts				
fresh	4 cups (30)	1 pound	Cut off wilted leaves. Wash. Halve large sprouts. Cook in 1½-quart covered casserole with 2 tablespoons water; stir once.	8 to 9 minutes
frozen		10 ounces	Cook in 1-quart covered casserole with 2 tablespoons water. Stir once.	9 to 10 minutes
Cabbage				
fresh, wedges	6 wedges	1½-pound head	Remove wilted outer leaves; cut in wedges. Cook in 2-quart covered casserole with 2 tablespoons water. Rearrange once.	10 to 12 minutes
fresh, shredded	4½ cups	1 pound	Same as above except remove core and shred. Use 1½- or 2-quart covered casserole with 2 tablespoons water. Stir once.	10 to 12 minutes

VEGETABLE	AMOUNT	WEIGHT	METHOD	TIME AT **HIGH**
Carrots fresh, sliced or diced	6 to 8	1 pound	Wash and pare; slice ½ inch thick or into ⅜ inch cubes. Cook in 1½-quart covered casserole with ¼ cup water. Stir once.	10 to 12 minutes
	4	8 ounces	Same except use 2 tablespoons water; 1-quart casserole.	6 to 7 minutes
frozen, cut	2 cups	10 ounces	Cook in 1-quart covered casserole with 2 tablespoons water. Stir once.	6 to 7 minutes
Cauliflower fresh, whole	1	1 pound	Wash; remove outer leaves. Cook in covered 1½-quart casserole with 2 tablespoons water.	7 to 9 minutes
fresh, broken into buds	6 cups	1 pound	Same as above but break into buds. Stir once.	7 to 8 minutes
frozen		10 ounces	Cook in 1-quart covered casserole with 2 tablespoons water. Stir once.	7 to 8 minutes
Celery fresh, sliced	6 stalks (4 cups)	1 pound	Remove leaves and root end; wash; slice. Cook in covered 1½-quart casserole with 2 tablespoons water. Stir once.	11 to 13 minutes
Corn on the cob fresh	1 ear	7 ounces	Remove husks; rinse. Cook on plate; cover with waxed paper. Or use covered baking dish.	2 to 3 minutes
	2 ears		SAME AS ABOVE	4 to 5 minutes
	3 ears		SAME AS ABOVE	6 to 7 minutes
	4 ears		SAME AS ABOVE	8 to 9 minutes
	5 ears		SAME AS ABOVE	10 to 12 minutes
	6 ears		SAME AS ABOVE	12 to 14 minutes
frozen	1 ear		SAME AS ABOVE	4 to 5 minutes
	2 ears		SAME AS ABOVE	6 to 8 minutes
	4 ears		SAME AS ABOVE	11 to 13 minutes
Corn, whole kernel fresh	2 cups (from 3 ears)		Rinse; cut from cob. Cook in 1-quart covered casserole with 2 tablespoons water. Stir once.	5 to 6 minutes
frozen		10 ounces	Cook in 1-quart covered casserole with 2 tablespoons water. Stir once.	6 to 7 minutes
Eggplant fresh	1 medium	1¼ pounds	Pare and cube or slice; cook in 2-quart covered casserole with 2 tablespoons water. Stir once.	4 to 5 minutes

COOKING FRESH AND FROZEN VEGETABLES

VEGETABLE	AMOUNT	WEIGHT	METHOD	TIME AT **HIGH**
Leeks fresh	3 medium	¼ pound	Cut off top to within 2 inches of white part. Halve if necessary. Remove outer leaves; wash. Cook in 1½-quart covered casserole with 2 tablespoons water. Stir once.	5 to 6 minutes
Mixed vegetables frozen	2 cups	10 ounces	Cook in covered 1-quart casserole with 2 tablespoons water. Stir once.	8 to 10 minutes
Okra frozen, whole		10 ounces	Cook in covered 1-quart casserole with 2 tablespoons water. Stir once.	7 to 9 minutes
Onions fresh, quartered	3 to 4 large	1 pound	Peel; quarter. Cook in 1½-quart covered casserole with 2 tablespoons water. Stir once.	9 to 11 minutes
frozen, small whole	2 cups		Cook in covered 1-quart casserole. Stir once.	5 to 6 minutes
Parsnips fresh, quartered	4 medium	1 pound	Pare and quarter; cook in 1½-quart covered casserole with ½ cup water. Stir once.	7 to 8 minutes
Peas fresh green, shelled	2 cups	2 pounds	Wash. Cook in 1-quart covered casserole with 2 tablespoons water.	7 to 8 minutes
	3 cups	3 pounds	Same except use 1½-quart casserole.	9 to 10 minutes
frozen, green	2 cups	10 ounces	Cook in covered 1-quart casserole. Stir once.	5 to 6 minutes
frozen green peas and carrots		10 ounces	Cook in covered 1-quart casserole with 2 tablespoons water. Stir once.	7 to 8 minutes
frozen, black eyed peas		10 ounces	Cook in 1-quart covered casserole with ½ cup water. Stir once.	12 to 13 minutes
Pea pods frozen		6 ounces	Make slit in pouch and place on plate or in bowl. Cook; rearrange once.	3 to 4 minutes
Potatoes baked	1 whole	6–8 ounces	Scrub; prick skin with fork. Arrange in spoke pattern, leaving 1 inch space between. Cook till slightly firm. Wrap in foil. Let stand 5 minutes.	4 to 6 minutes
	2 whole		SAME AS ABOVE	7 to 8 minutes
	3 whole		SAME AS ABOVE	9 to 10 minutes
	4 whole		SAME AS ABOVE	12 to 13 minutes
	6 whole		SAME AS ABOVE	16 to 17 minutes
	8 whole		SAME AS ABOVE	19 to 20 minutes

VEGETABLE	AMOUNT	WEIGHT	METHOD	TIME AT **HIGH**
Potatoes boiled, halves	3 medium	1 pound	Peel and halve. Cook in covered 1½- to 2-quart casserole with 1 cup water. Stir once.	11 to 13 minutes
	4 to 5 medium	1½ pounds	SAME AS ABOVE	14 to 16 minutes
Potatoes sweet or yams baked	1 whole	5–6 ounces	Scrub; prick with fork. Arrange in spoke pattern, leaving 1 inch space between. Cook till slightly firm. Wrap in foil. Let stand 5 minutes.	5 to 6 minutes
	2 whole		SAME AS ABOVE	7 to 8 minutes
	4 whole		SAME AS ABOVE	11 to 13 minutes
	6 whole		SAME AS ABOVE	17 to 18 minutes
boiled, halves	3	1 pound	Pare and halve. Cook in covered 1½- to 2-quart casserole with 1 cup water. Stir once.	10 to 11 minutes
Rutabaga, cubed	4 cups	1 pound	Wash; pare and cube. Cook in 1½-quart covered casserole with ½ cup water. Stir once.	12 to 13 minutes
Spinach fresh	12 cups	1 pound	Wash and trim; cook in 2-quart casserole. Stir once.	5 to 7 minutes
frozen		10 ounces	Cook in 1½-quart covered casserole. Stir once.	6 to 8 minutes
Squash, winter acorn, whole	2	8 ounces each	Prick with fork. Cook whole, rearranging once. Cut in half. Remove seeds to serve.	5 to 7 minutes
fresh Hubbard, whole	1	1½ pounds	Wash; halve and remove seeds. Cut in 2 to 3 pieces. Cook in covered 2-quart casserole with ¼ cup water. Rearrange once.	10 to 12 minutes
frozen Hubbard		12 ounces	Cook in 1-quart covered casserole. Stir once.	6 to 8 minutes
Squash, summer fresh zucchini or yellow crookneck	2 medium (4 cups)	8 ounces each	Wash; slice ½ inch thick. Cook in 1½-quart covered casserole with ¼ cup water. Stir once.	6 to 7 minutes
	2 small (2 cups)	4 ounces	Same as above except use 1-quart casserole and 2 tablespoons water.	4 to 5 minutes
frozen zucchini		10 ounces	Cook in covered 1-quart casserole. Stir once.	5 to 6 minutes
Succotash frozen		10 ounces	Cook in covered 1-quart casserole with 2 tablespoons water. Stir once.	9 to 10 minutes
Turnips fresh	4 medium	1 pound	Pare and quarter. Cook in covered 1½-quart casserole with ½ cup water. Stir once.	12 to 14 minutes

Forget to thaw the roast you'd planned for dinner? Are there unexpected guests at the door? Or did you just not think about dinner until now? All are good reasons for turning to your microwave oven for thawing help.

The chart below is a general thawing guide. Since the shape of the frozen package or meat cuts, the package weight, and the starting temperature may vary from the chart, expect the times shown to be close, but not necessarily exact.

1. Check the packaging material first. Freezer paper, plastic pouches, and freezer-weight plastic bags can go directly from freezer to microwave and are good choices for freezing. Avoid foil, which must be removed.

2. Leave the frozen food in the original unopened package (unless it's foil). Remove metal rings, clips, or paper-covered metal wires. On poultry, remove the metal ring that closes the bag; the large metal clip that holds the legs together may be left in place, however.

3. Place the food in a baking dish to catch juices.

4. Use **MEDIUM LOW** (3) setting for all items.

5. Turn the food over and rotate the dish as the chart directs; some items must be turned more often than others. Separate the pieces during thawing when possible. Chicken parts, burger patties, fish fillets, etc. thaw faster when parts are separated.

6. Times in the chart generally result in partially thawed foods rather than completely thawed. Food should be cool to the touch; edges should be uncooked or very slightly cooked. Center of the food should be icy. Suggested standing times are usually necessary for complete thawing.

7. Never leave thawed food at room temperature longer than the suggested standing time. Food that is not to be cooked immediately should be refrigerated. Never refreeze thawed uncooked food.

THAWING DONENESS TEST: With a long-tined meat fork, pierce the meat in the center and at the sides. If you can push the fork into the center of the meat using *moderate pressure,* the meat is ready for the suggested standing time. If foods are difficult to pierce, it means a few more minutes of microwave thawing time are needed.

FOOD	AMOUNT (weight, size)	DEFROSTING TIME AT **MEDIUM LOW** (3)	STANDING TIME	TIPS
Beef roasts				
beef chuck pot roast	4 pounds (2 to 2½ inches thick)	23 to 28 minutes	10 minutes	After 15 minutes, turn meat over.
boneless beef rib roast, rolled and tied	4 pounds (4-inch diameter)	32 minutes	10 minutes	After 16 minutes, turn meat over.
Beef steaks				
beef top round steak	1 pound (½-inch thick)	6 to 8 minutes	5 minutes	
beef round steak, whole	1½ pounds (½-inch thick)	10 to 12 minutes	5 minutes	
beef T-bone steak	1 pound (¾-inch thick)	5 to 7 minutes	5 minutes	
beef sirloin steak	2 pounds (1-inch thick)	12 to 15 minutes	5 minutes	
Beef, other				
beef stew meat	1 pound (1-inch cubes)	8 to 12 minutes	5 minutes	After 5 minutes, separate pieces.
ground beef	1 pound	9 to 10 minutes	5 minutes	After 5 minutes, turn meat over; remove any thawed portion.
	2 pounds	18 minutes	5 minutes	After 10 minutes, turn meat over; remove any thawed portion.
ground beef patties	4 (4 ounces each)	6 to 7 minutes	none	Use 8×8×2-inch baking dish. After 4 minutes, turn patties over and give dish a half turn.
	1 (4 ounces)	2 to 3 minutes	none	

FOOD	AMOUNT (weight, size)	DEFROSTING TIME AT **MEDIUM LOW** (3)	STANDING TIME	TIPS
Pork				
boneless pork loin roast, rolled and tied	4 pounds	18 to 20 minutes	10 minutes	After 9 minutes, turn meat over.
bone-in pork loin roast	4 pounds	30 minutes	10 minutes	After 15 minutes, turn meat over.
pork chops	2 (4 ounces each)	3 to 4 minutes	5 minutes	After 2 minutes separate pieces.
	4 (1 pound in all)	6 to 7 minutes	5 minutes	After 3 minutes, separate pieces.
	6 (1½ pounds in all)	8 to 10 minutes	10 minutes	After 4 minutes, separate pieces.
pork spareribs	2 pounds	12 to 15 minutes	5 minutes	After 6 minutes, separate pieces.
Poultry				
chicken, fryer, cut up	2½ to 3 pounds	18 to 20 minutes	5 minutes	After 12 minutes, separate pieces.
whole	2½ to 3 pounds	15 to 20 minutes	5 minutes	Cook 10 minutes breast up, then turn and cook 5 to 10 minutes breast down. Remove giblets.
roasting hen, whole	5 pounds	20 minutes	see tips	Cook 10 minutes breast up, then let stand 10 minutes. Cook 10 minutes breast down; remove giblets and let stand 10 minutes before using.
chicken breasts	1½ to 2 pounds (2 whole)	10 minutes	10 minutes	After 5 minutes, turn chicken over. Separate pieces before standing time.
Duckling				
whole	5 pounds	30 minutes	see tips	Cook 10 minutes breast up, then let stand 10 minutes. Cook 10 minutes breast down, then let stand 10 minutes. Cook 10 minutes breast up then let stand 10 minutes before using.
Cornish hens	1 (1¼ pounds)	12 to 15 minutes	see tips	Cook 6 minutes breast down; turn and cook 6 minutes breast up. Remove giblets and place hen in bowl of cool water for 10 minutes before using.
	2 (1¼ pounds each)	18 minutes	see tips	Cook 9 minutes breast down; turn and cook 9 minutes breast up. Remove giblets and place hen in bowl of cool water for 10 to 15 minutes before using.
	4 (1¼ pounds each)	28 minutes	see tips	Cook 14 minutes breast down; turn and rearrange. Cook 14 minutes breast up. Remove giblets and place hen in cool water for 10 to 15 minutes before using.
Boneless turkey roast	3 pounds	30 minutes	10 minutes	Remove from foil package; place in baking dish. After 15 minutes, turn meat over.

185

HOW TO DEFROST MEAT, POULTRY, AND MORE

FOOD	AMOUNT (weight, size)	DEFROSTING TIME AT **MEDIUM LOW (3)**	STANDING TIME	TIPS
Turkey breast	4 pounds	22 to 24 minutes	10 minutes	Cook 12 minutes breast up; turn over and cook 10 to 12 minutes breast down.
Whole turkey	up to 10 pounds	10 minutes per pound	see tips	Remove metal ring from wrapper. Rest 5 minutes after every 30 minutes of defrosting and give bird ¼ turn. (Cover parts that begin to brown with foil.) Let rest 30 minutes before use. Remove giblets and neck. Then cook at once.
Fish and seafood fish fillets	1 pound block	7 to 9 minutes	5 minutes	After 4 minutes, turn fish over. Open package and separate into fillets before standing time.
	2 pounds (2 1-pound blocks)	15 to 18 minutes	5 minutes	After 9 minutes, turn fish over. Open package and separate into fillets before standing time.
lobster tails	1 (8 ounces)	5 to 6 minutes	5 minutes	
shrimp, scallops	12 ounces	4 to 5 minutes	5 minutes	After 2 minutes, separate pieces.
	1 pound	6 to 8 minutes	5 minutes	After 2 minutes, separate pieces.
Other bacon	1 pound package	4 to 6 minutes	none	When slices can be separated, stop.
frankfurters	1 pound package	5 to 5 minutes	none	After 2 minutes, turn package over.
sliced luncheon meat	8 ounces	3 to 4 minutes	none	
frozen whipped dessert topping	4½-ounce carton	1 minute	none	
	9-ounce carton	1½ minutes	none	
frozen fruit	10-ounce carton	3 to 4 minutes	none	Remove one end of carton if metal. See other items on page 82 and 171.

HOW MUCH TO BUY?

PRODUCT	AMOUNT TO BUY PER SERVING
Large amount of bone (ribs)	½ to 1 pound
Medium amount of bone (chuck roast)	⅓ to ½ pound
Small amount of bone (steak or roast)	¼ to ⅓ pound
Boneless or ground meat	¼ pound
Chicken	½ pound
Duckling	2 pounds
Turkey	½ pound
Rolled turkey roast	⅓ pound
Fish, whole	¾ to 1 pound
Fish, large dressed	½ pound
Fish steaks, fillets	⅓ pound

HOW LONG IN THE FREEZER?

PRODUCT	STORAGE TIME AT 0°F
Bread	2 months
Cooked dishes	2 to 3 months
Fish and seafoods	3 to 4 months
Fruits	6 months
Juice concentrate	6 months
Meats	
Bacon	1 month
Pork roasts, chops	3 to 4 months
Sausage	1 to 2 months
Beef, veal, lamb roasts	6 months
Ground meat	1 to 2 months
Poultry	3 to 4 months
Vegetables	6 months

MICROWAVE OVEN ROASTING

Cooking times will vary according to size, shape, composition, and starting temperature of roast. You will have best results if you start with *completely defrosted* meat—generally you may have better results if you roast meats in the microwave oven that have been thawed conventionally. Use these cooking times merely as a *guideline*. Check *before* cooking time is up to see if roast is done. You will find a microwave oven meat thermometer, inserted in center of largest muscle (not touching fat or bone), your best judge of doneness. If any part of roast or bird is being overcooked, cover the area with a small piece of foil secured with wooden picks. Also turning the roast or baking dish more often is a good way to prevent overcooking in any one area. Generally microwave oven roasting may be less consistent than conventional oven roasting.

MEAT	WEIGHT	MINUTES PER POUND	METHOD
BEEF Standing Rib Roast	4 to 6 pounds	10 to 11 at **MEDIUM HIGH (7)**	Tie roast with heavy string. Cover ends of bones with foil. Place roast, bone side up, on microwave roasting rack or inverted saucers in 13×9×2-inch baking dish. Cover with waxed paper. Cook at **MEDIUM HIGH (7)** for *half* the cooking time. Turn roast fat side up and give baking dish a half turn. Cover with waxed paper and cook till meat thermometer* registers 125°F. Cover with foil (shiny side in) and let stand 5 to 10 minutes. Temperature should now read 130°F to 135°F. Roast will have rare center and a large surrounding area of medium-done meat. The outside will be well done. If you desire more well done meat, slice the roast, then cook the rare slices a few minutes at **MEDIUM HIGH (7)**.
Rolled Rib Roast	4 to 5 pounds	12 to 13 at **MEDIUM HIGH (7)**	Tie roast with heavy string. Place roast, fat side down, on microwave roasting rack or inverted saucers in 13×9×2-inch baking dish. Cover with waxed paper. Cook at **MEDIUM HIGH (7)** for *half* the cooking time. Turn roast fat side up and give baking dish a half turn. Cover with waxed paper and cook till meat thermometer* registers 125°F. Cover with foil (shiny side in) and let stand 5 to 10 minutes. Temperature should now read 130°F to 135°F. Roast will have rare center and a large surrounding area of medium-done meat. The outside will be well done. If you desire more well done meat, slice the roast, then cook the rare slices a few minutes at **MEDIUM HIGH (7)**.
LAMB Leg of Lamb	4 to 6 pounds	15 to 16 at **MEDIUM (5)**	Cap shank end of roast with foil; secure with wooden picks. Place roast, fat side down, on microwave roasting rack or inverted saucers in 13×9×2-inch baking dish. Cover with waxed paper. Cook at **MEDIUM (5)** for *half* the cooking time. Turn roast over and give baking dish a half turn. Brush roast with kitchen bouquet. Cover with waxed paper and cook till thermometer* registers 175°F. Cover with foil (shiny side in). Let stand 5 to 10 minutes. Thermometer should now read 180°F.
PORK Boneless Loin Roast	4 to 5 pounds	14 to 15 at **MEDIUM HIGH (7)**	Place roast, fat side down, on microwave roasting rack or inverted saucers in 13×9×2-inch baking dish. Cover with waxed paper. Cook at **MEDIUM HIGH (7)** for *half* the cooking time. Turn roast fat side up. Brush with kitchen bouquet. Cover with waxed paper. Cook till thermometer* registers 165°F. Cover with foil (shiny side in). Let stand for 5 to 10 minutes. Thermometer should now read 170°F.

Do not use a conventional thermometer inside the microwave oven. Special microwave thermometers are available. Do not use a microwave meat thermometer in a conventional oven.

MICROWAVE OVEN ROASTING

MEAT	WEIGHT	MINUTES PER POUND	METHOD
PORK			
Bone-in Loin Roast	4 to 5 pounds	11 to 12 at **MEDIUM HIGH (7)**	Place roast, fat side down, on microwave roasting rack or inverted saucers in 13×9×2-inch baking dish. Cover with waxed paper. Cook at **MEDIUM HIGH (7)** for *half* the cooking time. Turn roast fat side up. Brush with kitchen bouquet. Cover with waxed paper. Cook till thermometer* registers 165°F. Cover with foil (shiny side in). Let stand for 5 to 10 minutes. Thermometer should now read 170°F.
Ham, canned	3 to 5 pounds	9 to 10 at **MEDIUM (5)**	Tie ham with heavy string. Cap edges of ham on top and bottom with small strips of foil; secure with wooden picks. Place ham, fat side down, on microwave roasting rack or inverted saucers in 13×9×2-inch baking dish. Cover with waxed paper. Cook at **MEDIUM (5)** for *half* the cooking time. Turn meat over and give baking dish a half turn. Cover with waxed paper and cook till meat thermometer* registers 120°F. (Brush with glaze during the last 5 minutes of cooking time, if desired.) Cover with foil (shiny side in). Let stand 5 to 10 minutes. Temperature should now read 130°F. In larger hams, especially, the muscles may separate during cooking.
Ham, fully cooked formed	3 to 5 pounds	14 to 16 at **MEDIUM (5)**	Tie ham with heavy string. Cap edges of ham on top and bottom with small strips of foil; secure with wooden picks. Place ham, fat side down, on microwave roasting rack or inverted saucers in 13×9×2-inch baking dish. Cover with waxed paper. Cook at **MEDIUM (5)** for *half* the cooking time. Turn meat over and give baking dish a half turn. Cover with waxed paper and cook till meat thermometer* registers 130°F. (Brush with glaze during the last 5 minutes of cooking time, if desired.) Cover with foil (shiny side in). Let stand 5 to 10 minutes. Temperature should now read 140°F. In larger hams, especially, the muscles may separate during cooking.
POULTRY			
Chicken—*combination microwave and conventional roasting method:*			
	3 to 4 pounds	6 to 7 at **HIGH** then 5 in 350°F oven	*This method takes a few minutes longer than the all microwave method, but you'll have a browner, more evenly done bird.* In small bowl, melt 2 tablespoons butter at **HIGH** for 45 seconds. Stir in 1 teaspoon paprika; set aside. Tie chicken legs together and wings close to body. Cover legs and wings with foil; secure with wooden picks. Place breast side down on microwave roasting rack or inverted saucers in 12×7½×2-inch baking dish. Cut ½-inch slit in back skin. Brush with butter mixture now and after each turning. Cover with loose tent of waxed paper. Cook at **HIGH** for ¼ the cooking time. Turn one side up. Cook, covered, at **HIGH** for ¼ the cooking time. Turn breast side up. Remove foil from legs. Cook, covered, at **HIGH** for ¼ the cooking time. Turn other side up. Cook, covered, at **HIGH** for remainder of microwave cooking time. Remove foil from wings and waxed paper tent. Place in conventional 350°F oven and cook till thermometer* inserted in center of inside thigh muscle registers 185°F. Let stand 10 to 15 minutes before carving. If any portion of chicken is not quite done, return just that portion to the microwave oven and cook a few minutes at **MEDIUM HIGH (7)**.

Do not use a conventional thermometer inside the microwave oven. Special microwave thermometers are available. Do not use a microwave meat thermometer in a conventional oven.

MEAT	WEIGHT	MINUTES PER POUND	METHOD
POULTRY			
Chicken—*all microwave roasting method:*			
	3 to 4 pounds	2 to 3 at **HIGH** then 7 to 8 at **MEDIUM (5)**	Tie legs together and wings close to body. Place breast side down on microwave roasting rack or inverted saucers in 12×7½×2-inch baking dish. Cover with waxed paper; cook 2 to 3 minutes per pound at **HIGH.** Reduce setting to **MEDIUM (5)** and cook for ⅓ of the time at **MEDIUM (5).** Turn breast side up; give baking dish a half turn. Cover legs and wings with foil; secure with wooden picks. Cover with waxed paper and cook remaining ⅔ of time at **MEDIUM (5).** Thermometer* inserted in inside thigh muscle should read 175°F. Cover with foil (shiny side in). Let stand 10 to 15 minutes. Thermometer should register 185°F. If any portion of chicken is not quite done, return just that portion to the microwave oven and cook a few minutes at **MEDIUM HIGH (7).**
Cornish hens	four 1-pound 4-ounce hens	40 minutes total cooking time at **MEDIUM (5)**	Tie legs together and wings close to body. Place breast side down on microwave roasting rack or inverted saucers in 13×9×2-inch baking dish. Brush with butter and paprika mixture (see chicken, opposite page). Cover with waxed paper. Cook at **MEDIUM (5)** for *half* the cooking time. Turn breast side up. Brush with butter mixture. Cover with waxed paper and continue cooking at **MEDIUM (5)** till meat thermometer* registers 185°F. Cover with foil (shiny side in). Let stand 10 minutes.
Duckling	4 to 5 pounds	8 at **MEDIUM HIGH (7)**	Prick skin all over. Tie legs together and wings close to body. Place breast side down on microwave roasting rack or inverted saucers in 12×7½×2-inch baking dish. Cook, uncovered, at **MEDIUM HIGH (7)** for *half* the cooking time. Drain off fat. Turn breast side up; cook, uncovered, at **MEDIUM HIGH (7)** till meat thermometer* registers 175°F. Cover with foil (shiny side in). Let stand 10 to 15 minutes. Thermometer should now read 185°F.
Turkey—*combination microwave and conventional roasting method:*			
	6 to 9 pounds	4 to 5 at **HIGH** then 5 to 7 in 350°F oven	*This method takes a few minutes longer than the all micro-wave method, but you'll have a browner, more evenly done bird.* In small bowl, melt 2 tablespoons butter at **HIGH** for 45 seconds. Stir in 1 teaspoon paprika; set aside. Tie turkey legs together and wings close to body. Cover legs and wings with foil; secure with wooden picks. Place breast side down on microwave roasting rack or inverted saucers in 13×9×2-inch baking dish. Cut ½-inch slit in back skin. Brush with butter mixture now and after each turning. Cover with loose tent of waxed paper. Cook at **HIGH** for ¼ the cooking time. Turn one side up. Cook, covered, at **HIGH** for ¼ the cooking time. Turn breast side up. Remove foil from legs. Cook, covered, at **HIGH** for ¼ the cooking time. Turn other side up. Cook, covered, at **HIGH** for remainder of microwave cooking time. Remove foil from wings and waxed paper tent. Place in conventional 350°F oven and cook till thermometer inserted in center of inside thigh muscle registers 185°F. Let stand 10 to 15 minutes before carving. If any portion of turkey is not quite done, return just that portion to the microwave oven and cook a few minutes at **MEDIUM HIGH (7).**

Do not use a conventional thermometer inside the microwave oven. Special microwave thermometers are available. Do not use a microwave meat thermometer in a conventional oven.

MICROWAVE OVEN ROASTING

MEAT	WEIGHT	MINUTES PER POUND	METHOD
POULTRY Turkey—*all microwave roasting method:*			
	6 to 12 pounds	3 to 4 at **HIGH** then 4 to 5 at **MEDIUM (5)**	Make sure turkey is completely thawed. Tie legs together and wings close to body. Place breast side down on microwave roasting rack or inverted saucers in 13×9×2-inch baking dish. Cover legs and wings with foil; secure with wooden picks. Cover with waxed paper. Cook at **HIGH** for ½ the cooking time. Turn breast side up and cook at **HIGH** for ½ the cooking time. Turn breast side down and give baking dish a half turn. Remove foil from legs and wings. Cook at **MEDIUM (5)** for ½ the cooking time. Turn breast side up and cook at **MEDIUM (5)** for ½ the cooking time. Thermometer* inserted in inside thigh muscle should register 175°F. Cover with foil (shiny side in) for 10 to 15 minutes. Thermometer should now read 185°F. If any portion of turkey is not quite done, return just that portion to the microwave oven and cook a few minutes at **MEDIUM HIGH (7)**.

*Do not use a conventional thermometer inside the microwave oven. Special microwave thermometers are available. Do not use a microwave meat thermometer in a conventional oven.

TIPS INDEX

INDEX

197

199

MICROWAVE CHARTS

KITCHEN MATH AND METRICS

Measure	Equivalent	Metric
1 tablespoon	3 teaspoons	15 milliliters
2 tablespoons	1 ounce	30 milliliters
1 jigger	1½ ounces	45 milliliters
¼ cup	4 tablespoons	60 milliliters
⅓ cup	5 tablespoons, plus 1 teaspoon	80 milliliters
½ cup	8 tablespoons	125 milliliters
1 cup	16 tablespoons	250 milliliters
1 pint	2 cups	500 milliliters
1 quart	4 cups	1,000 milliliters or 1 liter
1 ounce (dry)	2 tablespoons	30 grams
1 pound	16 ounces	450 grams
2.21 pounds	35.3 ounces	1 kilogram

WARMING BREADS (see page 36)

Food	Amount	Time at **HIGH** from room temp.	Time at **HIGH** from frozen
Bread, loaf	¼	15 seconds	30 seconds
	½	20 seconds	1 minute
	1	30 seconds	2¼ to 2½ min.
Bread, slices	2	10 seconds	20 seconds
	4	20 seconds	40 seconds
	6	30 seconds	60 seconds
Large rolls	2	20 seconds	30 seconds
	4	30 seconds	50 seconds
	6	40 seconds	1 min. 10 sec.
Doughnuts	2	15 seconds	35 seconds
	4	25 seconds	60 seconds
	6	35 seconds	1½ to 1¾ min.

BOILING WATER

Amount water	Time at **HIGH**
¼ cup	40 seconds
½ cup	1 minute 15 seconds
¾ cup	1 minute 45 seconds
1 cup	2 minutes 30 seconds
1½ cups	3 minutes 30 seconds
2 cups	4 minutes 15 seconds
2½ cups	6 minutes
3 cups	7 minutes 30 seconds

HEATING ROOM TEMPERATURE COFFEE

Number of coffee cups	Time at **HIGH**
1	1 minute
2	2 minutes
3	3 minutes
4	4 minutes

HEATING MILK FOR COCOA (see page 48)

Amount milk	Time at **HIGH**
1 cup	2 minutes
2 cups	3 minutes
3 cups	4 minutes
4 cups	5 minutes

BACON (see page 48)

Number of slices	Time at **HIGH**
2	2 to 2¼ minutes
4	4 to 4¼ minutes
6	5½ to 5¾ minutes
8	6½ to 7 minutes

HOT DOGS (see page 87)

Number of hot dogs in buns	Time at **HIGH**
1	30 seconds
2	50 seconds
3	1 minute 20 seconds
4	1 minute 30 seconds
5	1 minute 50 seconds
6	2 minutes

INDEX OF CHARTS

SCRAMBLED EGGS (see page 48)

Number of eggs	Amount of milk	Amount butter	Time at MEDIUM HIGH (7)	Stir
1	1 tbsp.	1 tsp.	¾ to 1¼ min.	once
2	2 tbsp.	2 tsp.	1¾ to 2¼ min.	once
4	¼ cup	4 tsp.	3 to 3½ min.	twice
6	⅓ cup	2 tbsp.	4½ to 5½ min.	twice

EMERGENCY SUBSTITUTIONS

Product called for	Substitute
1 tablespoon cornstarch (for thickening)	2 tablespoons flour or quick-cooking tapioca
1 package active dry yeast	1 cake compressed yeast or 1 tablespoon active dry yeast
1 cup whole milk	½ cup evaporated milk plus ½ cup water or 1 cup reconstituted nonfat dry milk plus 2½ teaspoons butter
1 cup sour milk or buttermilk	1 tablespoon lemon juice or vinegar plus sweet milk to make 1 cup (let stand 5 minutes)
1 ounce (1 square) unsweetened chocolate	3 tablespoons cocoa plus 1 tablespoon butter
1 tablespoon fresh snipped herbs	1 teaspoon dried herbs
1 small fresh onion	1 tablespoon instant minced onion, rehydrated
1 teaspoon dry mustard	1 tablespoon prepared mustard
1 clove garlic	⅛ teaspoon garlic powder

BASIC MICROWAVE RECIPES

HOW MUCH AND HOW MANY

2 tablespoons butter = 1 ounce
1 stick or ¼ pound butter = ½ cup
28 saltine crackers = 1 cup fine crumbs
14 square graham crackers = 1 cup fine crumbs
22 vanilla wafers = 1 cup fine crumbs
1½ slices bread = 1 cup soft crumbs
1 slice bread = ¼ cup fine dry crumbs
4 ounces macaroni (1 to 1¼ cups) = 2¼ cups cooked
4 ounces noodles (1½ to 2 cups) = 2 cups cooked
7 ounces spaghetti = 4 cups cooked
1 cup packaged precooked rice = 2 cups cooked
16 ounces American cheese = 4 cups shredded
4 ounces blue cheese = 1 cup crumbled
1 medium onion, chopped = ½ cup chopped
1 cup whipping cream = 2 cups whipped
1 square chocolate = 1 ounce

SIZING UP CANS

Can Size	Contents	Name
8 ounces	1 cup	
10½ to 12 ounces	1¼ cups	Picnic
12-ounce vacuum	1½ cups	
14 to 16 ounces	1¾ cups	No. 300
16 to 17 ounces	2 cups	No. 303
20 ounces	2½ cups	No. 2
29 ounces	3½ cups	No. 2½
46 fluid ounces	5¾ cups	No. 3 cylinder
6 lbs. 8 ozs. to 7 lbs. 5 ozs.	12 to 13 cups	No. 10

(equal to 7 16-ounce cans or 5 20-ounce)

Part No. 309601